EDWARD CULLINAN
ARCHITECTS

EDWARD CULLINAN ARCHITECTS

KENNETH POWELL

Aᴅ ACADEMY EDITIONS

ACKNOWLEDGEMENTS

The author wishes to express his gratitude to the many members of the extended 'family' created by Ted Cullinan over thirty years of practice. In particular, Mark Beedle was a constant guide, supporter and source of inspiration, who chauffeured me to many of the key Cullinan buildings, and was never lost for an answer to my questions. Hardly less crucial was the contribution of Claire Herniman and Louise Potter, while Robin Nicholson, Johnny Winter, Roddy Langmuir and Mary-Lou Arscott at ECA were equally enlightening on the work of the practice. Among others I have to especially thank are Sir Denys Lasdun, Julyan Wickham, Tchaik Chassay and Sunand Prasad for their reminiscences, and many owners of Cullinan buildings for permitting free access. Michael Spens at Academy, a true advocate of the best of modern British architecture, fired me with enthusiasm. Above all, I am grateful to Ted Cullinan, not only for his unstinting commitment to this book and generous hospitality on many occasions, but for his steadfast defence of a modern architecture of place, history and human identity which this book celebrates.

Cover: Media Centre for the Cheltenham and Gloucester College of Higher Education, Pittville Campus, Cheltenham.
Frontispiece: San Miniato al Monte, Florence, drawn *in situ* by Edward Cullinan, 1952.
Page 6: Entrance to Bell Tout Lighthouse

Attempts have been made to locate sources of all photographs to obtain full reproduction rights, but in the very few instances where this process has failed to find the copyright holder, apologies are offered. All illustrative material is courtesy of the practice unless otherwise stated. Photographic credits: John Allan/Avanti Architects, p8 (below); John Bethell p63 (below right); Jerry Bragstad, p58 (above and below left); Geremy Butler, pp41 (below), 42, 129-131; Graham Challifour, p85; Martin Charles, pp20 (below), 21, 23 (above), 25, 48, 51, 52 (above), 94, 95, 96, 97, 98, 103, 106-111, 115, 119, 123, 126, 128, 132, 133, 135, 138, 140, 162-167, 175 (above), 176, 177 (above right), 181, 200; Paul Cullen, p28; Paul Dixon, p63 (above); English Heritage, p191; Dennis Gilbert, front cover, pp50, 52 (below), 53, 114, 125, 127, 136 (above right), 137, 152, 153, 170-171, 179, 186; Brian Housden, pp6, 9 (above), 10 (below), 55 (below), 57 (above), 113; R. M. Leonard, p77; JJ Photoservices, pp120-121; National Gallery, p195 (above right); National Monuments Record, p89; National Trust Photographic Library/Oliver Benn, p34; Nils Obee, pp33 (above), 169 (above and below right); Tim Rawle, pp122, 124; Seeland, p30 (below); John Sturrock/Network, pp93, 134; Bill Toomey/AR, pp18, 67, 68, 70-71; Julyan Wickham, p49; Mark Wickham, pp11 (below) 12, 61 (above), 64, 65, 73 (above and centre); David Wild, pp75, 77 (above left, below left, right); Philip Wolmuth, p24 (above); Charlotte Wood, pp30 (above), 136 (above left).

Certain articles and images in this book have previously been published, and in such cases, we would like to thank those who have made it possible to reproduce them. Visual credits: p7 (centre) Greene & Greene, Gamble House interior and p147 (above centre), photographs by Marvin Rand, from *Five California Architects* by Esther McCoy, Praeger, New York, 1960; p8 (above), Gerrit Thomas Rietveld, Child's Trolley, photograph by Giorgio and Valerio Lari, from *Rietveld Furniture*, p53, Daniele Baroni, Academy Group Ltd, © Gruppo Editoriale Electa SpA, Milan, 1978; p10 (above), Rudolf Schindler, Lovell Beach House, from *Schindler*, p84-85, by David Gebhard, Thames and Hudson Ltd, 1971, © Architectural Drawing Collection, University Art Museum, University of California, Santa Barbara; p41 (above), engraving of Covent Garden Piazza c1717-28 by Sutton Nicholls, from the British Museum, Department of Prints and Drawings, in *Covent Garden Market*, p11, by Robert Thorne, Architectural Press, GLC, 1980; p94 (below left) from *Detail*, Institut für Internationale Arkitektur-Dokumentation, Munich, March/April 1985; p147 (below), Gerrit Thomas Rietveld, Schroeder House from *Rietveld, Schroeder House*, pp26, 29, pictures 19, 20, 32, C Blotkamp and B Mulder, Uitgeverij Impress, Utrecht, The Netherlands, 1984; p149 (above), Tecton plan of Highpoint 1, from *Lubetkin and Tecton*, p120, Peter Coe and Malcolm Reading, Arts Council with the Department of Architecture, University of Bristol, 1981; p149 (centre and below), Olivier Theatre, p86 and Hallfield Primary School, p21, from *A Language and a Theme*, RIBA, 1976; p151, Pilgrimage Chapel, Ronchamp, photographs by Robert Winkler and Bernhard Moosbrugger, from *Oeuvre Complet, Volume 1952-57*, W Boesiger, Les Editions d'Architecture, Zurich, 1957.

Drawing credits: pp46 (above), 157, perspectives of Morrison Street, Edinburgh by Peter Hull; pp78-81, illustrations for 'A Question of Style' by Giles Oliver, from *Spazio e Societa* No. 15/16, GC Sansoni Editore Nuova SpA, Firenze, Italy, September/December 1981; p85, illustrations from 'House, Architecture, the Cocktail and the Dry-Stone Wall', from *The Toshi-Jutaku*, Urban Housing No. 156, Tokyo, October 1980; p170, illustration of Bedfont Lakes by Michael Hopkins & Partners. Other drawings were done by various members of the ECA teams involved in the buildings.

Quotations are taken from: p147 from *CR Ashbee: Architect, Designer and Romantic Socialist*, p152, Alan Crawford, © Yale University, 1986; p184 from *The Moment of Cubism and Other Essays*, p133, John Berger, Penguin, 1969. Previously published articles: p104 'Hang-Gliders and Sailing Surfboards' from *What is a Designer?*, Norman Potter, Hyphen Press, Reading, 1980; pp142-151 'Where Does My Baggage Come From?' from the *RSA Journal*, No. 5366, Volume CXXXV, January 1987.

Editor, art director and co-ordinator at ECA: Mark Beedle

CONTENTS

BEGINNINGS: THE YOUNG CULLINAN

'I am totally committed to making architecture with people and for people', Edward Cullinan declared in 1986. It was a statement which surprised nobody, an expression of a theme which is fundamental to Cullinan's work over the last thirty years, and nobody doubted its sincerity. But, he continued, there is more to architecture than the fundamental matter of addressing the needs of people, whether individual or social. Architecture is an art. 'I am convinced', Cullinan insisted, 'that if architects bring no understanding, no commitment, no ego even, and only their obedience . . . there will never be any risk *but neither will there ever be any architecture again*.'

Edward (whom everybody calls Ted) Cullinan and his practice, Edward Cullinan Architects, occupy a unique place in late twentieth-century English architecture. Their work is widely characterised as socially-minded, responsive to place, landscape and history, and rooted in a respect for materials and a fascination with the mechanics of construction. It represents a progressive and critical restatement of the tenets of the Modern Movement. Yet it is equally inventive, expressive, sometimes colourful, and on occasions frankly decorative (though never in a way which obscures form and structure). As such, Cullinan's architecture belongs centre-stage in any discussion of world architecture at the end of the century, when old shibboleths and orthodoxies have withered away in the face of a defiant re-emergence of the art of architecture. Though nearly all the work of the Cullinan office to date has been in Britain, there is nothing insular about it. It belongs to an honourable and creative tradition of intelligent dissent within the Modernist tradition which long predates the Post-modernism with which it is sometimes linked (to Cullinan's annoyance, even disgust). Gaudi, Greene & Greene, Wright, Rietveld, Lubetkin and Lasdun are in Cullinan's pantheon of heroes, alongside Corbusier – but so too are Charles Rennie Mackintosh and Philip Webb, towering figures of the Arts and Crafts tradition who were once (rather misleadingly) seen as 'pioneers of modern design'.

Ted Cullinan never knew the Arts and Crafts architect Percy Morley Horder (who died while Cullinan was still a boy), but 'Holy Murder' (as his assistants called him) was a distant relation and, to some degree, a role model. Cullinan's uncle, Mervyn Horder, spoke of Morley with admiration, and encouraged his nephew to take an interest in architecture. 'I was taught to distinguish pseudo-Tudor from the real thing at an early age, on car journeys to Hampshire along the Kingston bypass,' Cullinan recalls. 'I was indoctrinated – and soon wanted to be an architect.'

Born in London in 1931, Cullinan grew up in a comfortable, distinctly artistic, middle class world. His father, a doctor who served as senior

FROM ABOVE: Philip Webb, Joldwyns, 1873; Greene & Greene, exterior and interior of the Gamble House, 1908

physician at St Bartholomew's Hospital, had no great interest in the arts – though he was a brilliant amateur conjuror – but his mother (Slade-trained painter and daughter of the royal physician, Lord Horder) was an enthusiast for modern architecture and filled the nursery with Aalto furniture. He was taken as a child to see the new Penguin Pool at London Zoo: Anthony Chitty, a partner in Tecton from 1932 to 1936, was a family friend and godfather to Ted Cullinan's brother.

Cullinan's world was transformed with the outbreak of war. His father went into the Army medical corps and the family (three boys and a girl with their mother) was evacuated to Canada. It could have been a traumatic time, but was actually memorable and even enjoyable. Cullinan remembers Montreal with enormous affection and still loves Canada: 'a place of welcoming, frank, outgoing people and of wilderness, space, snow and definite seasons.' In 1943 Cullinan and one of his younger brothers returned to school in England: 'The officer class had to be sustained', he jokes. The journey back across the Atlantic took three months, via New York and Bermuda, on a Royal Navy cruiser. Britain came as a shock, a place of blacked-out windows and austerity. Cullinan had been brought up as a Roman Catholic and was bound for Ampleforth, the Catholic public school on the edge of the North Yorkshire Moors. 'I was obsessively religious', he says.

Cullinan never entirely liked Ampleforth, finding its boy-centred social life alien, but loved the ritual of Mass, the choir offices and the great ceremonies of the Christian year. He took to rugby 'as a means of survival'. (He became an adequate player and has maintained his active interest in sports and outdoor pursuits ever since, setting a pace that many younger colleagues find hard to match.) Having established his standing in the school, he was allowed to spend much of his time in the art room. 'We used to go out painting with Father Raphael on the moors – sometimes it was so cold, the paints froze. Father Raphael claimed that this improved the quality of sedimentary washes.' He was impressed by the austere but majestic abbey church at Ampleforth, designed by Sir Giles Gilbert Scott, but found even more inspiration in the great historic buildings of Yorkshire. One place, in particular, remained a strong memory: Fountains Abbey, near Ripon. The Benedictine monks of Ampleforth were considering the restoration of the ruined shell of the abbey, and perhaps even reopening the monastery there. The idea was never really practical, but Cullinan was taken to see the abbey, set in a fantastic Georgian landscape – which was then sliding into dereliction. When, forty years later, the chance came to build there, he was to seize it with relish.

Regarded as something of an academic failure, Cullinan was allowed to spend a lot of time on art; his proficiency at drawing, rather than more 'serious' subjects, took him to Cambridge. But first came National Service: Cullinan joined the Royal Engineers, spending most of his time on the Longmoor Military Railway, a branch line which served the big army depots on Salisbury Plain. One of his jobs – perhaps it counts as the first Cullinan design – was to work on plans for a new heavyweight rail truck, intended to carry the massive, new 'Centurion' tank. The

FROM ABOVE: Rietveld, Child's Trolley, 1918; Lubetkin and Tecton, Penguin Pool, 1934 truck was a success, but proved so heavy that the track beneath it gave way as a bevy of senior officers watched in horror.

Leaving the army with a commission – 'it took me three attempts' – Cullinan went to university. He enjoyed his time at Cambridge; rowing for his college, taking up skiing, and designing sets for the May Balls, but found the department of architecture an undemanding place. 'It was like the remains of a school left over from the Arts and Crafts era. We spent weeks detailing sash windows.' Gropius had been rejected for the headship of the department, and some of the staff were far from Modernist in outlook. However, David Roberts was 'a marvellous teacher', Cullinan recalls: 'and we also educated ourselves'. The first Cullinan building (leaving aside childhood tree-houses) dates from this time – a garden shed constructed for an aunt who lived in Cambridge.

After Cambridge, the Architectural Association School in London (Cullinan was there between 1954-56) came as a revelation. 'It was brilliant, a great experience. We had first-rate teachers who were actually building, and on a large scale'. They included John Killick, Arthur Korn, Peter Smithson and Denys Lasdun, who was to play an important role in Cullinan's career. Cullinan has always believed that architects must build: 'make buildings' is the way he puts it. Significantly, his first 'real' project was not an entirely new building, but a substantial re-creation of an existing one. His father, intending to retire to the country, had seen the remains of a lighthouse, wrecked by wartime target practice, on the edge of the South Downs in Sussex. It was no more than a shattered remnant, but in 1954 Cullinan senior managed to secure a ninety-nine year lease (as a gift, on the condition that he repaired it). 'It was my first experience of making a building', says Cullinan. Still at the AA, he went to the site most weekends and during vacations. 'I found that to build things oneself and with friends was a source of inspiration; partly for the simple pleasure that it provides but also because it draws out the building process and gives one time to cogitate on the way that materials might join one another to enclose the spaces that surround life', he later recalled. Cullinan learned a lot about the practicalities of construction from the local master mason, a Mr Viner, who carried out most of the work. The Bell Tout Lighthouse may have been a youthful and far from perfect work, but the mix of careful reconstruction and uncompromisingly new additions was an augury of some of Cullinan's best mature work.

The lighthouse reflected the influence of Corbusier, at that time the idol of all young and progressive architects but already the subject of a critical response from what was to become Team 10 – with Peter and Alison Smithson and Aldo van Eyck (another architect who influenced the young Cullinan) on the cutting edge. Cullinan, however, was removed from the world of European architectural polemics in 1956 when, having won a prestigious King George VI Memorial Fellowship, he found himself crossing the Atlantic again, this time in the relative comfort of the liner *Queen Mary*. He flew on from New York to California, since he had elected to spend his year away at Berkeley: 'It was the most thrilling time of my life', he recalls, 'and it gave me a new

FROM ABOVE: Bell Tout Lighthouse, 1956; on the road, Mojave Desert, 1957

view of the world.' These were the early days of the 'Beat' poets –
Ferlinghetti lodged in the same building as Cullinan. Modern jazz and
marijuana were the fashion: when Cullinan set off to hitchhike across
America, he used Jack Kerouac's *On the Road* as a practical manual.
Later, he acquired a car, a classic 1949 Ford V8 (as featured in the James
Dean movie *Rebel Without a Cause*) – 'I went to places and saw things
that touched me.' There was also the architecture; Greene & Greene
(who became near-gods to the young Cullinan), Maybeck, Neutra,
Wright. The latter, the grand old man of American architecture, lectured
at Berkeley, and Cullinan was briefly introduced to him: 'he laid his
hand on my shoulder and said simply "my boy". It felt like a blessing!'.
Above all, there was Rudolf Schindler, who had died in 1953. Esther
McCoy had already published the first of the pioneering articles which
effectively established Schindler's canonic reputation. Cullinan was
impressed by Schindler's way of making houses from 'bits and pieces'
and by his obvious love of materials: 'he was a great architect who
loved building things himself.'

'I was amazed by the fact the Americans didn't just talk, but got things
done', says Cullinan. When he needed extra money at Berkeley, he got
a labouring job digging out foundations for a new house for a doctor
and his family. Then, as now, he enjoyed physical work, but he longed
to design buildings: 'I went round telling people how good I was and
how much I needed work.' Among the potential clients he met were
Mariah and Stephen Marvin, with whom he became friends. For the
moment, however, Cullinan's Californian idyll was over and he was
back in London. Britain seemed flat and 'deeply disappointing' after
Berkeley, though the growing critique of Corbusian orthodoxy in AA
circles provided interest. He discovered Rietveld through Peter Smithson,
and saw how abstract European Cubism shared something of the open,
experimental spirit of the West Coast architects he had come to admire.

In 1958 Cullinan began working for his former AA tutor, Denys
Lasdun, a former partner in Tecton who was to become one of the
dominant figures in British architecture during the 1960s and 70s. With
Peter Ahrends, another of Lasdun's talented assistants, he worked on
Fitzwilliam College, Cambridge. Cullinan came to admire Lasdun, who
became something of a father figure to him and was to provide practical
help with his career. The Horder house, however, built for his uncle
Mervyn in 1959, helped Cullinan keep in touch with the hands-on
realities of building: 'It was influenced by Wright and Schindler',
Cullinan concedes, 'but there was more to it than that.' The site was
located in the grounds of the Horders' large house at Ashford Chace in
Hampshire, tucked away from public view (which helped when it came
to obtaining planning consent).

'I never had a theory of architecture: I just *did* things', says Cullinan.
For the Horder house, as he calls it, Cullinan was joint contractor with
Horace Knight, a seventy-five year old gardener on the estate; he still
remembers the sheer tactile pleasure of putting together the house – an
accretive process which mixed traditional techniques with the use of
ready-made, typically twentieth-century components. Meanwhile,

Cullinan's Californian friends, the Marvins, had resolved to construct a new house adhering to his designs and he returned to the USA in mid-1959 to build it. It was to be a simple house for two people, overlooking the sea in Marin County. The living space was contained in a long, timber-construction gallery, while the kitchen, bathroom and other ancillary spaces were tucked into a series of small compartments along one side. Cullinan sees them as 'green rooms' serving a 'stage'. There were also plans for a guest house, but the Marvins later gave up the house, and it was subsequently destroyed.

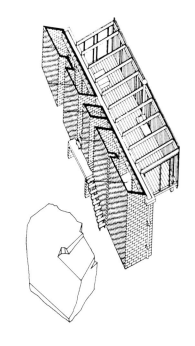

In 1960, back in England, Cullinan returned to Lasdun's office on a part-time basis. Lasdun was busy with major commissions, including an extension to Christ's College, Cambridge, and the new University of East Anglia at Norwich. Cullinan worked on both these jobs and stayed in the office for four years, doing a four-day week and trying to establish his own practice in the remaining time. Denys Lasdun remembers the journeys he and Cullinan made to the UEA site: 'We'd take a first class compartment and use the floor to lay out the drawings, sketching as we went along. Ted was close to me temperamentally. He also seemed to represent the kind of bright young person for whom I was building the university.' A secure job allowed Cullinan to marry Rosalind Yates in 1961 and start a family. There was never any question that Cullinan would want to build his own house – he finds it disappointing, if not surprising, that so many architects are happy to adapt old ones. The Cullinan house in Camden Mews was built 'in two years of Sundays', between 1962 and 1964 by Ted and Ros with the help of various friends. Money was relatively scarce – the blue bricks used to pave the entrance courtyard and ground floor were rejects from Lasdun's Royal College of Physicians. The site was a tight one; twenty-five feet wide and forty-six feet long, but Cullinan made optimum use of it by building against a parti wall on the northern boundary and erecting a line of concrete columns to form the southern edge of the house. The roof was supported on these columns and the rest of the building gradually infilled below it. The ground floor is faced in stock brick. The top floor, containing a large living/dining/kitchen area, is of timber ('sticks' is Cullinan's term) and glass and contains a single, intense living space. It is superficially a simple and economical house, but Cullinan sees it as 'an interpenetrating indoor/outdoor world, perceived in many ways, that one can move through from boundary to boundary'. It is a commentary on the nature of materials and on the modern use of space. It is also a family house, designed for the various, overlapping activities of different generations, unlike the Marvin and Horder houses. Cullinan has lived there for over three decades (though weekends and holidays are often spent at his retreat in the North Staffordshire Peak District). It is well-worn and much-loved; Cullinan recalls several Japanese architectural students asking 'but why is it so *derelict?*' Relatively simple and cheap as it was, the house at Camden Mews contained key themes and ideas which have re-emerged in Cullinan's work over the ensuing three decades.

FROM ABOVE: Marvin House, California, 1959, axonometric; Cullinan House, London, 1963

FROM HOUSES TO HOUSING

FROM ABOVE: Kawecki House, 1964; Law House, 1967

The Californian houses Ted Cullinan had seen on his two visits to the West Coast had been a crucial influence on the early development of his architecture. Houses have a strong resonance for him. He sees them as places which have the flexibility to respond to the changes which mark the lives of everyone. Cullinan's houses embody a view of the family which, though positive, is not strictly traditional. There are compartments, but they are not rigid. There is scope for the individual as well as for the life of the family as community: Cullinan is nothing if not an individualist.

'I started with houses for individuals and single families, but I always wanted to build groups of houses', says Cullinan. The next house he designed was, in fact, hardly opulent or elaborate. The Kawecki House was designed for a musician and, like Camden Mews, was fitted into a small, left-over space in a typical Victorian street in inner London. Designed with an upper gallery intended for chamber music, it was eventually completed for a fellow architect in the Lasdun office. The Garrett house was designed for Ted Cullinan's great friend, the Labour MP John Garrett, and finished in the election year of 1966. The Kawecki and Garrett houses were both single aspect structures and the latter took up the theme of Camden Mews, a lightweight timber superstructure sitting on a solid brick base. The Law house was altogether grander: located on the South Downs and 'technically a conversion' of a small cottage, it elaborated the ideas that Cullinan had developed in his London houses – sticks and bricks, in effect – and on a larger scale. The site was strikingly beautiful. The plan was quite formal, reflecting the tastes of the clients. In all the early houses, Cullinan was experimenting with the relationship between structure, plan and section and the life that the building was to contain. The makings of a radical and accommodating public architecture were already apparent in schemes that provided for purely private needs.

From 1965 onwards, Cullinan taught in the department of architecture at Cambridge. Teaching has always been important to him, and his academic activities have enriched the life of his office. From Cambridge came, in due course, key members of the Cullinan practice such as Giles Oliver, Mark Beedle, Tony Peake, Philip Tabor, Sunand Prasad, Robin Nicholson and Richard Gooden. The teaching job provided Cullinan with the possibility, at last, of going solo, and the practice of Edward Cullinan Architects dates from 1965. After a brief partnership with Guy Jervis, he set up his own office. Cullinan's first collaborators were Ian Pickering, Julyan Wickham (from 1966), Julian Bicknell, and Michael (Tchaik) Chassay (from 1968). Julyan Wickham was still at the AA when he joined Cullinan's office to work on the Law and Garrett houses: 'Ted was a house architect at that time', he recalls. Wickham was encouraged to contribute to the design process and had participated in the Knox house at Colchester. (This relatively large house consisted of two wings, one intended for the children of a large family, connected by a kitchen and dining area.) 'Ted is an optimist, who has tremendous faith in people – he gave me a lot of freedom and encouraged me to develop schemes', says Wickham.

Julyan Wickham remained with Cullinan (whose office was then in Henrietta Street, Covent Garden) until 1971, by which time the practice's first major non-domestic projects (the Minster Lovell conference centre and the various schemes for Olivetti) were in hand. Cullinan was heartened by the Labour election victories of 1964 and 1966, and excited by the events of 1968, when students in Paris, Berkeley and even London took to the streets. 'It was a kind of fulfilment for me,' he says, 'and the spirit of California seemed to be alive in Britain.' Though his political views had always been radical, Cullinan had no sympathy for authoritarian collectivism of the Marxist variety. He describes himself as a libertarian socialist: 'I concluded in 1968 that socialism needed to be done, not talked about', he says. In this spirit, he proceeded to turn his practice into a co-operative; everyone who worked there became a member, receiving an agreed percentage of fees, with no 'hidden' profits. The system still operates: today all permanent members are made directors of a limited company, deciding whom to employ and how much they and their colleagues should be paid. From that time on, 'Cullinan' was effectively a collective noun.

Cullinan's growing interest in housing (as opposed to houses) was opportune. The Wilson government was intent on building large amounts of housing for rent, both in established urban areas and in new towns. Milton Keynes was the newest of the latter, a bold experiment in social and planning terms, while in the northwest, Runcorn was being developed. The practice eagerly entered a competition for a big housing scheme at Runcorn. They did not win (James Stirling was appointed) but the project provided valuable experience. Cullinan's individual houses, though generally modest in size and often built on small, awkward sites, were spatially rich. A house needs to be a secure, reassuring place but Cullinan provided not just security but light and transparency too. (In the words of Brendan Woods, Cullinan's houses, 'combine a fascination for the cave dwelling and the bird's nest'.) Lightweight construction and a radical approach to the section produced domestic interiors of unique quality.

Working with Denys Lasdun on the UEA and Christ's College projects, Cullinan developed stepped sections, with interlocking spaces that provided the inhabitants of the buildings with access to light, views and open space. The results were rigorously geometrical – and typical of Lasdun, who maintained a firm control on the design process – but Cullinan advanced the approach when he came to design substantial buildings.

The Highgrove housing scheme at Hillingdon in London was certainly substantial. A Labour council had been elected and had promised

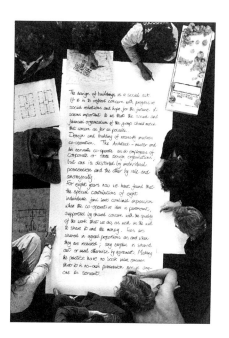

Trying for a co-operative manifesto

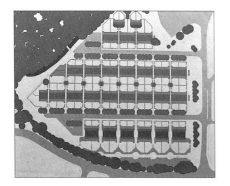

Highgrove, ground plan

to build 1,000 houses a year. When Cullinan was approached in 1973 by Hillingdon's Borough Architect, Thurston Williams, an AA graduate who had cut his teeth in the housing section of the London County Council, 'it seemed like a dream come true – at last, something worth returning from the USA for.' The site in Ruislip was possibly the best in the borough, set amongst typical streets of owner-occupied semis and acquired, at considerable expense, as part of a deliberate policy of providing rented housing in middle class areas and achieving a healthy social mix. A relatively high density (seventy people to the acre) was demanded, but the form of the housing was an open question. The early 1970s had seen a growing reaction against the high-rise, system-built housing of the 1960s. Several Labour councillors in Hillingdon believed that council tenants should have semis, closely modelled on those built by the private sector.

Ted has always admired the garden cities of the early twentieth century – places like Hampstead Garden Suburb, Welwyn and Letchworth. Helped by a cordial relationship with the chairman of the Hillingdon housing committee, the Cullinan team pursued the idea of 'giving people territory' (co-designers for this and all subsequent projects are listed at the back of this book). Each house was to have its own private garden, with car parking provided separately in areas away from the houses. This was achieved by building the houses in blocks of four on a 'back to back' principle, an arrangement prohibited by public health legislation. ('We discovered that you were allowed to build "tenements" on a back-to-back plan', says Cullinan, 'so we described the houses as tenements!') The residents of Highgrove have no back doors, but they do have plenty of light and views from windows extending the full width of the broad fronts of the houses. The sections of the Highgrove scheme derive from Cullinan's smaller houses, though the architects concede the influence of Aldo van Eyck and Herman Hertzberger too: 'We saw the scheme as houses, not "housing" – it was to be a neighbourhood, a community', says Mark Beedle, one of the co-designers. Taking their cue from van Eyck's loathing of 'the boredom of hygiene', the architects wanted 'order, but with scope for randomness and individuality'. Beedle sees Highgrove as proof 'that you can do good value, interesting houses for the many without resorting to stereotypes'. With its blue metal roofs (intended to be cheerful and to lift people's eyes to the sky) and other bright colours, together with the network of pedestrian ways and tree-lined streets, Highgrove seemed to offer a genuinely new way of creating not just housing units but also harmonious communities.

Other housing schemes followed Highgrove in the years before the Thatcherite revolution shattered the public housing programme. At Westmoreland Road, Bromley, a job which came to the office in 1974, Cullinan was working not for a local authority (indeed, the attitude of the planners seriously delayed the scheme), but for a housing association called Solon. The team initially proposed a low-rise, Highgrove type development spreading across the leafy suburban site and carefully preserving its mature trees. The Bromley planners had very

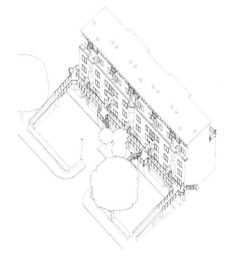

different ideas, proposing that the housing should be concentrated in one substantial block and the rest of the site left empty. There were to be no fewer than eight versions of the scheme before it received planning permission – it was finally completed in 1979. (Cullinan hints that the Conservative-controlled council might not have wanted rented housing in the area at all.)

The Westmoreland Road housing as built (a mixture of thirty-five houses and flats cleverly combined in one six-storey block), provides an opportunity to examine the approach to design that prevailed in Edward Cullinan Architects at that time. The section of the block, which makes clever use of the fall of the site, is typically Cullinan, designed with his usual fervour for light and air. The garden elevation has plenty of 'sticks' to lighten the effect of the solid walls – balconies, trellises, planters and lots of what Cullinan calls 'the paraphernalia of house life'. The street front is much more formal and embodies what Sunand Prasad describes as 'the cerebral preoccupations' of Brendan Woods, whose approach tended towards the formalism of Jeremy Dixon, Edward Jones and others of the 'Grunt Group'. The details were entrusted to Prasad, working with Brendan Woods. Prasad also supervised the job on site: 'it was an amazing opportunity: I was really thrown in at the deep end', he says.

The office by this time consisted of eight people, with Tchaik Chassay, Philip Tabor, Tony Peake, Brendan Woods, Sunand Prasad and Mark Beedle practising alongside Cullinan, all of them bringing strong ideas to bear on the work. (The office had, in fact, already been obliged to learn to function without Cullinan for some months, when he suffered a serious – indeed, near-fatal – skiing accident.) There was a particular tension in much of the work done in the mid- to late 1970s between the Cullinan dictum that 'the section is all', allied to an intuitive, accretive approach to composition, and a growing reductivism, which implied a more formal view of composition. Most of the architects of the Cullinan generation were seeking positive alternatives to the established Modernist tradition, but it was not obvious where these lay. On the one hand, the expressive, socially minded humanism of Aldo van Eyck seemed entirely consistent with Cullinan's architectural and social vision. Others in the Cullinan office felt that a more disciplined approach, reining in the detailing and elevating the cerebral over the sensual, offered a better way forward. Inevitably, given the nature of the practice, both philosophies found expression in completed buildings.

At Leighton Crescent, Camden, where the practice had to produce a housing scheme for a gap site in a Victorian crescent, a degree of formalism was inevitable. 'It was the first of our urban buildings' says Cullinan. The five-storey block was like a Highgrove in the air, with wide-fronted apartments placed back to back around a stepped section. Staircases were concentrated at the centre of the building, where the flats have their front doors. Demountable partitions allow residents a degree of control over their living space – it was typical of Cullinan to apply this classic Rietveld device to mass housing. 'People have a right

Westmoreland Road, forecourt and balconies

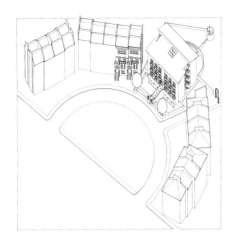

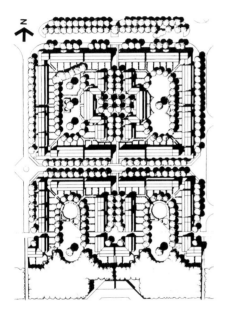

to proper space', says Cullinan. Balconies on the street and garden fronts have proved popular. When the doors from the living room are thrown open, they shelter and enclose the external space. The Solon scheme at Selhurst Road, South Norwood, built between 1974-76, took another Victorian setting and slotted in a block of four houses in an unselfconscious manner: balconies overlook the garden.

The housing at Bradwell Common, Milton Keynes (the largest of Cullinan's residential schemes with 158 units), consists of long terraces with street corners signposted by taller blocks (some containing shops) laid out on a typical Milton Keynes grid, which it used to the full. The scheme exploits the landfall and orientation to produce particular places within a predetermined urban order. There are private gardens behind each house, but beyond these are shared open spaces, secure areas where children can play. Garages are integral, with direct access to the street. The details were kept simple, but the scheme has contributed to an area which (according to the *Buildings of England: Buckinghamshire*) is 'particularly successful'. There are no fewer than seventeen house types, reflecting not just the variety of the site but the differing needs of the people who live there. Cullinan succeeded in wading through 'a knee-deep river of jargon', as he puts it, to produce an human-scaled development with a purposeful sense of place.

Bradwell Common was not completed until 1982. It was the last of the groups of 'houses called housing' produced by the practice. By the early 1980s, Cullinan had largely ceased to be a 'house architect' and the practice was exploring new areas of building. The determination to build with and for people remained, but the social dimension was tempered by a deepening concern for place and history which struck a chord in the conservation-conscious Britain of the period.

FROM ABOVE: Leighton Crescent, axonometric; Bradwell Common, site layout

COMING TO TERMS WITH HISTORY

The Minster Lovell conference centre was the first Cullinan building to achieve wide critical attention and it remains an icon of the art of combining old and new. Minster Lovell established Cullinan's reputation for sensitively combining old and new. It led to many commissions for what he calls 'holy places'. Equally, it set a stamp on Cullinan which has proved a mixed blessing for the practice in subsequent years – that its architecture is, above all else, 'contextual'. Intended as a term of approval, 'contextual' has become a jaded concept, sullied by its implications of deference, compromise and timidity (none of which is in tune with Cullinan's architecture). Yet Minster Lovell was a far more radical project than it seems at first sight – and could have been more radical, had not the planners intervened.

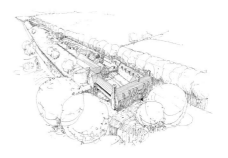

The commission coincided with Cullinan's departure from the Lasdun office and allowed him to set up his own practice and employ staff. Lasdun had, in fact, originally been approached (in 1965) with a view to taking on the job: 'I was offered the job, but decided against it, so I gave Ted his chance', Lasdun says, 'I believe that you should send people from your office with a blessing – and a building'.

The client at Minster Lovell (completed in 1976) was Tony Ambrose, who had inherited a fortune made in the concrete business and wanted to turn his childhood home (a former mill on the river Windrush, deep in the Cotswolds) into a residential conference and study centre for his private educational foundation. In this venture, he was helped by a charismatic Oxford doctor, Kit Ounstead. Cullinan was asked to convert the existing house, barn and malthouse as communal spaces and add a number of bedrooms in new additions. His first scheme for the new buildings was a restatement, in effect, of the principles behind the Lasdun 'ziggurat' residential blocks at UEA – the approach was completely modern and in striking contrast to the existing buildings. A lecture theatre was housed in a circular structure, clearly Corbusian in inspiration. The local planners were not impressed and the scheme had to be greatly revised – Julian Bicknell joined Julyan Wickham in the Cullinan office at this time and played a key role in this process. The redesigned conference centre was an almost seamless mix of old and new, the new embracing and extending the old, faced in recycled Cotswold stone with stone slate roofs. Cullinan saw it as a natural extension of the village of Minster Lovell and added to the old buildings in a completely unselfconscious way, creating 'a place to be in and move through'. Cullinan argues that Minster Lovell is 'terrifically disciplined – there are simply no literal uses of the Cotswold vernacular'. Inside, of course, the buildings, both new and converted, are full of Cullinan devices – including stepped sections and inhabited roofs:

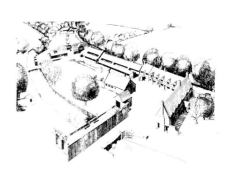

Minster Lovell, cloister

designed for flexibility and movement. Ounstead encouraged Cullinan to think about routes and about the balance between communal activity and privacy. The results were anything but traditional: the spatial qualities were entirely modern. The plan was skilfully resolved, turning a diverse group of buildings into a unity, a sort of lattice with more than one way to every part. But the external image of the scheme was to strike a chord with a public disenchanted with Modernism, and, rightly or wrongly, Minster Lovell had a strong influence on the evolution of the neo-vernacular style of the 1970s.

The motives behind this movement of taste were mixed. There was much in the architecture of the 1960s, especially in the fields of housing and commercial development, that justified the public reaction against Modernism. Yet there was also an element of unthinking nostalgia, a yearning for an ill-remembered past. Cullinan has always deplored this way of thinking: 'The strange thing about a living tradition in architecture', he declared in 1984, at the time of the Prince of Wales' first interventions into the realm of architecture, 'is that it needs to be inventive and energetic, to be liberating, to respond to the present, to create futures – quite the opposite of the debased use of the word "traditional" to mean "nostalgic".'

Recovering in hospital from his serious skiing accident, Cullinan was cheered by a visit from Julyan Wickham, who brought good news. James Stirling, having won a commission from Olivetti for a major new training centre at Haslemere in Surrey, had invited Edward Cullinan Architects to collaborate with him. The job had arisen through a chance conversation at a party, where Wickham was introduced to Stirling by Eldred Evans, a mutual friend. Stirling asked how much work the Cullinan office had in hand. It emerged that he did not relish the task of converting a large late Victorian house which formed part of the Olivetti site – would Cullinan take it on? The conversion (completed in 1972) linked the old house to the new buildings, creating circulation routes, and adding light, glazed elements to the solid core to rationalise what had been a rambling and inconvenient plan. The principles were essentially those of Minster Lovell. (Olivetti, in fact, became Cullinan's main client over the next few years, commissioning four new buildings.)

Minster Lovell had been acclaimed as a model of the marriage of old and new from the time of its completion and the European Architectural Heritage Year Award it received in 1975 reinforced its iconic status. When the parish church of St Mary, Barnes, was half-destroyed by fire in June 1978, Edward Cullinan Architects might have seemed the ideal practice to undertake its rebuilding. Although St Mary's was basically an ancient village church and retained a fine seventeenth-century brick tower, it had been more or less submerged under a dull, late Victorian rebuilding by the largely unknown Charles Innes. Not even the Victorian Society wanted to retain the Innes work in the post-fire reconstruction. Indeed, a prominent member of the society's committee, the architectural historian Dr Roger Dixon, was an active parishioner chairing the rebuilding committee up to the time of his early death, and was to prove a good ally to Cullinan. Yet there were some in the parish who wanted a literal reconstruction and the Barnes job was to prove one of the most difficult the office ever faced. It produced one of Cullinan's finest buildings, one which (he says) 'takes a complicated built history and powerful local feeling as inspiration, not as encouragement to nostalgia and pastiche'.

Ted Cullinan recalls the interview for the commission – some thirty architects had been initially listed. Faced by a committee chaired by the vicar, the Reverend Basil Whitworth (an idiosyncratic High Churchman of socialist leanings), Cullinan had to admit that, though raised as a Roman Catholic, he was no longer a believer. 'The vicar asked me how I saw the Beyond – I was so nervous, I assumed he was talking about the extent of the nave'. Nor had Cullinan ever built a church, though he had worked on an abortive scheme for one at Ashford and had carried out repair work at St John's, Downshire Hill, Hampstead. But he was appointed – to his considerable surprise – and rebuilt Barnes with Mark Beedle and Alan Short. The Parochial Church Council (PCC) was immensely supportive, with positive ideas of its own: 'They'd decided that the Victorian additions could be sacrificed in favour of a building which was full of light and space.' But opposition to this idea was swift to move into action: 'There were terrible arguments – so many meetings where we were attacked as vandals, screamed at and cursed', says Cullinan. Sir John Betjeman, the Poet Laureate, was persuaded to join the anti-Cullinan camp and published a poem attacking the proposals. The rebuilding plans had to have the approval of no fewer than eleven bodies, ranging from the PCC to the Southwark Diocesan Advisory Committee, the Greater London Council, Royal Fine Art Commission and, of course, the local planning committee. Every national amenity society was assiduously consulted, though the conservationists were reassured by an undertaking that every surviving pre-nineteenth-century element would be preserved, and that the new church would be sited to the north of the old and be invisible from the street.

When Innes rebuilt St Mary's in the 1900s he simply added a new church, on the conventional nave and chancel plan, alongside the old (which was reduced to the status of an aisle). Basil Whitworth and the PCC wanted a church which reflected the new approach to the liturgy stemming from the Second Vatican Council (which had implied a breakdown of the division between priest and people). The altar was to be clearly visible, with the chance for the congregation to gather round it, rather than isolated at the far end of a chancel, and balanced by provision for reading and preaching. Better facilities for the congregation and clergy were needed – vestries, meeting rooms, lavatories: the church was seen as a place to use daily and not just for a few hours on Sundays.

The opposition at Barnes was ill-tempered and (on the whole) ill-informed; Cullinan and colleagues went home from some of the public meetings feeling shaken, but the process of consultation and debate probably produced a better building. Cullinan's first ideas were for a new church running north from the old, on the site of the Innes additions. This large, square building would have featured a striking

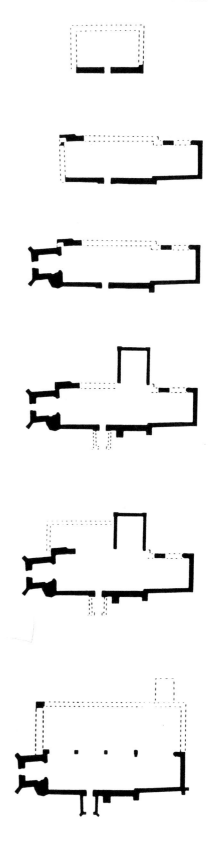

FROM ABOVE: Plans of St Mary's Church, Barnes, through the centuries

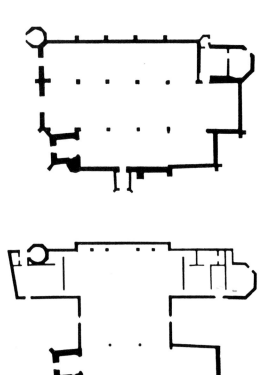

FROM ABOVE: Plans of St Mary's Church, Barnes, through the centuries; interior of St Mary's

roofline, its drama deriving in part from the presence of big solar collectors. 'Nobody seemed to like that idea much', says Cullinan, though he personally felt it was the right solution: 'My son, who was ten at the time, said to me, when he heard that we'd dropped that idea: "dad, you gave in." It really hurt.' The architects explored a less radical approach, working within the gutted walls – a tactic intended, perhaps, to galvanise the support for a radical rebuilding. What was eventually built was both radical and 'contextual'. The plan was emphatically modern, yet the great new roof which dominated the interior contained memories of the English vernacular tradition – of the great barns which inspired William Morris, and of America's West Coast (specifically, Bernard Maybeck's Christian Science Church at Berkeley). Externally, the roof reads as a vast, over-sailing canopy that embraces the retained old church and sweeps across the appended vestries and meeting rooms – 'Pitched roofs were reassuring to people', Mark Beedle comments. The key to the roof structure is the use of long-span trusses which sit on two new columns. At the suggestion of Roger Dixon (then terminally ill), these columns replicated their fire-damaged predecessors. Responding to a request from the PCC, Cullinan retained and reset the original east window as a backcloth to the altar, while other Gothic Revival fragments created an interesting palimpsest around the vestries. All these historicist elements could have compromised the integrity of the new work, yet they read as part of a dialogue between old and new and help to tie the new building into the old church. Despite the strength of the opposition and the sad death of Dixon (he was replaced by Roger Squire, a property developer and architectural enthusiast), the scheme was carried out in full, and Cullinan was commissioned to design all the furnishings. Mark Beedle still attends to the church, carrying out the requisite quinquennial inspections.

The interior of Barnes church is, says Beedle, 'a wonderfully subversive space'. It is not conventionally religious and certainly not numinous (in the way that Corbusier's Ronchamp – which the young Ted Cullinan had cycled through France to see – is numinous). It is cool and rational; perhaps puritan, rather than catholic (though, in the post-Vatican II world, such distinctions have become less meaningful). It is, without question, beautifully crafted. The building has transformed parish life; congregations have grown and the church is regularly used for concerts because of its excellent acoustics. Appropriately enough, Basil Whitworth, Cullinan's firm supporter who died shortly after leaving office, was later succeeded by a young priest, Richard Ames-Lewis, who had originally trained as an architect at Cambridge. His tutor there had been Ted Cullinan.

While Barnes was being designed, the Cullinan office was invited (in 1979) to enter a limited competition for a new residential block at Worcester College, Oxford. The site was close to the lake which straddles the college which comprises a mix of fairly modest medieval buildings and rather grand early Georgian ones on the edge of the historic centre of Oxford and close to the railway station. The building was to function as a normal part of the college, but (with an eye to out-of-term conference letting) it had equally to work as a self-contained unit with a separate entrance from the town. The original intention was to commission a new building from the firm of Phippen, Randall & Parkes, which had already completed other work for Worcester. The promise of extra funding from the Sainsbury family encouraged the college to set up a limited competition, with Cullinan, Arup Associates, MacCormac & Jamieson and David Thurlow invited to present their ideas alongside those of Phippen et al. MacCormac & Jamieson won the competition – this was the first of a series of Oxbridge buildings by their practice – but Edward Cullinan Architects' proposal remains one of the most significant and most influential of their unbuilt projects.

'Worcester was a lovely scheme', says Ted (using one of his favourite adjectives): while Arup envisaged the new building as 'an object in the landscape' and MacCormac took his inspiration from the spreading house plans of Frank Lloyd Wright, Cullinan (working with Sunand Prasad) was, in some ways, more conservative and proposed to create a new quadrangle for the college. This approach was, however, entirely logical – it provided for the development to be split into two distinct phases, and would have given Worcester a modern equivalent to the tight, intense spaces found in some of the more glamorous Oxford colleges. It offered a rational transition between the institution's verdant grounds and the workaday streets beyond, addressing both with equal conviction and, by implication, criticising the rigid town/gown division. (The mix of materials, typical Oxford stone and ordinary local brick, emphasised the determination of the architects to address not only the college but also its urban context.) Cullinan's rationalism was tempered by a strong dose of romanticism – the scheme rejected the relative uniformity and symmetry of some of the other competition entries in favour of variety and incident. The study bedrooms were to be in groups of six (like the rooms of a family house) with shared communal spaces. Most had window views in more than one direction. But the essence of the Cullinan scheme was its use of the tower theme. As the buildings rose from the cloistered surround of the quadrangle, they would have become very recognisable towers, where residents would enjoy wonderful views and have access to rooftop terraces. Although beautifully planned and 100 per cent practical, the proposals were probably too romantic to gain acceptance, yet they represented a logical development of the concept underlying Lasdun's UEA residences and reflected Cullinan's intense dislike of conventional institutional design. For Cullinan, the individual always has to have a place, whether he or she is rich or poor, young or old, healthy or not. The Worcester College scheme would have been an important contribution to the discussion on tradition which gained momentum during the 1980s. MacCormac's Sainsbury Building, which was constructed as a result of the competition, has its own qualities, not least a close empathy with the landscape, but it is significant that his later Oxford buildings, including the additions to St John's and Wadham, break away from the Worcester formula and make use of the tower motif.

Worcester College, Oxford, new quadrangle

MINDS AND BODIES

The Lambeth Community Care Centre, completed in 1985, is another landmark in the history of the Cullinan office. The building, which contains clear echoes of the unbuilt Worcester College proposal (not least in the use of flat roofs as open-air rooms), challenged conventional notions of institutional design and equally embodied a view of society diametrically opposed to that of the ruling Thatcher government. Mrs Thatcher had stated unequivocally that 'there is no such thing as society' – there were only individuals. But how should those individuals be treated, if they lacked the means to buy health care (as the government believed they should)? Ted Cullinan's response was clear; he wanted to make a special place for the sick, whoever they were.

The Lambeth project (the introduction came about through Ted Cullinan's doctor-brother) was the first major contribution by Robin Nicholson, who had joined the office in 1979. A Cambridge graduate – the Cambridge/AA nexus was still strong – Nicholson had previously worked with James Stirling. The project overlapped with Barnes church and with Nelson (later known as Beechwood) Lodge at Basingstoke ('Basingstoke and Lambeth were virtually brother and sister', says Nicholson.) The commission came about as a result of major changes in the organisation of the National Health Service. Community Health Councils (CHCs) had been set up in the early 1970s and, under the Labour government, were given enhanced powers over the care provisions in their areas. When the closure of the dismal Victorian pile that was the old Lambeth Hospital was proposed, there were few local objections. Serious cases would in future be treated at St Thomas's, a major teaching hospital only a mile or two distant. But there were other patients (not yet accorded the unctuous, post-Thatcher title of 'customers') who, while not critically ill or needing surgery, did require constant care – the infirm elderly, for example, or people recovering from major operations and not fit to look after themselves. Local general practitioners also wanted a centre where physiotherapy and other forms of therapy could be economically provided in one place, close to the homes of their patients.

The Lambeth Centre happened because local GPs and other community activists fought for it, and because the architects helped them to develop their ideas of what was needed. Edward Cullinan Architects was not a practice known for expertise in health care buildings – indeed, it had no experience in that field whatsoever. But neither had Berthold Lubetkin when he took on the commission for the Finsbury Health Centre, that 'icon of social deliverance' (as Lubetkin's biographer, John Allan, describes the building). If anything, inexperience, and

FROM ABOVE: Lambeth Community Care Centre, site from the north; model

the resulting freedom from preconceptions and well-worn formulae, seemed an advantage to the Lambeth clients.

'The NHS establishment probably hated the ideas behind Lambeth', says Nicholson. But Sir George Young, the minister responsible, backed the project, which moved steadily forward. 'It was soon after the Toxteth riots', says Cullinan, 'I think the government was really worried about the inner cities'. Inner-city funding came to Lambeth: 'We had to go and talk to nurses, who were far more used to listening than talking', Nicholson recalls. Nurses, therapists, and CHC representatives (led by Sue Thorne) joined the local GPs in regular meetings between 1980-82 with the architects, who spent a lot of time just listening and drawing, sketching out ideas for the building in the usual Cullinan way. When a first scheme was produced (in September 1981) it was criticised for its over-rigid, symmetrical plan and separation of functions. A drawing by Ted Cullinan suggested ways in which these problems could be addressed. Six months of work – consultation, discussion, and a rapid reduction in the overall size of the building when funding was cut – produced the final scheme as built.

The Lambeth Centre stands in a nondescript south London street: there is no obvious context, save for the prevailing vernacular of London stock brick. The former nurses' home of the Lambeth Hospital survives next door as offices; the rest has been razed. The main street front, where a superstructure of glass and steel emerges from a solid brick base, is instantly recognisable as a Cullinan design. The great glazed entrance canopy is a striking, perhaps exaggerated, gesture. (Locals claim that it is even now occasionally mistaken for a filling station!) Inside, day-care facilities are located on the ground floor, with wards for in-patients above. The long, straight corridors found in old-style hospitals have been dispensed with, instead favouring more irregular spaces which flow through large openings into the wards. The balance between communal and private space is crucial – this was an issue Cullinan had addressed at Minster Lovell. In one private ward, a person may be near death; across the way, a small ward of elderly people do not want to feel shut away – they want to communicate with the people passing by. Of course, the Lambeth Care Centre is a typically Cullinan 'inside/out' building. Pulling the top floor back on plan allows for a broad terrace overlooking the garden.

The garden is a work of art in itself. Wonderfully maintained by a first-rate gardener – via a generous endowment and the support of volunteers – it is complex, varied, compartmented, and very English; a Sissinghurst for south London. The building opens up to it and the contours are skilfully used to create routes around it for wheelchairs.

The centre is a resource not just for the sick, but for the local community more generally. Local people value and support it, and use it as an educational and social resource – the sick are embraced by the wider community, not shut away. In contrast to most modern health care buildings, it promotes integration rather than segregation. Its success results from a process of consultation, from which both brief and design emerged. Is it then an example of 'community architecture'?

FROM ABOVE: Lambeth Community Care Centre, the building opens on to the garden; the mature garden

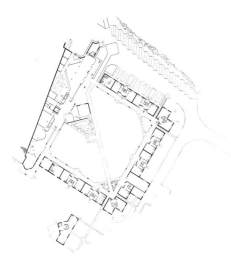

Ted Cullinan hates the term: 'it's too often an excuse for third-rate design', he insists, 'the architecture wasn't generated in some mysterious way from the dialogue with the client. We got to understand their needs and then produced our ideas.' Robin Nicholson speaks of 'low-key solutions to difficult problems'. There is a simplicity and directness about the Lambeth Centre which is not compromised by the 'eagerness' and over-detailing which the critic Peter Buchanan (author of a generally laudatory review) saw in the building. It is an intensely enjoyable, highly durable community resource, which has worn well over the last decade and looks set to serve Lambeth well for many decades yet. It is a worthy successor to Lubetkin's Finsbury building.

Beechwood Lodge represents a rare intrusion of distinctly 'social' architecture into the bland commercial landscape of the new Basingstoke. Admittedly, it is discreetly sited (next to a West Indian social club): a recent commercial block looms over it, discharging the effluent from its air conditioning system at the residents with arrogant disdain. But it seems amazing that it is there at all – how could a residential hostel for homeless men be allowed to exist in this corporate preserve? The answer is that many of the men were amongst the builders of the twentieth-century corporate Basingstoke, and were employed in the construction industry. The institution came into existence as a hostel for building workers and developed into a hostel for homeless men of all trades (and none), housed in a ramshackle collection of huts, replaced by the Cullinan building. Many of the residents are long-term unemployed, the rejects of the corporate society. Some are disabled, others have spent periods in mental hospitals. About half are constant residents, the rest stay for a couple of nights or a week. Cullinan's client was the Stonham Housing Association, which took over the site from the local authority. The brief was for 100 bedrooms, plus communal facilities.

The Cullinan office launched into the project in its usual critical spirit. The social – and, by implication, political – agenda was obvious: 'We aimed to make the building pleasurable and connected, rather than utilitarian and compartmented', the Cullinan team commented in the *Architects' Journal*. Instead of thinking of the building as a hostel, it was envisaged as 'some houses and a hotel'. The form of the scheme, a quadrangle with towers, has clear analogies with the Worcester College project and there are links too with the Nationwide Building Society conference centre, a concurrent project. The architects were clearly uneasy at the very idea of an 'institution', with its implications of control and dependency. Fortunately, the clients shared this view and the scheme was developed in close liaison with them.

The 'hotel' is a five-storey block set up against the road – partly to shield the site but equally to advertise the presence of the place – and containing the communal facilities and reception area. The accommodation in this block is consciously designed to avoid the institutional effect of long corridors and uniform cell-like rooms and to give residents their own territory. All the bedrooms face into the quadrangle

FROM ABOVE: Beechwood Lodge, 'covered way' and residents; plan

varying widely in size and shape, with special provisions for the disabled. The remaining three sides of the quadrangle contain nine shared houses for long-term residents – these were designed to be occupied by family groups, should a new pattern of demand emerge, but equally there was the intention that the people occupying the houses would hopefully become supportive 'families' of a sort. Three-storey pavilions mark the corners of the quadrangle – they may seem an arbitrary gesture, but they are special places, like the towers at Worcester – why should homeless men not have spaces as special as those given to Oxford undergraduates?

In an assessment of the building, written in 1987 when it was new, Jeremy Seabrook commented: 'homeless men . . . are rarely accommodated in such a clearly cherishing environment.' Seabrook wrote of 'the concern for the people that lies behind the new building; the aesthetic and spiritual, as well as the more sternly material, impulse behind it' but mused on what the architecture signified. 'The style of the building', he continued, 'is such that it will not strike the people of Basingstoke as representing excessive comfort or luxury.'

The aesthetic of Beechwood Lodge is, in fact, spare, lean, expressive. The usual Cullinan contrast between solidity and lightness, structure and superstructure, is there in the contrast between brick and render, steel and glass. But the steelwork is used with a degree of bravado uncommon even by Cullinan standards. The metal roof of the 'hotel' block almost takes off; those on the corner pavilions have an equally aeronautical look. The roof structures are economically done – aluminium cladding on timber rafters – and sparingly detailed. The roofs at Beechwood Lodge provide an object lesson in economy and elegance, but they are far more than functional. There was much talk in the 1980s about the emergence of a 'free spirit' in architecture: this is surely the spirit behind Beechwood Lodge. Like Bernard Tschumi, Frank Gehry and Zaha Hadid, Cullinan draws on history – De Stijl and Purism especially – and transfigures it in a specifically late twentieth-century way. Beechwood Lodge is a work of art which works hard to earn its keep: the two are not mutually exclusive – 'social' architecture can be innovative and beautiful. It should have been the first of many such buildings in Britain's towns and cities, but there were, it seems, higher priorities in 1980s Britain than housing the homeless.

The Architectural Review, February 1985, contained an enthusiastic review of 'two school refurbishments in Hampshire'. The Hampshire schools in question were Winchester College – one of the two or three most prestigious and ancient public schools in England – and the less famous (and not at all ancient) Calthorpe Park secondary school at Fleet. Calthorpe school was not a Minster Lovell or a Barnes, a fine old building needing extension and restructuring to meet present-day needs, but a mundane 1960s structure, built on the SCOLA system, with flat roofs and timber clad walls, like 200 other schools of the period. After little more than twenty years, the roof of the three-storey science block was leaking, and the cladding had rotted because the original materials

Beechwood Lodge

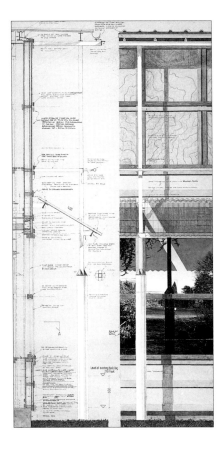

Sheltering a 1960s system-built school

had been of poor quality, and used with little thought as to maintenance. Lack of insulation was a particular problem: the building was often very hot in summer and expensive to heat in winter. It posed a problem both for users and for the education authority; demolition was out of the question, but Edward Cullinan Architects was asked by Hampshire's renowned county architect, Colin Stansfield-Smith, to give Calthorpe a new lease of life. The science block had to be upgraded, and new blocks for teaching drama and mathematics were to be added.

'This was the secondary school for "Silicon Valley"', says Ted Cullinan. 'I recalled Californian high schools set in acres of car park – here there were bicycle racks for a thousand!' Cullinan's transformation of Calthorpe was far more than functional: the look of the place was radically altered: it became somewhere very special.

Practically deficient as the 1960s block was, Cullinan saw some merit in its undemonstrative minimalism. 'We needed to humanise the box', says Mark Beedle, 'and we also wanted to give it more complexity and depth.' What was done was quite simple: a new roof, an insulated 'umbrella', was constructed over the 1960s flat roof, with a generous overhang to provide shading and protection from rain. The two lower floors were also given canopies to protect the surface of the building from the weather. All this was supported on a new steel frame standing outside the original cladding. The result: 'like moving the school to Spain', says Ted Cullinan. In summer and winter, conditions inside the building are pleasant, and running costs have been slashed.

The new blocks are designed to be in keeping with the existing buildings. The budget for them was not great, but the architects were naturally anxious to avoid the mistakes of the past, laying up problems for future generations. Thus the relatively cheap cladding and glazing system is protected by a bold framework of steel, supporting oversailing roofs. The new buildings have a classic elegance lacking in the refurbished block, but the harmony of the site has been maintained. The Calthorpe scheme offers significant insights into the issue of coming to terms with the legacy of 1960s Modernism and revitalising buildings which, though of ordinary quality, have plenty of life left in them.

At Winchester, the issue was rather different. The college dates back to the fourteenth century; at its centre is William of Wykeham's splendid chapel and cloister, at the heart of a dense collection of historic buildings which backs on to Kingsgate Street. Behind lies the college meadow (known simply as Meads), a lovely place which seems to merge into the country beyond. Deliberately tucked away in a backwater off the meadow were the former gymnasium and sanatorium, both the work of the highly original Victorian architect William White: these were to be converted into the school's drama and art departments. Winchester had a headmaster, John Thorn, who placed great value on the arts; the old tradition that no Wykehamist should waste his time on anything as frivolous as art or music, was being challenged. Cullinan has always admired the work of the Victorian Goths – Burges, Street, Butterfield – and warmed to White's tough polychromatic style.

The theatre came first (in 1982-83, with the new art school completed in 1985), formed from the old gymnasium – a relatively straightforward job which prefigured the more elaborate studio theatre at Carshalton. The bare interior of the old gym was made into an effective, intimate auditorium. The former sanatorium consisted of two almost parallel blocks (strictly separated to avoid infection), Gothic in style and free in composition. Sometime during the 1950s, the two blocks had been joined by a mean single-storey structure, little more than a hut. Clearly, the blocks had somehow to be linked to suit them to their new role, but the existing hut was quite unworthy. They were listed buildings and the way in which any new link was achieved might have been a matter for considerable debate. Luckily, the local planners were highly supportive.

The link between the two blocks takes the form of a bridge at first floor level, but it is not a functional bridge any more than the Bridge of Sighs in Venice is 'functional'. It takes the form, in effect, of a small, cubic building, standing on steel legs, joined at each side by a passageway. The whole space is used as a gallery. The cube has a lofty gabled roof, metal-clad. Cube and linking passages are clad in metal-framed ceramic tiles which take up the polychromatic theme of the White buildings. A new path passes under the bridge between Kingsgate Street and Meads, crossing the ground-level route between the two blocks. At the crossing point, there is a gathering place, with seats under cover. The interiors of the White buildings have been radically, but not unsympathetically, remodelled. Much of the ground floor of the north block is used as further gallery space, plus office, lecture room and library. Upstairs, printing studios flank a painting studio. In the south block, potters and sculptors are downstairs, with more painters above; the two floors are joined by a spiral stair. The top studios are spectacular: the plastered ceilings were removed to expose White's fine roof structures and the gables filled with glass to increase light levels. An orthodox Modernist might worry about the way in which these large glazed areas are treated, but Cullinan had no qualms and introduced a form of geometrical wooden tracery which might almost be High Victorian. Never willing to miss an opportunity for a piece of visual wit, the architects contrived a 'shadow' on the west wall of the bridge which corresponds (it is claimed) with the shadow cast by the setting sun on Midsummer Day. Cullinan's libertarian spirit also emerged in the tractor seats attached to the corner staircases used by pupils – a place for a surreptitious cigarette? Perhaps not, but they were soon removed: frivolity is apparently still frowned on at Winchester.

In contrast to these refurbishment and extension projects, Farnborough Grange Primary School, built in 1989-90, also in Hampshire, was completely new. The existing 1960s building had been judged beyond economic repair and was demolished. Ted Cullinan sees the new school as a fusion between ideas which go back to his early houses, and the inspired contributions of his partner, Sasha Bhavan. The school is a spreading single-storey structure containing eight classrooms, plus library, music room, hall/dining room and administrative offices. The first impression gained here is of a remarkable, almost attenuated elegance – recalling the best schools of the 1930s (like Oliver Hill's

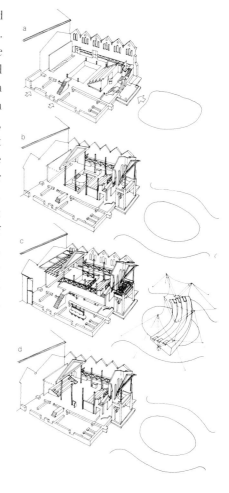

Winchester theatre development

Farnborough Grange primary school

Whitwood Mere). The classrooms fan out in symmetrical wings facing south, making good use of passive solar gain. They have large doors which can be thrown open in fine weather and glazing at ground and clerestory level – the overhanging roof provides the necessary shade. The mix of timber, steel and glass contrasts with the solid brick facades to the north. A typical Cullinan touch is provided by the staff room, hidden away in a little tower up a circular staircase away from the children. It provides a welcome sanctuary for the teachers, who have access to a small balcony in fine weather. And it is used: a random visit revealed an off-duty teacher quietly reading the paper and enjoying a mid-morning coffee and bun.

RETHINKING THE WORKPLACE

Ted Cullinan quotes with approval the words of William Morris on the dignity and purpose of labour:

> let us work like good fellows trying by some dim candlelight to set out a workshop ready against tomorrow's daylight – that tomorrow, when the civilised world, no longer greedy, strifeful and destructive, shall have a new art, a glorious art, made by the people and for the people, as a happiness to the maker and the user. (*Arts of the People*, 1879)

Morris had in mind not the wage-slaves of the Victorian factory system, but the free craftsmen whom he saw as the foundation of a better society. The factory system (as Morris knew it) is dead, but the capitalism of the late twentieth century, superficially benign, is corporate, faceless, global. Cullinan, libertarian socialist though he is, has never eschewed commercial work. He is happy to work with major companies who recognise that better workplaces mean happier workers – and better results. Yet all his best work in this field has resulted from a close dialogue with the clients – in the person of creative individuals, not faceless boards.

The various schemes for Olivetti which followed on from the Haslemere training centre between 1969-73, were produced in consultation with one of these inspired clients, Carlo Alhadeff. A number of the commissions were for conversions, the best-known of an elegant early nineteenth-century chapel in Hove. The Olivetti branch offices in Dundee, Derby, Carlisle and Belfast were new-build, and all built on a system. In each case, the structure consisted of a solid base of concrete, housing services and parking. The main floor sat on top, with offices, showrooms and workshops, and was constructed from a 'kit of parts', consisting of steel and wood. A U-shaped plan was employed in each case. These were straightforward, cheap buildings, designed for unprepossessing sites on industrial estates or ring roads. They have the raw elegance of early Cullinan – with an aggressive edge which suggests the influence of Stirling alongside more usual Cullinan sources. A distinctive feature of the buildings was the area set aside for the workers to meet, relax and eat in their breaks – this was not hidden away but located close to the main entrance used by customers: a typical Cullinan move.

The projects which Edward Cullinan Architects undertook for the MacIntyre organisation, a charity which set out 'to provide a creative, purposeful and dignified way of life for mentally handicapped children and adults', could be classified as educational or therapeutic in function. The architects, however, tackled them as workplaces – the essence of the MacIntyre approach is integration, allowing people to do 'real'

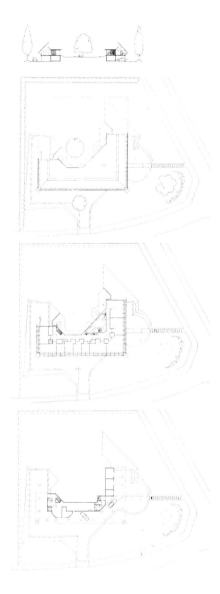

Olivetti at Dundee, section and plans

jobs. MacIntyre acquired Westoning Manor, Bedfordshire, and the approach to Cullinan came through a fellow architect, the late Theo Crosby, the charity's chairman at the time. The existing house was to become the centre of a complex of residential buildings and workshops, ranged around a quadrangle. Cullinan's new buildings are externally discreet, but the workshop has an elegant, light-filled interior which is made for serious work. There is not a whiff of 'institution' about Westoning.

The MacIntyre development at Great Holm, Milton Keynes (opened in 1988), was the charity's most ambitious project. The brief to Cullinan provided for three shared houses for thirty-six residents, and a community building which became known as the 'Moot Hall'. The houses are quite simple but their integrity stands out amid the routine new housing of Milton Keynes with its superficially 'vernacular' dress. They stand on sloping ground, with entrances at two levels. The Moot Hall block is altogether more ambitious. The hall itself, the centre of the Great Holm community, is at its hub, but there are also studios and a bakery, serving a cafe and shop which are open to the public. Because of the fall in the site, a lower ground floor level can be utilised as workshops and garden centre. The steel frame, timber clad and supporting a pitched, tile-covered roof, rises above – the 'bird's nest' over the 'cave' There are memories of Scandinavia, as well as West Coast America in the extravagant sweep of the roof towards the great 'beak' – or is it a 'prow'? – which faces the street. The interior of the building is white, light, slender, calm; yet it is a place for activity. The top-floor weaving studio is a particularly successful and purposeful space.

The Uplands conference and training centre at Hughenden, High Wycombe (completed for the Nationwide Building Society in 1984) is, in effect, a residential college, though its teaching is strictly linked to the practical commercial operations of Nationwide. The initial discussions with the clients took place in 1979. The practice was probably chosen because the project involved retaining, converting and extending an existing historic building – a 'Gothick' house which looks c1800 but is actually of 1859. Though the client saw the centre as a very serious workplace, the architects were determined that there should also be a clear element of enjoyment. Socialising and relaxing, they argued, were important to the success of the events taking place there. Tony Peake played an important role in the scheme: he had come to Cullinan from Evans & Shalev and had a justly deserved reputation as a good organiser and strategic thinker, though his vision of architecture was perhaps less radical than Ted Cullinan's.

Nationwide was, in fact, prepared to think quite radically, since they particularly wanted a low-energy building that was economical to run. They responded positively to Cullinan's notion that the centre should have something of the character of a university, a place with character and identity which would inspire the employees who stayed there. The completed scheme is finely balanced between formality and informality, expressiveness and discipline. (Cullinan wonders whether the formal mood should not have been broken by placing one of the enc pavilions at an angle.) It is radical, rigorous and completely modern, but very much rooted in the site and in the landscape around it.

The old house remains the centre of Uplands. It was completely refurbished inside with an eclectic mix (largely chosen by Ros Cullinan) of Morris papers and fabrics and classic Modern Movement furniture. A wing was pushed out at the back to contain the reception area and new staircase, certainly a place for socialising with its ample supply of places to sit and chat. The visitor enters the centre from the car park on the side, passing along a covered cloister which forms the main axis of the whole complex and joins the house to the new, symmetrical wings. The new buildings are generally two storeys high, building up to four in the corner pavilions which frame the front elevation. The section provides for rooftop terraces and the materials; timber, steel and glass on top of a mix of rubble and red brick, expresses the process of growth and accretion. The detailing is consistent and sharp: 'dainty' is Mark Beedle's description. Uplands, looked at in plan, is undeniably highly formal – the idea of the wings is Palladian in concept – but it does not *feel* formal. It is very English – 'of the soil' – yet not obviously historicist or referential. It has worn well – indeed, it has matured – the Cullinan buildings now seem a more natural part of the site than the Victorian house. The control which the architects (working with the landscape architect Georgina Livingston) were given over the setting has paid off, and buildings and gardens form a happy totality. Here is a truly modern place, designed with the user in mind and with a strong concern for context but quite lacking in sentimentality or nostalgia. It exemplifies the Cullinan office on top form.

As much might be said of the RMC headquarters at Egham, Surrey (built in 1988-90). Edward Cullinan Architects was approached by RMC – the world's largest concrete company – after various development options had been explored and a number of architects interviewed. The site had come to RMC with adjoining land which had been excavated for gravel pits. There were two old houses there: Eastley End House, early Georgian with a substantial Victorian stable block known as Meadlake House, and The Grange, a pretty Arts and Crafts house of the 1900s. RMC had used these buildings as a conference centre but eventually decided to develop the site as its new headquarters. The proposal flew in the face of local planning policies: compromised as the site was by gravel digging, it was nonetheless in the green belt. A public inquiry had to be won before the plans could proceed, and RMC saw that its case would be strengthened if the development proposals were of special quality. With this in mind, it asked William Whitfield, a respected senior architect and member of the Royal Fine Art Commission, to suggest some suitable names. That of Edward Cullinan Architects was among them.

'I sketched out the scheme the first day I went down there', says Ted Cullinan, 'It was clearly a matter of respecting the old houses and giving them some kind of meaningful setting'. New buildings obviously had to be low-rise and the client was anxious to keep energy costs to a minimum. The ideas behind the scheme emerged from these requirements.

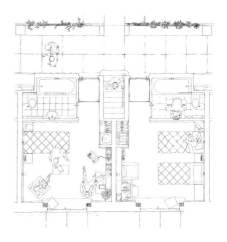

Uplands Conference Centre, part plan, study bedrooms

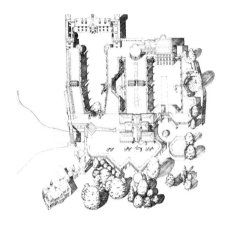

Ted Cullinan is famous for his ability to charm and enthuse clients. Having sailed through the interview and won the job, he formed an amicable relationship with John Camden, then RMC's chairman. Camden was a forthright conservative in political terms, but the two men got on well from the start and Cullinan got the backing he needed to realise the scheme. 'I stressed the gardenesque aspects', he says, 'Gardens are the way to an Englishman's heart – they help you to get quite radical ideas across.' RMC is, in some ways, far from radical: the organisation is very hierarchical – separate dining rooms for directors, executives and the rank and file of the staff were considered essential. Eastley End House was, in fact, fitted out expensively, in a highly conservative taste, as a sanctum for the directors. The house is given a formal setting in a grassed court focused on a rectangular pool and enclosed by part of the new single storey offices, 3,500 square metres of them. Two further courts, the larger of them addressing Meadlake House, punctuate and light the office floors. The offices are covered with a huge roof garden which allows them to blend into the surrounding landscape. The executive dining rooms break though from below to look across to the more exclusive directors' dining room opposite – doubtless an encouragement to those with aspirations to promotion – but planting, pergolas and 'follies' (like the famous chess piece ventilators) provide visual interest and a very practical amenity for RMC's employees.

The architecture of the RMC project is wonderfully varied, exemplifying the essential quality of the scheme – creating not so much a building as an object *in* the landscape, but one which *is* the landscape. The team of architects was large, led in the latter stages of the project by Ted Cullinan, Richard Gooden and Alec Gillies, and was able to cast aside the moralising fears about 'pastiche' to 'keep in keeping' and extend the wings of Meadlake House in an entirely natural, unjokey manner. Elsewhere, the aesthetic is relaxedly modern, with a predominance of plain glass and white steel. 'In our dull climate,' argues Cullinan, 'we need to make maximum use of the precious light.' White coated steelwork provides a unifying theme across the site. In the intimate little Fern Court, lighting columns burst upwards, bearing more than a passing resemblance to the exaggerated forms of Charles Rennie Mackintosh. RMC may look episodic and picturesque, but there is a rigour behind the plan which belies superficial impressions: the scheme is an excellent illustration of Ted Cullinan's plea for a humanistic modern architecture which 'uses industrial production in the service of particularity as opposed to using its methods as a guide to an aesthetic of sameness and repetition'.

A company like RMC, hierarchical though it was, was an ideal Cullinan client. (Its sincere paternalism extended to the provision of a swimming pool and squash courts for staff, located next to the main reception area.) Working in the field of speculative commercial development, for unknown users, was harder for the practice. The Chilworth Research Centre was jointly developed by Southampton University and MEPC Development Ltd, a company whose chairman, Roger Squire, had become an important Cullinan client with the

FROM ABOVE: RMC, aerial view; offices and gardens

ebuilding of Barnes church. The Chilworth site adjoined the gardens of hilworth Manor and the formal landscape of the development takes its ue from them. There is a real sense of place, not just the usual ollection of 'units' dumped down in landscaping and parking areas. here was not the generous budget which had been available at RMC: ie six blocks are simple enough (and typical of Cullinan's approach to ich economical buildings). It is making buildings, and the space bet-een them, part of a balanced composition that makes this a real place.

MEPC was also joint developer at the Bedfont Lakes business park ear Heathrow. The master plan for the site was drawn up by Michael lopkins and Partners, who laid out the huge square (with landscaped arking areas) around which the buildings stand. These were divided etween Hopkins and Cullinan. Hopkins proved to be the antithesis of ullinan: his blocks, very much separate objects in the landscape, are legantly, if blankly covered in repetitive steel and glass cladding. The ullinan buildings are much more animated and form a unified compo-tion, a clear sequence. The facades have a brick base with white metal ladding above; the roofs are given proper weight. The corners of the locks are emphasised – a typical Cullinan device which might be aced back to Denys Lasdun's major works. The entrances are stressed o: there is no difficulty in finding the way in through human-scaled paces. Even inside, as far as the strict constraints of the brief allowed, iere has been an attempt to provide variety and identity. 'Bedfont is ery much our architecture – not a compromise', Cullinan insists, 'it's omposed with a kit of parts, like all our work.' He compares the roblems of designing speculative commercial buildings with the prob-ems the practice faced when it moved from single, one-off houses for nown clients to 'housing'. It is, Cullinan says, a matter of dealing with lients who have 'control without desire'. Their primary concern is that ie building is on time, on budget and 'lettable'. 'It's a deathly process i some ways', Cullinan concedes, 'but satisfying the criteria of the ommercial market is no worse than meeting the housing cost yard-ticks'. Cullinan's colleague, Johnny Winter, recalls 'a feeling that this /as not our kind of job. We disagreed totally with that view and set out o prove that the sceptics were wrong'. In fact, the project went without hitch and the Cullinan office showed its ability to manage a large ommercial project. 'People are people,' says Winter, 'though not nowing the end user is a challenge – one, I believe, which we esponded to well'.

The modern business park could hardly be further away from the /orld of the small craftsman evoked by William Morris. The idea of 1aking buildings for unknown users was not obviously appealing to 1e Cullinan office, but Bedfont proved that it was capable of reworking 1e corporate mould. Ted Cullinan has always derived enormous pleas-re from working with clients to get buildings right, to develop the esigns out of the brief. A distant corporate body has little time for such ne tuning. If schemes that the practice has worked on for clients of 1is sort sometimes seem to lack the passion of its best work, it isn't ard to see why.

FROM ABOVE: Chilworth, detail of solar shades; Bedfont Lakes, overview

BUILDING IN THE LANDSCAPE

Mention of Fountains Abbey takes Ted Cullinan back to his schooldays in the 1940s, when he first saw the great medieval ruin amid the mouldering landscape of Studley Royal. Studley was saved from utter dereliction to the credit, firstly, of the former West Riding County Council, which bought the park and opened it to the public, and (more recently) of the National Trust, which acquired Studley in 1983 and has developed it as its most popular property, investing large sums in restoration work. When Cullinan heard that the Trust was considering the idea of a visitor centre there, he was determined to be involved. Edward Cullinan Architects was duly interviewed (one of six practices short-listed) and subsequently appointed.

Studley Royal was laid out by two members of the Aislabie family; John and his son William. John Aislabie was sometime Chancellor of the Exchequer, and had inherited the estate *c*1699, retiring there after his political downfall in 1720. William acquired the remains of the Cistercian abbey in 1768 and incorporated them into the landscape of water and woods, of wild rocks and secluded pastures. When the National Trust acquired Studley, it did not acquire Fountains: having been a 'monument in care' in the hands of the government, the abbey had been vested in English Heritage. A car park to the west of the ruins, beyond the seventeenth-century Fountains Hall, catered for visitors. For those who wished to 'do' the landscape in the proper Georgian manner, by arriving at the abbey as the climax of the gardens, another parking area existed at the east end of Studley Royal, where the Trust provided a small tearoom and shop. With visitor numbers growing – the present figure is around 300,000 annually – parking was becoming a problem. The villagers of Studley Roger, east of the park, were complaining about the growing volume of traffic along their narrow main street. The old Fountains Abbey car park had become grossly inadequate and was approached via the narrow, winding road which was entirely unsuitable. The view in the Trust was that a radical reworking of traffic arrangements was needed and that this provided an opportunity to create a visitor centre, a new building type which had emerged at other Trust sites during the 1970s and 80s.

This period was one of massive growth for the Trust. Its membership increased from 540,000 in 1975 to 1.3 million ten years later (with a further million joining over the next decade). From its early days as a loose alliance of interested people, the Trust developed a complex system of management and decision-making. The everyday administration of its land and properties is regionalised, with powerful regional directors in charge of every aspect of the Trust's work in their areas. One of the longest-serving of the regional directors is John Garrett (in

Fountains Abbey, eighteenth-century gardens

the Yorkshire area); effectively Cullinan's client at Fountains. Policy-making and strategy are concentrated in London where the Trust's central secretariat is based. The Trust's council meets here, which in turn reflects the views of the regions through elected members, like Sir Marcus Worsley, sometime chairman of the Trust's Yorkshire Region and another player in the Fountains saga. In 1986, the chairmanship of the National Trust passed to Dame Jennifer Jenkins, something of a radical in her own right, who became closely (and generally supportively) involved in the Fountains project.

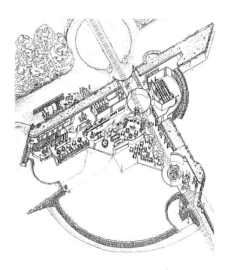

The Fountains visitor centre represented a test of the Trust's commitment to new design. Its historic buildings secretary, Martin Drury, believed that the project should go to the best contemporary architects for new buildings, and his views were endorsed by the Trust's powerful architecture panel. For others, the Cullinan building projected an image of the National Trust which they found disturbing and distasteful – many members, it was argued, joined the Trust because they loathed modern architecture.

'The opposition came from the new country people', Ted Cullinan argues, but on the other hand, the regional management of the Trust was highly supportive. Cullinan recalls exploring the projected site for the building and pointing out to John Garrett how close the tower of the abbey was, though only the top portion was visible above the trees. Determined to take traffic out of the valley, the National Trust had found a site off the main Ripon to Pateley Bridge road, on the high ground to the north of the gardens. Climb up here and you pass from a lush Arcadian world into a harsher, bleaker, almost moorland landscape. This is the landscape of the dry-stone wall, that symbol (as Cullinan once described it) of a certain sort of natural modern architecture, of buildings 'that enjoy limited means and hope for honesty, truth to materials, architecture as a democratic experience'. (Cullinan's weekend and holiday house is, significantly, in the dry-stone wall territory of the Peak District.) The access road to the new centre would necessarily pass close to the church of St Mary, built as a pious memorial to a Victorian youth murdered by Greek brigands – this fantastic and exuberant example of the work of William Burges stands yards from the obelisk erected by William Aislabie in memory of his father. (Indeed, it replaces the latter as the climax of the great avenue leading from Ripon.)

Cullinan's first scheme developed the initial idea of a building close to Abbot Huby's great tower. Arriving along the new track, the visitor would have parked in an area shrouded by woods and itself softened by extensive tree planting. The visitor centre would have straddled the path from the car park to the abbey, a compact building on a most satisfying plan. The restaurant, lavatories, and exhibition/audio visual area clustered round a circular court, repeated further on where a ticket desk marks the entry to the park. The visitor would have become aware of the presence of the tower before entering the centre, leaving the building and proceeding to the edge of the valley, the great ruin suddenly appears, albeit through a veil of foliage, and the visitor might

FROM ABOVE: Fountains Abbey, first scheme axonometric; first scheme *in situ*

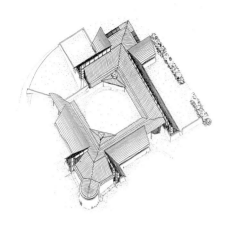

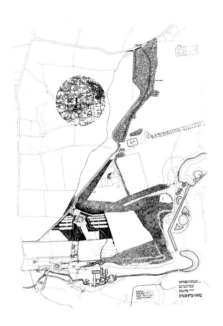

FROM ABOVE: Fountains Abbey, built scheme, axonometric; plan

sense the drama below. The architectural form of this first Fountains scheme was both forceful and delicate. The solid base is clad in dry-stone walling or sunk into the earth; the timber and steel superstructure rises above with great elegance. On the eastern elevation, the zinc-covered roofs, sail-like in form (in the spirit of Lubetkin's Dudley Zoo), erupt in flight. Lubetkin might seem an unlikely source, yet Cullinan captures the spirit of relaxation and enjoyment in a way which few British architects since the 1930s have been able to. The spirit is that of other modern architects who pursue the ideal of 'natural' building – Glenn Murcutt, Sverre Fehn, and Stanley Saitowitz, for example, as well as Cullinan's Californian masters.

Cullinan fought hard for this scheme, yet it was abandoned. The National Trust was concerned that the building might be visible on the skyline, if not from within the park, then at least from the back road to Harrogate which lies to the south. A second proposal, to develop the visitor centre around existing farm buildings northwest of the abbey, also foundered. 'There was a lot of opposition, especially from the archaeologists', says Cullinan – the farm had been a grange of the abbey during the Middle Ages. The chance of a 1980s version of Minster Lovell was thus lost. What was actually built at Fountains was Cullinan's third scheme. The site was much further back from the valley edge, so that the immediate relationship between the abbey tower and the new building was lost. Working with Alec Gillies and others, Cullinan rethought the building. What had been one block became two, confronting each other across a courtyard (or is it a cloister?). The whole scheme grew in scale to contain a large restaurant, shop, auditorium and exhibition/ticketing area. The architects wanted to cover the roofs with red clay pantiles, a material common enough in the nearby farms and villages, but local planners feared the material would be too strident, and suggested recycled stone slates instead. The architects were surprised when the National Trust caved in on the matter. ('We were simply *told* by the Trust that the roofing material had been changed', says Cullinan.) The dry-stone walls remain, as does the timber superstructure. Lead-covered roofs around the courtyard sweep and dive gently, but the consistency of the first scheme is compromised.

It is the use of stone slates which probably gives some critics the idea that Fountains is 'very English'. Cullinan is adamant that it is essentially a cosmopolitan modern building, 'free-form even', he says. 'But then the English tradition of design isn't about freedom or even enjoyment - talk about enjoyment and the English will think your work is light weight, frivolous'. The Fountains visitor centre is certainly enjoyable though there is much in it that demands a response from the users which cannot always be forthcoming. Perhaps Cullinan idealistically expects more from the National Trust and its visitors than either can give. There are times when the building seems overdone, and busy trying to kindle a spark that is not there, yet it is one of the monuments of the new humane modernism – a building which exemplifies Ted Cullinan's own tactile, sensual approach to building in tune with place. It marked a clear restatement of the intuitive, expressive Cullinan taking the opportunity to cast aside the growing formalism which had characterised much of the work of the 1980s.

The Cullinan way is to work *with* a landscape, to draw out the qualities of a place. An unexecuted project of the mid-1980s, for Copped Hall, a derelict late Georgian house close to the M25 in Essex, shows the confidence of the Cullinan approach. New single-storey, grass-roofed wings were to project from the house, while another new building was to close off the Victorian garden – famous of its kind – to the east. The scheme was not greeted with enthusiasm by the various conservation lobby groups and was never built.

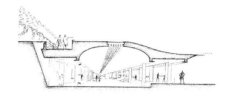

Although the Cullinan practice has been praised for its way with old buildings, its outlook is not narrowly conservationist. Indeed, Ted Cullinan himself has more than once castigated the 'heritage' lobby and criticised the constraints imposed by the planning system. 'We should protect the rights of individuals to self expression more than we protect the rights of the existing home owners to stop it', he argues.

The impact of Fountains was reflected in Cullinan's success in the invited competition to build a new visitor centre at the most famous heritage site in England; Stonehenge. The idea was first made public in 1992 – Jocelyn Stevens had become Chairman of English Heritage (which ran the site) in April of that year, and had focused attention on Stonehenge, making the construction of the visitor centre one of his prime objectives. (A Commons select committee had described the setting of Stonehenge as 'a national disgrace'.) An architectural competition was launched – twenty practices were short-listed, then six, including Edward Cullinan Architects, Dixon & Jones, Future Systems and the young but much-respected Birds, Portchmouth & Russum. The competition brief stipulated that the centre was to be sited at Larkhill Plantation, due north of the monument. From the first, it was clear to everyone involved that the entire Stonehenge site, included on the World Heritage Register and largely owned by the National Trust, needed a radical rethink. The vast majority of visitors arrived by car, turning off the main A303 London-Exeter road on to the A344, which runs disturbingly close to the stones, and entered the site through a car-park, a dismal 1970s ticket office and a foot tunnel beneath the road. The A344 was dispensable, but the A303 was earmarked for upgrading as a main route to the west. Cullinan and team found that their vision of a road-free Stonehenge struck a chord with Jocelyn Stevens and the other competition judges.

The competition-winning scheme provided for a long, low building; a shelf' scooped out of the landscape. Parking in a heavily-planted area to the north, the visitor would pass through the building on a clear axis which recalled the first Fountains scheme). Exhibition, restaurant and retail areas lay to either side along an east-west axis – and could be avoided by a visitor determined to proceed direct to the monument. The interior was arranged on a classic 'nave and aisles' plan. The south aisle' was glazed but shaded, with fine views out. That to the north was 'cave', with no view over the car park. The main space recalled in

FROM ABOVE: Arriving at Stonehenge; understanding Stonehenge

form the galleries of Louis Kahn's Kimbell. The palette of materials was rigorously chosen – high-quality concrete, oak and glass – nothing else. The building positively encouraged visitors to go outside – to ascend to the roof terrace for a splendid view of the stones or visit the external display areas.

Cullinan's scheme (again developed with Georgina Livingston) was a clear winner, but was not built. Like all the competition schemes, it required an awkward new access road, close to Ministry of Defence property (and a big ammunition depot) and across archaeologically sensitive land. The proposals to upgrade the A303 seemed to offer an opportunity for the sweeping changes which Cullinan and his clients thought vital. Eight possible sites were examined. In the end, the choice fell on Countess Road, on the edge of the small town of Amesbury and close to a big traffic roundabout where the A303 meets the A345. This location lay outside the World Heritage site, more than a mile from Stonehenge itself. The advantages of keeping any new building well away from the monument are clear, but the scheme drawn up for this new site also recognises that many visitors will not want to walk such a distance. Fortunately, a change of heart by the Department of Transport, spurred on by English Heritage, is likely to see the A303 diverted northwards, partly in a tunnel, and the World Heritage Site totally cleared of roads. Visitors will either walk to Stonehenge or use a form of rapid transit, terminating at a 'lookout point', a small new building at New King Barrows which will be discreetly sunk into the contours. The setting of Stonehenge will be retrieved and visitors will enjoy 'a voyage of discovery' in the ancient landscape.

The exact architectural form of the new visitor centre remained uncertain at the beginning of 1995, though some clear principles had been established – notably in terms of the relationship between the building and the necessarily large area of parking. Cullinan's approach to the project is rooted in two principles – firstly, that the approach to Stonehenge should be free and unfettered by development and that people should be encouraged to explore the entire Heritage site – preferably on foot – and not bowl up in their cars, look at the stones briefly, perhaps find them an anticlimax, and move on. Secondly, that a new building of quality can itself help to filter and even partly deflect the mass of visitors which threatens to destroy what people come to see. Cullinan believes in 'holy places', in the magic they possess and in its beneficial powers. The Stonehenge project is a bold attempt to come to terms with the forces of mass tourism and channel them to positive ends.

Roddy Langmuir, a Scot by birth, has combined work on Stonehenge with the development of the Archaeolink project at Berry Hill, Oyne, in the Grampian Region. The beautiful landscape here is rich in ancient sites and there are plans to re-erect a Neolithic village, accurately constructed on the basis of archaeological research. The Cullinan visitor centre will form the core of the site, a very simple building of 'glass and grass' partly buried beneath an enigmatic circular mound.

Edward Cullinan Architects is generally thought of as a very British

FROM ABOVE: Walking around at Stonehenge; Archaeolink

practice. But it is an accident of history, rather than a deliberate policy, that all Cullinan's executed buildings are in Britain (the Marvin house in California has been destroyed). Cullinan's expressive Modernism is anything but insular. Oddly, both the foreign projects with which the office has been involved in the last few years are masterplans for large areas, rather than single buildings.

In summer, 1992, the Cullinan practice welcomed a group of Japanese visitors from the Tama Forest area, a hilly region close to Tokyo, partly included in a national park, but inevitably under severe development pressure from the populous capital, for which it formed a much-visited 'lung'. Edward Cullinan Architects was subsequently invited (with two other foreign firms) to go to Japan and produce a preliminary report on the potential for combining development with the protection of the magnificent natural landscape. A further visit took place early in 1993, following which a second report was drawn up.

Cullinan's beautifully produced report is both a vivid record of Japan, seen through the eyes of architects who naturally empathised with Japanese architecture and design, and a passionate plea for an intelligently planned, inhabited landscape as an alternative to random sprawl. The Cullinan team was amazed to find imitation American-style 'log cabins' being built for tourists, when a wonderful way of building in wood was central to the Japanese tradition – 'calm, well proportioned and economical . . . like all good architecture, a celebration of necessity'. On one site, an estate of new houses was proposed, on a regular suburban grid, spread across the bottom of a fertile valley. Why not, Cullinan asked, leave the valley floor free for agriculture and dispose the houses informally amongst trees on the neighbouring slopes? He has always been critical of the 'aesthetic controls' which (he claims) encourages half-hearted pastiche rather than vigorous new design. He had no wish to urge the imposition of such policies on the Japanese, but wanted to build on traditional Japanese ways to encourage a way of developing in harmony with nature. He urged, 'Design your developments with care; compose them well and consciously and allow industry, forestry, houses, shops, commerce, farms, horticulture, education, quarries, sport, fishing, tourism, climbing, biking, sailing, surfing, natives and visitors to contribute to one another's enjoyment in well-designed mixed developments.' The formula typifies Cullinan's view of a landscape which meets both social and individual needs and aspirations.

The second trip to Japan was followed closely by Cullinan's visit to the University of North Carolina, Charlotte, in March 1993. With two other British architects, Christine Hawley and Piers Gough, he was there to lead a master class at the architecture school (headed by Professor David Walters and Dean Charles Hight). The theme of the master classes was very real – ideas for the expansion of the university itself. Charlotte is the fastest growing city in the United States and expanding the university is seen as a priority. In a decade, it will grow from 15,000 to 25,000 students. A visit to Cullinan's master class by the university chancellor, Jim Woodward, resulted in Edward Cullinan

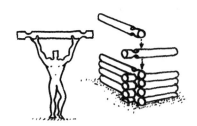

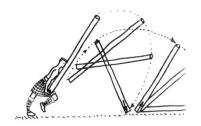

FROM ABOVE: Tama forest, wasteful use of wood; careful use of wood

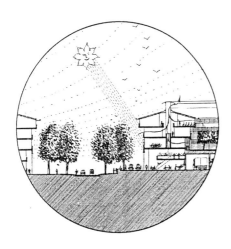

University of North Carolina at Charlotte: naturally ventilated, sheltering buildings, quadrangles and boulevards

Architects being invited to present concrete ideas for planning the campus.

None of the campus buildings at Charlotte is more than thirty-five years old. Although the university site is large – more than a mile across – and well-wooded, the need for a strategic plan was obvious if random development was not to create havoc. 'Our approach to master planning is like our approach to buildings', says Ted Cullinan, 'we identify the right pieces and then put them together'. Proposing some great planning 'idea' and fitting the uses into it is not Cullinan's way. The Charlotte master plan seeks firstly to protect the marvellous site, secondly to accommodate new development in reasonable walking distance of the university's heart (around the library), and thirdly to make the university a memorable place. A great lake at its heart, forming a majestic frontispiece to the buildings, will give it the image it so much wants. 'It will be a dense urban place, surrounded by fine green space', says Johnny Winter, who has been developing the plan with Cullinan and Robin Nicholson, implying that the campus could become a model for the boom town of Charlotte beyond.

CULTURE AND THE CITY

Ideas for a major refurbishment of the Royal Opera House in Covent Garden emerged as early as 1970, when a report by the Department of Education and Science proposed a considerable extension of the building and providing a second, medium-sized auditorium. It was not until 1983, however, that the 'selection procedure' to find an architect for the Royal Opera House (eventually won by Jeremy Dixon/Building Design Partnership) was launched. The development brief laid down early in 1984 allowed for a substantial amount of commercial development on land adjacent to the Opera House together with major backstage and front-of-house improvements which would be funded by that development. The government of the day believed that by giving the land to the ROH, it had conveniently acquitted its funding responsibilities. The onus of devising a scheme which balanced artistic and commercial considerations and took into account the interests of the Covent Garden community, fell on the ROH board. Ten years later, with the property boom of the 1980s gone, the Opera House development remained unbuilt.

The appointment of Jeremy Dixon proved to be the beginning of years of bitter conflict over the plans, which were strongly opposed by the Covent Garden Community Association and other local interested parties. Cullinan, ironically, despite his belief that 'community architecture' was a rather meaningless term and sometimes a cover for poor design, believes that he might have fared better. Had not the Prince of Wales described him as 'a man after my own heart' and praised his brand of social architecture?

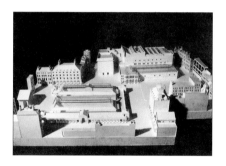

Ted Cullinan recalls that 'we were very excited about the Opera House competition'. The short list of competitors was steadily whittled down – from twenty-one to eight, and finally to just four: Dixon, Richard Rogers, the Toronto-based Jack Diamond practice and Edward Cullinan Architects, with Ted Cullinan, Tony Peake, Robin Nicholson and Mark Beedle comprising the team. 'We were the favourites', Cullinan believes, 'We really thought we had cracked it – losing was a major blow.' Though it had never built in the heart of London, or any major city, the Cullinan office had thrown itself wholeheartedly into the competition. There was no question of challenging the prescription for commercial development. The Cullinan team focused instead on the positive potential of the development – the idea of 'apartments in the sky' in the atrophied historic centre of London appealed a great deal. There were even to be apartments on top of the fly-tower. The Cullinan proposal was, in some respects, the most radical of the final four. Inigo Jones' famously pioneering piazza had long vanished, though the Victorian architect Henry Clutton had resurrected its format in his

FROM ABOVE: Inigo Jones, Covent Garden, c1630; Covent Garden today

Bedford Chambers. The ROH competition brief provided for the rein-statement, in some form, of the rest as a frontage to the new development. Richard Rogers, surprisingly, opted for a literal re-creation, which would have provided a striking contrast to the rest of his scheme. Dixon's projected new facades were certainly Classical, but not literally so – they reflected the influence of twentieth-century progressive Classicists like Plecnik and Asplund. Cullinan proposed to exactly rebuild Inigo's arcade at piazza level. Above, however, the new building would have been essentially modern. True, the first two storeys were recognisable as a *piano nobile* and attic, although the modern constructional system of steel, clear glass and glass blocks was clearly expressed, the desired element of reference and continuity was provided. On top, however, sat three further storeys, each set back to allow for broad terraces seen as 'gardens in the sky'. There was a bold and generous quality to the scheme which suggested that the Prince of Wales, who seemed to be continually demanding deference and discretion from architects, had found the wrong man in Ted Cullinan. Cullinan used steel and glass above the reconstructed arcade, rejecting literal historicism in favour of an abstracted reinterpretation which had nothing in common with the commercial Post-modernist style then gaining ground in London. In its rigour and austerity, Cullinan's ROH scheme had more in common with Lasdun's National Theatre than with the large London commercial schemes of Terry Farrell (though Farrell, interestingly, took up the idea of 'gardens in the sky' for his MI6 building at Vauxhall Cross).

Covent Garden lies in the heart of London – at least as far as most visitors to the capital are concerned. Quarry Hill is an awkward appendage to the great provincial city of Leeds. Lying to the east of the city centre, the area had developed as a densely-populated industrial suburb at the end of the eighteenth century. It had subsequently degenerated into a slum. Between the wars, it was completely cleared and replaced by a massive block of council flats modelled on the Karl Marx Hof in Vienna. This heroic development had itself been destroyed in the 1970s, leaving the Quarry Hill site empty and purposeless. The decision to move the Leeds Playhouse there (subsequently renamed the West Yorkshire Playhouse) from its temporary site next to Leeds University was seen as a vital element in the regeneration of the area. In 1985 a competition was held for the design of the new theatre. Edward Cullinan Architects' only completed theatre was that at Winchester College, a small and informal studio space, but the Royal Opera House competition had given the practice a further grounding in the mechanics of theatre design. The Leeds Playhouse was to include two auditoria, one containing a modern thrust stage to seat approximately 800, the other a small and adaptable studio which could adapt to a wide range of performance styles.

The Cullinan competition entry took as its starting point the place of the theatre in the city. At first sight, Quarry Hill seemed to have been scoured of any visible links with the past. The new Playhouse would have as its neighbours a sprawling bus station and a brutal 1970s police headquarters. Yet a surviving street name – St Peter's Square – suggested that Quarry Hill *was* part of the city. The old square had disappeared in the 1930s but Cullinan proposed to give it new substance by placing the smaller theatre there, addressing a new square which would accommodate various administrative and production spaces. The two theatres were to be 'unwrapped' from the usual coating of foyers, workshops and offices and treated as dramatic objects in the urban landscape. The large theatre was placed on the highest part of the site and given a circular form – the architects saw it as a 'castle keep'. Fly-towers are a perennial problem for theatre architects. Instead of trying to conceal the Leeds fly-tower, Cullinan proposed to celebrate it – it became a real tower, 120 feet high, with clock and flagpoles, a marker at the east end of the city centre as is Brodrick's splendid 1850s Town Hall to the west.

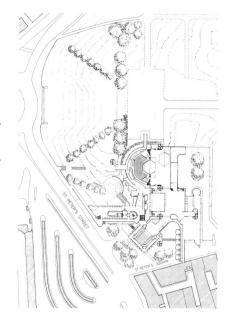

The *parti* of Cullinan's Leeds scheme was distinctly modern, both in architectural terms and in its view of the role of a theatre. The theatre was envisaged not as an internalised, highly specialised place, set aside for devotees, but as a lively component in the urban scene, a marker of civic values. An open-air performance space overlooked by the restaurant, a cloistered way around the main theatre, a system of glazed access galleries – stairs were dispensed with in favour of ramps – with views over the city, and a foyer conceived (in good Leeds fashion) as an arcade, all reflected a dynamic view of the role of the theatre as a generator of city life. 'Our building was considered too expensive', Ted Cullinan concedes. The ambitions behind the Cullinan scheme seemed too great. A far more modest (and rather dull) proposal by the Appleton Partnership was chosen instead (locally, the new building is compared to an Asda superstore). Leeds gained an efficient working theatre: the winning scheme, in fact, virtually replicated the main auditorium layout in the old Playhouse – but lost the chance of a new city quarter where the arts would be integrated with urban life.

If Quarry Hill was a rather lifeless quarter of a lively city, the City of London is definitely the most inert area of London, a maze of commercial buildings, mostly banal and post-war, with surviving Wren churches and a few other old buildings struggling to be seen among them. One building elevates the City and asserts more lasting values: St Paul's. Even the great cathedral, however, is surrounded by buildings of generally poor quality. Wren had intended that St Paul's be given a dignified, formal setting. His proposals were ignored and the City grew piecemeal around it. St Paul's Churchyard, to the south, developed in the nineteenth century as a major road, destroys any sense of seclusion or specialness. A number of twentieth-century planners wrestled with the problem of giving the cathedral a dignified setting: Lord Holford, who masterminded the new Paternoster Square to the north, wanted to create a completely traffic-free precinct. Not until the mid-1980s, however, did the City Corporation incorporate proposals for restricting traffic in St Paul's Churchyard into its official plan.

When the developers MEPC looked at the possibility of demolishing

Leeds Playhouse, ground plan

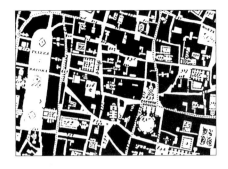

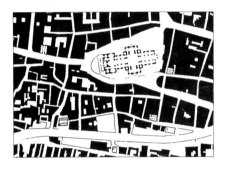

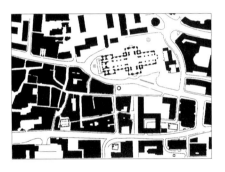

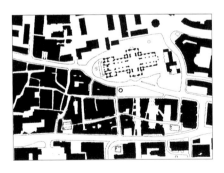

FROM ABOVE: Rome, mapped by Noli, subject; pre-war Petershill, after Noli, subject; post-war Petershill, object; proposed Petershill, subject

Petershill House, a poor quality 1960s block south of St Paul's, and building new offices on the site, it soon became obvious that a large development scheme of this sort would have to address the wider problems of the St Paul's precinct. MEPC was not deterred, however, and in 1988 it proceeded to organise a limited architectural competition. The very strong short list of competitors included not only Cullinan but also MacCormac, Jamieson, Prichard & Wright (as the victors of the Worcester College competition had become), Edward Jones (not yet in partnership with Jeremy Dixon) and Michael Hopkins, with whom Edward Cullinan Architects worked at Bedfont Lakes, also for MEPC. The competition was well run (by Dr Frank Duffy, later President of the RIBA) and effectively resulted in a dead heat. 'I think they liked our elevations, but Hopkins' plan', says Ted Cullinan. Maybe the two practices could work together, as at Bedfont. Collaboration on a large site, involving a number of different blocks, was one thing, but the Petershill site was too small to be shared by two powerful architectural personae: Hopkins retired, and Cullinan continued.

The competition judges had liked Hopkins' 'very rational' scheme, and especially his idea of developing the site as a group of independent blocks, separated by re-created streets. Cullinan was praised for offering 'external spaces which offered a great variety of interest to the public as well as the office users'. Like Hopkins, Cullinan proposed to reinstate the lost line of Knightrider Street across the site: on Petershill itself, running from St Paul's to the river, the Cullinan submission proposed a line of low-rise buildings intended to be let as small office suites or possibly as club or guild premises – another case of Cullinan's asserting the small-scale and the individual in a corporate context. With its varied skyline – there were even plans to rebuild the tower of a lost Wren church – and rich mix of materials, the Cullinan scheme offered the City a building of unusual quality.

The City was supportive of the plans – seeing an opportunity to resolve the issue of St Paul's Churchyard. As the scheme was developed, the idea of a ceremonial way across the churchyard, in place of the busy road, was developed and generally welcomed. But the City planners wanted more: St Paul's was a major tourist attraction and many visitors arrived by coach. The coaches generally waited in an area close to the south transept, an arrangement which nobody thought very satisfactory. The City wanted MEPC to include an underground coach park in the Petershill scheme, but neither the developers nor their architects warmed to the idea. Cullinan came up with the idea of using the site of the Festival Garden (a 1950s public space close to the east end of the cathedral) as a landscaped coach park and even, perhaps, building over it. The redesigned space, it was argued, could provide a setting for the historic Temple Bar, removed from Fleet Street by the Victorians and rotting in a Hertfordshire park. Suddenly Petershill became not just a commercial development project but a vision for revamping one of the most visited (and least attractive) areas in London. 'It would have been wonderful', says Cullinan. But the scheme foundered between the views of bodies like English Heritage and the

Royal Fine Art Commission (who did not want a coach park under the building) and the City (who did). Discussions dragged on for over a year. Meanwhile, the property boom of the 1980s showed every sign of coming to an abrupt end. The Petershill scheme was dropped; had it been built, the image of Edward Cullinan Architects might have changed markedly, but it did not in the event join the ranks of the leading 'developers' architects' of the 1980s.

Cullinan's return to the City came a few years later at Ludgate, where the City (owner of the site, west of St Paul's and directly abutting on to the main processional route to the cathedral) wanted to see an appropriate development there. Cullinan was directly commissioned to design a speculative scheme of offices and shops, incorporating an existing railway station, the intention being that the City Corporation would either seek a development partner or even carry out the development itself. Cullinan himself is a realist when it comes to commercial buildings. 'The market basically determines the shape of the buildings', he admits, 'You have to get to know the animal, as it were, and see what positive gains can be got from the development'. Cullinan always starts with the kit of parts. At Ludgate this includes a steel frame, a lot of glass and cladding materials – brick, stone and terracotta – which reflect the character of the better buildings in the vicinity, one of them a handsome late Victorian bank by TE Collcutt. The cladding will be visibly hung on the frame, providing a rich and highly articulated screen (which reduces solar gain and noise) 600 millimetres in front of the glazing. The Ludgate scheme is highly modelled and expressive, though disposed on a rigorous rectangular grid which brings to mind Arup Associates' Broadgate. Its skyline is constrained by the strict guidelines governing buildings close to St Paul's. The two blocks in the scheme differ markedly in character. That on Ludgate Hill is regular in form, but behind lies a second block which responds dramatically to the historic City-scape, accommodating old pedestrian routes and stepping down to embrace small scale buildings. Ludgate may finally bring the City the positive benefits which Petershill offered.

The Morrison Street goods yard development, designed for a large site in the West End of Edinburgh, is (like Petershill) an example of Cullinan's ingenuity in bridging the gap between commercial imperatives and wider urban issues. The practice had begun work on Morrison Street, in fact, before the Petershill competition was launched. The site was empty, used as a huge parking lot, but its importance to the Scottish capital was clear. Potentially, it formed a gateway to the city for those arriving from the airport and was close to the new conference centre (designed by Terry Farrell). Offices, apartments and a hotel were included in the brief from the developers, working on a joint-venture basis with the local authority. The housing was to include low-cost, rented accommodation and a new public open space was also to be provided. The centrepiece of the Cullinan scheme was a great crescent of housing, recognisably in the Scottish mould, with a new garden separating the housing from the offices. The architecture was emphatically

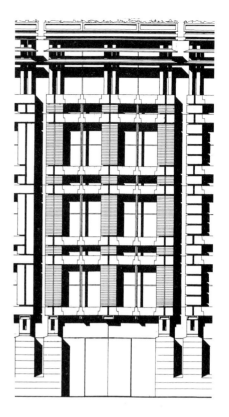

Ludgate, elemental, deep elevation: steel, stone, terracotta, brick

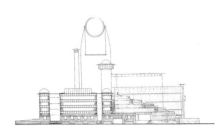

in the Cullinan mould, layering a rich pattern of metal and glass on to stone-faced elevations. But the project had a cool assurance and sobriety which confirmed the practice's ability to build on local traditions and to make a new mixed quarter with overall benefits to the city. Even so, the scheme foundered.

Cullinan's urban projects have, for a variety of reasons, fared badly. Covent Garden, Leeds Playhouse, Petershill and Morrison Street were all outstanding in their way, and demonstrated that the Cullinan practice is not anti-urban or incapable of thinking on a large scale. The failure of these schemes was, in several cases, seen as a major blow to Cullinan, but the practice is well placed to take a prominent role in the very different development scene of the 1990s, where the macro has given way to the micro, the general to the particular, and where the property lobby is no longer able to sweep aside community and social arguments as it did so effectively in the 1980s.

After all these disappointments, the failure of Edward Cullinan Architects to be short-listed in the competition (won by Zaha Hadid) for a new opera house at Cardiff Bay was not a major blow. Amid dozens of other unsuccessful proposals, the Cullinan scheme might easily be overlooked, but it deserves to be remembered, however, for its combination of common-sense practical planning, excellent audience provision and appropriate monumentality. Cullinan would have made the auditorium at Cardiff – like that at Leeds – into an 'object' in the landscape. The backdrop to the new opera house is a flat expanse of waterfront, a mile or so from the centre of the city. At the Royal Opera House, flats would have perched on the fly-tower. At Cardiff, it would have been capped by a restaurant and terrace – a memory, Cullinan says, of the courtyard which sits on top of William Burges' Cardiff Castle. Grand staircases set in glazed foyers lead up to the various levels of the auditorium, and up on to the roof. 'We unwrapped the significant public spaces and set them against a background block of offices, stage and rehearsal spaces', Roddy Langmuir explains. The rectangular 'backdrop' block contains the dressing rooms, stores and offices: the backstage domain. The scheme illustrates Cullinan's sheer versatility. 'We took the view that a night at the opera can become a performance in itself', says Langmuir. A major cultural building is still a prime objective of the practice and it can hardly be long before it is realised.

BACK TO THE FUTURE

Most architectural practices are hierarchies, rigidly stratified and with a small group of partners or directors taking not only the decisions but also the greater share of the profits. They are no different in this from other businesses – indeed, the predominant ethos of the architectural profession in Britain is that of business. In contrast, a select group of architects has been promoted over the last decade or so as leading cultural figures, pursuing their careers increasingly on an international stage. It is an unhealthy dichotomy. When Edward Cullinan Architects initially took its own idiosyncratic course as a co-operative, many scoffed and suggested that this radical policy would not last. It has worked well for over quarter of a century.

Ted Cullinan is, of course, an architect of world stature who enjoys being in the limelight as much as anyone else, but at heart he distrusts the pervasive cult of personality which turns architects into media stars and he always stresses the co-operative nature of the work done by the office. As the constant factor in the practice over thirty years, however, he occupies a unique position and his overview of the work has always been critically important. Understanding Ted Cullinan is fundamental to understanding the work of Edward Cullinan Architects. He certainly inspires loyalty: Sunand Prasad recalls his first day in the office in 1976: 'I arrived to find one person holding the fort – the rest had gone to the airport to wave Ted off on a lecture tour in the USA'.

Cullinan is a radical spirit and has always attracted those of a similar outlook – like Giles Oliver, who, rejecting the comprehensive redevelopment projects he was expected to undertake at Cambridge in the 1960s, spent his time making agitprop posters instead. The Cullinan office in the early days was, by all accounts, a great adventure, a place where ideas mattered and where the debate could become quite heated on occasions. Julyan Wickham recalls that the back room of Cullinan's first office in Covent Garden contained a judo mat. Both Cullinan and Wickham had taken up the sport at the time and a particularly knotty problem was sometimes the occasion for a bout. 'That's typical of Ted', Wickham says, 'He has a very physical approach to things – he tempers ideas with action'. Tchaik Chassay, another veteran of the early years, says of Cullinan: 'he is intense, physical – he can be mischievous, but behind the surface there is a very determined brain. Ted likes to keep tabs on everything that goes on in the office'. Claire Herniman joined the office in 1975 when it had just moved to Jamestown Road, Camden Town: 'I was hooked from the moment I walked in there', she says. Herniman recalls that the office was then, 'a very male, rather boisterous environment – there was a definite lack of women'. (This situation was subsequently rectified – much to the benefit of the practice.) She

Office trip, Orkney, 1990

RMC, new fronts old

has administered the practice ever since.

Ted Cullinan's vision of modern architecture has remained remark-ably intact over the years. He remains a profound optimist – his optimism finds expression in an architecture which rejects the nostal-gic, referential and the replicatory elements which came to the fore in the Post-modernism of the 1980s. Equally, the drift towards the arbi-trary, the self-indulgent and the illogical, which typifies much of the fashionable architecture of the 1990s, is incomprehensible to him. Cullinan's consciousness was forged by memories of the Arts and Crafts which fed into his schooling in the ways of the Modern Movement, and were rekindled by his youthful exposure to the expressive style of America's West Coast. While he rejects wilful eclecticism, he is anything but a purist – Philip Webb, Mackintosh, Bruce Goff, Greene & Greene, Schindler, Rietveld, Wright and Aldo van Eyck are as much a part of his make-up as Corbusier, Lubetkin and Lasdun. Cullinan found the 'mod-ern versus traditional' debate, which took place in Britain during the 1980s, completely pointless and irrelevant. Although the Prince of Wales described him as 'a man after my own heart', Cullinan is a Modernist through and through, in the sense that he believes that the literal revival of past styles and ways of building leads nowhere. Yet he is a strident critic of many of the products of the Modern Movement. Of the slabs and towers which disfigure most large cities he declares: 'it is a puritan architecture which takes from the modern idea only those parts of it which are to do with mass production, the idealisation of a standard solution, generalisation, and such necessary matters as the perfection of light angles and cross ventilation: and the cold douche of a stripped down aesthetic'. Rejecting the standardised, the generalised and the mass-produced in favour of the individual and the particular, could imply a rejection of modern industrial society – the path followed by Morris and the Arts and Crafts. Philip Webb and Bruce Goff, for example, built only one-off commissions for wealthy clients – their works were effectively handmade. Cullinan's social imperative tells him that good architecture is for everyone, not just the rich. The tension in his work is reconciling his desire to create special places for individuals with the constraints imposed by cost guidelines, design formulae, developers' briefs and (in the end) a society which tends to regard short-term cost as a higher priority than long-term value.

Cullinan's commitment to 'an expressive and a responsive architec-ture' singled him out from the run of young architects in the 1960s but a handful of exceptional clients allowed him to apply the philosophy of the early houses to larger buildings. The rising tide of public dissatisfac-tion with conventional Modernism fuelled Cullinan's successes of the later 1970s and 80s. The Lambeth health centre, Barnes church, and the unbuilt schemes for Covent Garden and Worcester College at Oxford were bursting with a sense of purpose and a clear confidence. The RMC headquarters showed that the conservative bastions of commerce could be breached by the Cullinan approach to 'places for people' Ted Cullinan's own personality has always counted for a good deal when it comes to commercial clients. He is simultaneously capable of

allaying their anxieties and yet making them aware of issues and problems which never occurred to them; setting up a creative dialogue from the start. He would not pretend that working in the commercial sector does not involve compromises on occasions, but Cullinan's pre-emptive approach usually means that the essential ideas in his projects survive into the completed buildings. An essential part of the Cullinan mythology is the adage that 'Ted always wins through'.

Cullinan is certainly a pragmatist. Some years ago, he was character-ised as a 'romantic pragmatist', a nebulous categorisation which he finds meaningless. The Arts and Crafts (and, further back, Pugin and the Gothic Revival) may be part of his 'baggage', but he is a Modern, a rationalist, a humanist who cannot accept that, to be modern, architec-ture has to be formulaic and bloodless. His Modernist belief in the doctrines of honest construction and truth to materials is tempered by a conviction that the look of things matters. His relish for the varying qualities of metal, stone, brick, wood and glass is legendary, and a modern rationalism emerges especially strongly in the plans of his buildings. He is insufficiently recognised as a rigorous planner, but he is never a predictable one – the plan always comes from the perceived needs of the users, but there is also a delight in the sensual, tactile, spatial qualities of buildings which is rare in contemporary British architecture and is founded on his unswerving admiration for Corbusier. (Ronchamp is unquestionably the European building which has always meant most to him – 'I would love to approach such a wholeness of composition, such a logical sequence, in my own work', he once wrote.)

The reputation of the Cullinan practice for creating buildings which sit comfortably in the natural landscape has its roots in Ted Cullinan's own love of the British countryside. As a boy in the years immediately after the Second World War he loved travelling around the country on his father's canal boat during vacations – 'a constant delight'. His school days in Yorkshire opened his eyes to a grander, wilder terrain of moors and peaks. Cullinan still derives immense satisfaction from the time spent at his country retreat on the gritstone of the Peak District. The vast landscapes of the USA, where he formed his mature views on architecture, and Canada are also dear to him, but the British country-side is richer in the layers of history and tradition which inform the kind of architecture he has always striven to make.

Cullinan is sometimes described as 'a very British' architect. The description often has a pejorative thrust, implying insularity and even parochialism. Cullinan's architecture belongs, in fact, squarely in an international tradition of alternative, humane modernism with its roots in Team 10 and its branches in the flowering of free and inventive design which followed the collapse of the old Modernist hegemony. If Cullinan is parochial, so are Van Eyck, Hertzberger, Erskine, Sverre Fehn, Saidowitz, Siza, Carmen Corneil, the Patkaus, and Murcutt. The emergence of regionalist themes within modern architecture has pro-vided a necessary corrective to the universality of the International Style. Perhaps the charge of parochialism could only arise in Britain,

Peak District, smallholding

FROM ABOVE: Carshalton, Scenery Workshop; Charles Cryer Studio Theatre

where the High Tech style has been dominant for over a decade. Cullinan's Modernism leads him to conclude that the living tradition of British architecture expired before the First World War. Britain, having retreated into dead-end insularity, only became reconnected to 'an architecture of hopeful invention' in the 1950s, the starting point for Cullinan's own creative odyssey. Cullinan understands 'tradition', not in static terms – as a constant reservoir of knowledge and wisdom waiting to be rediscovered by successive generations – but as a dynamic force. A tradition must be alive: 'a shared and continuous development of a way of doing things towards practical and artistic and social ends'. Cubism, for instance, did not destroy artistic traditions, but unearthed those which had been buried beneath a welter of academic and historicist rhetoric.

Cullinan speaks for the practice when he says 'we want to be considered as modern architects, but as part of a romantic stream of Modernism which seeks to build with spirit'. He concedes that there have been 'diversions' in the work of the last thirty years – a certain formalism, for example, which crept in during the 1980s – but the basic themes have never changed. Cullinan's accretive style is closely related to his belief in making special places, and every Cullinan building has a 'kit of parts' at the very beginning – the final designs grow out of the details, allowing for great flexibility in the creation of spaces. Cullinan believes that users will have a far greater role in the buildings of the future: 'architects will have to learn to like the process of consultation', he says. But his own way of making buildings and places provides for the individual, for growth and change.

Cullinan's architecture is diverse, rich, various – the antithesis of the reductivism which has become one of the most loathed features of modern design. It is capable of enriching an historic context or creating a context of its own. It is never predictable.

Far from being timid or middle-of-the-road, the architecture of the Cullinan office can be irreverent to the point of transforming a very ordinary place into somewhere remarkable. Nobody with an eye for buildings can pass the Charles Cryer Studio Theatre in Carshalton (a small Surrey market town now subsumed within greater London) without being puzzled, even a little disturbed. Is the building old, or new? More to the point, where does the old work end (the theatre is basically a public hall from the 1870s), and the new begin? The theatre (opened in 1991) is the only visible result so far of a major study carried out by Edward Cullinan Architects for Sutton Borough Council, which envisaged Carshalton town centre as the main focus for new arts developments in its area. (Cullinan designed a large new theatre for a striking parkland site.) The old public hall had been converted into a cinema between the wars and given a pleasant, rather flat, new facade in a version of the late Arts and Crafts style.

Here the Cullinan team (led by Roddy Langmuir and Mary-Lou Arscott) warmed to the building's eccentricities and finished by accentuating them. The street gable was rebuilt in fanciful Gothic form; below is a projecting metal balcony. The facade has been given dept by extending the aisle roofs of the building to form sheltering porches. At either side, the ground floor has been opened up to provide access to offices, shops and a restaurant – originally fitted out by the architects but recently overlaid in a suburban version of the oriental style. The first-floor theatre has to cope with a wide variety of uses, from keep-fit classes and conferences to concerts and plays and is a heavily used community resource. The theatre workshops are in a separate, cruciform building on axis with the theatre and hidden from the street. Metal-roofed and timber clad, this small building is a Cullinan classic, at once completely functional and logical yet with serious presence and quiet monumentality. Only a few mannered details – the tricksy, over-elaborate treatment of the doorway, for example – detract from a remarkably assured performance. Above all, this is a completely 'natural' building, using good materials without extravagance or false display to create an excellent workplace. Together the two buildings make a place, a 'cultural quarter' far less ambitious than that which Cullinan originally envisaged, but a location with real identity, where old and new are fused not reverentially, but with magnificent verve.

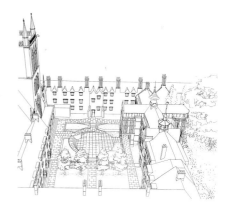

At St John's College, Cambridge, Cullinan was faced with a site which might be conventionally described as 'sensitive'. Cambridge University and its colleges have a generally excellent record of commissioning new buildings in the post-war era. St John's, the second-largest college with 800 students, had itself built one of the best of them, the 1960s Cripps Building by Powell & Moya. Good as Cripps was, however, it was discreetly detached from the main college complex, which contains buildings ranging in date from the early sixteenth century to the 1930s.

The building which St John's wanted from Cullinan (after informally interviewing many other firms) could not be tucked away on the edge of the college site. It was to contain the main undergraduate library and had to be linked to the original, seventeenth-century library, which it proposed to refurbish as a repository for the college's rare books and archives and a place where the incunabula and manuscripts could be studied by scholars. There seemed to be only one place where the new library could go: on the site of a large Victorian Gothic block designed by a relatively obscure (but interesting) nineteenth-century architect, FC Penrose.

In the event, the Penrose building was not destroyed but underwent, in the words of Mark Beedle (who led the Cullinan team) 'a transformation' as radical as that which took place at the Carshalton theatre. The Penrose block faces the west end of Sir George Gilbert Scott's vast Victorian chapel, a building which it was once fashionable to despise, but which Ted Cullinan justly compares to the choir of a great French cathedral – the court can be imagined as the site of a vanished nave. The north side of the court is closed by the 1930s residential buildings designed by Sir Edward Maufe in a timid semi-modern style.

Much of the Penrose building was already occupied by the library, which had spread haphazardly into it, creating an untidy maze of spaces convenient neither for readers nor for staff. By night and for much of the weekend, the library was closed and totally inaccessible to

FROM ABOVE: St John's College, Chapel court transformed; working interior of library

FROM ABOVE: St John's library, lantern; Cheltenham, oversailing

students. With rare books in a separate place, however, the college wanted to create a twenty-four-hour library, protected by electronic security devices, where students could go and read at 3.00am if the fancy took them.

The principles behind the Cullinan scheme were to retain most of the external walls of the existing building but to extend it on an east-west axis, into Chapel Court and behind into the Master's Garden. This made sense not only in terms of gaining space, but was equally part of a strategy for low-cost natural ventilation which demanded a tall, thin building. These principles were accepted by the client, but the first proposals for the treatment of the Chapel Court addition – an elevation of wood and glass – proved (in Cullinan's words) 'too much for the dons'. The college took the view that the predominant materials should be brick and stone – even a proposal for an exposed steel lintel over the entrance was subsequently vetoed. The Cullinan team's revised designs, as built, are far more referential and contextual. Both the gable and the flèche on the Penrose building are blatantly echoed in the new work. At the rear, an apsed addition breaks into the Master's Garden – it is a freer composition than that on Chapel Court, but has clear roots in the Gothic Revival.

The building would have been bolder had the architects been given free rein, but securing approval for, and completing the first new building to be put up in a Cambridge quad since the 1930s is something of an achievement. The real quality of the new library is best seen, however, in its interiors, which provide a remarkable variety of places to read. Mark Beedle sees it as 'a sociable place', where there are corners for quiet chats away from those studying. Any doubts about architectural authenticity raised by the external treatment of the building, fade when you enter it. It is a serene, light, cheerful place which provides a striking contrast to the traditional crowded gloom of other college libraries. But it is not an obviously radical statement. Its radicalism lies in its servicing strategy, which revolves around the central duct housed in the extraordinarily fanciful new flèche: 'a return to a natural environment, but all managed by a microchip', as Mark Beedle puts it.

Cheltenham and Gloucester College of Higher Education lacks Oxbridge-style glamour, but it has a notable record in teaching art and what is today known as 'media studies'. The Cheltenham campus is a typical 1960s complex, decent but a little dull – 'sub Hunstanton' – as Cullinan describes it. In extending it, Cullinan, Mary-Lou Arscott and Seán Harrington, showed a clear respect for what existed, seeking neither to outface it nor to provide a disjunction in style. The new Media Building grows out of the 1960s structure, logically complementing the existing plan.

The brief was quite complex: exhibition space, studios, a video production suite, small theatre, offices, and even a range of study bedrooms. The concept behind the building is simple and effective: working spaces are distributed around a generous central glazed court – a place of passage but also used for exhibitions and displays – of lightweight steel construction, clear and precise. Bridges give access to rooms at upper level; corridors are eliminated. This is a lively place, where the various disciplines taught in the building (fashion, photography, film and graphics) meet and interact. The usual Cullinan interest in section is apparent in the southern wing of the building, which rises four storeys to perch a run of student rooms in a jettied top floor structure which is clad in wood shingles; a rather American device. These rooms look out and away from the workspaces behind, but the building is a clear statement about the virtues of mixing working and living accommodation.

Ingeniously planned and decisively detailed – to a fairly tight budget – the Cheltenham Media Building is, by any standards, an uncompromisingly late-twentieth century design. It would never be commissioned by a Cambridge college – nor permitted in Cheltenham's Regency Centre for that matter (the college site is a safe distance away). It is contextual in the sense that it takes up elements of the 1960s college and builds on them. But the great sailing metal roof has a sheer exuberance which few architects in that decade could even have contemplated. The range of materials is equally unfettered and used with great gusto. It is not surprising that the Cullinan office is in demand for educational buildings. The International Manufacturing Centre at Warwick University is another addition to a 1960s campus and the architects have again deferred to what they see as the quiet dignity of the existing buildings. A further phase of the Cheltenham campus is in hand and a new college at Runcorn will build on the success of the Cheltenham atrium idea.

Ted Cullinan places great importance on continuity, and is pleased that the office can still produce beautiful small houses – like the one Roddy Langmuir has built in the Scottish Highlands – together with radical housing projects (like the timber residential buildings currently under construction at Hooke Park, Dorset), as well as large buildings and ambitious master-plans. Cullinan views the future of architecture not in terms of stylistic fashion (a matter which has never interested him much) but in the context of a changing society. He foresees a new generation of low-cost housing schemes which will be designed in consultation with the residents. Control and involvement are vital issues, he says: 'architects will have to justify what they do'. Energy-saving and ecological issues will come ever more to the fore. Architects have to learn to be responsible, to build for people, but this does not preclude a new flowering of the art of architecture. If there is to be a renaissance of expressive, even romantic modern architecture at the end of the twentieth century it will owe a good deal to Cullinan and he will, one hopes, play a leading role in it. His particular skills have never been so urgently needed.

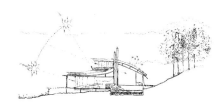

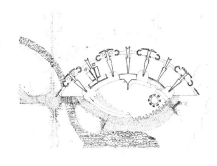

FROM ABOVE: Cheltenham, student rooms above movie studios; Hooke Park, greenwood High Tech house

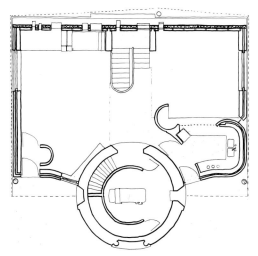

RIGHT: Upper floor plan

BELL TOUT LIGHTHOUSE
1955-56

Discounting the efforts of childhood – numerous tree houses, a stone igloo for a girlfriend Shirley at the age of ten, one half-built houselet at thirteen, a boathouse at seventeen, Bailey bridges and other constructions during National Service, one garden shed and a redwood sleeping platform in California – the Bell Tout Lighthouse was my first completed building. The magnificence of the site, atop a 300-feet high chalk cliff on the southern edge of England, was almost enough to compensate for the youthful inexperience of the architect, and for the fact that he had been further hobbled by cycling to Ronchamp halfway through the design process. The cycling was fine; Ronchamp was the problem, for the power it exerted on visitors (especially the interior) when it was first built, can never be forgotten. So although the plan of my part responds to the form of the round, stumpy granite tower of William Hallett's 1830s lighthouse, and the form of the new first floor was decided before pedalling to Ronchamp, there are certain details, directly lifted by myself, awestruck. These pale by comparison, which I regret.

But in the 1950s people were less reverent about the past than they are today, less inclined to pussy-footing where historic buildings were concerned. So I was free to compose a completely new top floor to go on to Hallett's ground floor. In this way the old lighthouse became the first of a long series of conversions, alterations and additions to historic buildings and places which I have done with many partners during the subsequent thirty-eight years. In all these projects we have attempted to compose radically; resulting in contemporary buildings which add positively to our inheritance from the past, without pastiche. For copying the past insults the past.

While the Bell Tout Lighthouse was under construction I graduated from the Architectural Association to Berkeley in California. During the course of an eye-opening year and while being reborn a Beatnik, I wrote a splenetic thesis called *Gap*: ie, the gap between ideas (those of today, plus the fundamental precepts of the Modern Movement) and the quite arbitrary design of consumer economies. In one part of this thesis I wrote,

> Likenesses are the source of most troubles; for to design or make anything somewhat like anything else is to have foreknowledge of the end result which immediately stifles useful inventiveness.

> Modesty in building has nothing to do with designing modest little structures; rather it is in the strength to search out and accept the necessary, to 'do', without knowledge.

> Knowledge is knowing all the possibilities, understanding all the approaches, and is gleaned at school and only confuses and hinders the contact with what must be. Knowledge allows one to compose buildings from a catalogue of bits, an encyclopaedia of features; it leads to disaster. Hence Peter Smithson's wish to teach style or dogma so that choice is removed and submission or reaction remain.

This final point is probably due to interdisciplinary slippage, since the other subjects I signed up for at Berkeley were abstract expressionist painting and wrestling. The whole so-called 'thesis' was a youthful effort to resolve the experience of a highly academic, classical education in England with Beatnik (Californian) 'stream of consciousness' ideas, via the unveiling by Smithson and others of the precepts of the early Modern Movement at the Architectural Association.

This is where I come in.

HORDER HOUSE
1958-60

Modernism has often been described in terms of tech-nological progress and sometimes (more dangerously) in terms of social progress: true enough, but not enough. It was and is far more interesting when seen as a liberating system of composition, derived from that great period which John Berger describes as 'the moment of Cubism': a liberating system for making interpenetrating spaces, for breaking down the barrier between inside and out (and other barriers), for the expressive use of planes and sticks, opaqueness, transparency, colour, being true to materials and so on: much of it loosely covered by the word 'abstraction' in architecture.

I can see no reason to depart from these inspiring ideas, but contained within them are a number of smaller concerns of my own, which are first exhibited by the Horder House in Hampshire and the Marvin House in Marin County, California. Both houses react to their specific sites and use the climate, rearranging the spaces within them from those normally associated with houses, they are concerned with the method of their realisation, and they use simple but expressive details. These ideas have interested me ever since.

The Horder House, for my uncle Mervyn Horder, basks long, thin and south-facing in a crease in the landscape of Hampshire where a steep-wooded bank joins a flattish, grassy valley floor. It is a single big space – the 'there' there – served by a tiny kitchen. It has a bedroom and showers at either end, in both of which the beds are on enlarged window sills cantilevered over the wild garden; so by sliding open the windows you can 'sleep out'. It stands alone in its valley, with no road access and was built in the following manner.

- Horace Knight (a retired gardener) and I dug ten holes down to the chalk in two rows of five, put asbestos pipes in the holes and filled them with concrete.
- Eight concrete beams from Bison came by tractor and we placed them in two lines along the tops of the pipes. On top of the beams went a rectangular floor deck of precast planks.
- On the deck Horace and I formed two large concrete

door frames, and when they had set we pulled them upright with a tree winch, 'tilt up' fashion. The door frames led into the house from terraces at each end; holding pivoting doors to allow breezes to flow through immediately behind the south-facing glass. The door frames needed solidity because,

- they braced the walls which Horace then built from six feet thick insulated (slightly in today's terms) blocks which were tarred black on the north side and 'Snowcemed' white on the south.
- The roof was put on, forming a warped plane which channels all the water to a single spout on the north side. The roof overlapped the walls and was finished with silver.
- Patent glazing was fitted over the kitchen and on the south front, and,
- Horace and I bolted pre-made Allday sliding windows onto the bedroom ends.
- All the plumbing, drainage and wiring was installed after the house was built, screwed to the underside of the floor deck.

It was fascinating to think of a house as a series of simple self-contained pieces to be added by different people at different times. In this way of thinking I was vastly helped by discovering Schindler in the exhibition of 1956, *Five California Architects*; Schindler, who was also fascinated by the bits and pieces, the various parts that might go to make a new architecture; Schindler, who took 'tilt up' concrete from Californian warehouses and used it to make his sophisticated houses of cards.

Today the Horder House might be called a passive solar house, gaining from its southern aspect, protected by bamboo screens from over-powering summer sun, through breezes provided for. But then it suffered, as it might now, from looking 'different' in the eyes of the local planning officers who passed it only after a map was drawn to prove that it would not be visible from any other house or even from any public road or path. The best way would be to accept this as a tribute to the strength of feeling that architecture can arouse in human beings.

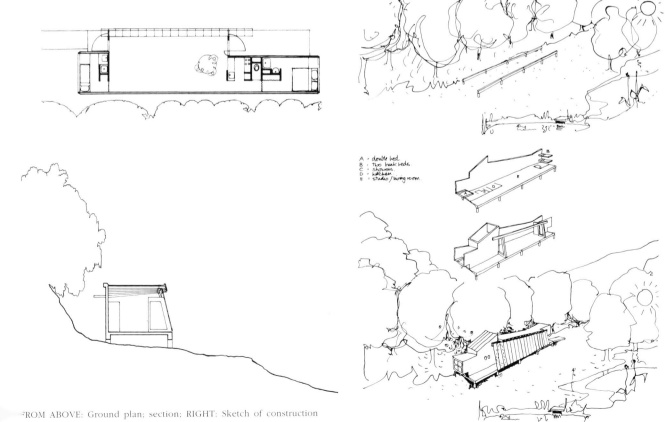

FROM ABOVE: Ground plan; section; RIGHT: Sketch of construction

A = double bed.
B = Two bunk beds.
C = showers.
D = kitchen.
E = studio/living room

MARVIN HOUSE
1958-60

I lodged the plans of the Marvin House with the Marin County (California) Planning Departments one morning, and two afternoons later they passed it. I then built this house for my beloved friends the Marvins, with a Mexican medical student and with Stephen Marvin, who turned up late each afternoon after teaching high school.

In the Marvin House the old concept of rooms, with names behind doors leading from corridors, vanishes altogether. Instead a series of 'green rooms' made from concrete masonry, serve a single 'stage' made of sawn Californian redwood (tilted up).

The green rooms are top-lit except for strategically placed, tiny viewing windows, made from concrete blocks laid sideways and glazed. The house comprises the green rooms, two dressing rooms with a giant-sized shower between them, a guest's shower and WC, an entrance, a study and a kitchen. The green rooms serve a stage of life containing a bed at one end, a fire with couches round it in the centre, and dining table and chairs at the other end by the kitchen. The redwood walls of the stage room have fixed glass in chinks; large and small redwood panels can be opened in summer and shut in winter (a device directly lifted from Le Corbusier's Maison Jaoul), which makes for lovely differences between lighter breezy open-air summers, and darker, more enclosed winters.

The original plan was to have another two of these houses, one for guests, another for a greenhouse, set further down the hill and served by a driveway of cobbles running straight up the hillside like a San Francisco Street. But it was not to be, for illness forced the Marvins to move – this little house became the entrance hall for a vast hyperbolic paraboloid and now the whole place has been pulled down. I loved building these houses, I still love building things myself and with friends, and I still do it.

a long gallery of rough Californian redwood, contains a bed, a hearth for sitting around and a table to eat at.

the light in the gallery is warm and ruddy and comes through windows that are like chinks in its wooden sides.

beside the gallery, a row of service rooms

the service rooms are white and brightly lit from above.

and later they will add a greenhouse.

and a guest house going on down the hillside.

and a drive goes straight up the hill like the roads do in San Francisco.

path   road.

Since I have mentioned the matter of control, and because I do not want to dwell on it throughout this brief history, I shall say here what I have come to think about it. To illustrate the point I shall use the example of 'one-off' houses.

In Britain, during the period since the Second World War, the Town and Country Planning Act has again and again been used by planners (among others) as a licence to control the design of houses, often more or less extraordinary houses by young architects. For example, in my final year at the Architectural Association I designed a house for the (brave to employ me) parents of a friend in Devon. It was rejected for being 'out of keeping with the character of the locality and detrimental to the amenities of the district'. We made a written appeal – whilst at Berkeley in 1956-57, I used to write elaborate proofs of evidence about prickly little aesthetic matters, and elaborate replies to myriad objectors from the other side of the world in wide-open California. This appeal felt very different. We lost: I designed them a more Devonish, white-walled and Delabole slate roofed house, but it was turned down again saying that 'traditional' meant more Sussex style, half-timbered maybe. We appealed again, and won: the first house was by far the best, and sadly, this experience is all too typical for young (and old) architects.

When I read that the Secretary of State said that aesthetic control or taste policing was not the intention of the Town and Country Planning Act, and would not stand up at appeal, I was happy. But many secretaries of State have said that and it seldom sticks. Today there are two situations which effectively licence aesthetic control. The first is that it is allowed in conservation areas and there are far too many of these; the second is consultation by local home owners who nearly always reject odd newcomers.

The next part of my argument depends on your thinking that architecture is an art, the mother of the arts perhaps, an art that has inspired, enlarged and enlivened our kind throughout our time, an art of extreme necessity which can at the same time achieve extremes of poetry; an art which needs careful nurturing and tending.

If architecture is such an art, then surely it should be encouraged to grow and develop in the strange ways that it will in the hands of young architects, designers and many other thoughtful eccentrics; like music does or poetry or painting or sculpture, dance, drama and movies. As in those arts, there will be many dead ends, much so-called vulgarity but there will also be invention and creation and progress to make it all worthwhile.

In the ordinary streets and avenues of our towns, cities and suburbs we should protect the rights of individuals to self-expression more than the rights of the existing home-owners to stop it. As a start we need to relieve single houses in most places of the need to have planning permission at all, asking only that they conform to the least possible number of height and alignment requirements. The results would be very interesting and quite unfrightening: far more enjoyable than the timidity of most houses and housing today.

Having cleared the air somewhat for houses in ordinary places, we might then take a new look at the larger scale of our cities. For many years we have tried to plan our surroundings as though we lived in the eighteenth century, when our cities and towns were owned and laid out by aristocrats who could naturally insist on order and uniformity. Today we live in a time of separate and even individual freehold tenure, which means that such uniformity is not naturally attainable, and any attempt to impose it can result in emasculated mediocrity. Therefore we should celebrate and enjoy our difference instead. We should attempt to make cities whose well-considered public or shared places (squares, streets, places) are framed by many different, and many different kinds of building; thereby moving towards an urban scene, and with it an urban architecture of expressive but collective diversity.

In the eighteenth century, the dressing of people was rather uniform and accorded to class and rank: in the twentieth century, the dress and the self-expression of the crowds that throng our city streets is varied and individualistic – that is how buildings are going to be, for better and for worse.

CAMDEN MEWS
1963-64

At the beginning of the 1960s I worked for Denys Lasdun. With him I designed the student ziggurats at the University of East Anglia, which form the foothills along the southern edge of his total plan. Denys had taught me at the Architectural Association; I admire him, I love the fact that he worked with Lubetkin, who worked with Ginsberg, who was one of the fathers of modern architecture. I think that Lasdun's Royal College of Physicians in Regent's Park is one of the masterpieces of twentieth-century architecture. With clarity and grace the Royal College sees the blackness of the roofs and the creamy white walls of the surrounding Nash buildings (early nineteenth-century): it uses the blackness to make the flowing, moving lecture theatre, floors, routes and stairs, and the creamy parts for the more static parts of the composition. These two elements together make a building which works within itself and creates understandable and useful public spaces between it and its neighbours.

The Royal College is always and completely itself, and lifts no details from the surrounding buildings; yet it completes most beautifully the whole composition of the corner of the park. Besides being a fine piece of architecture in the original Cubist stream of modern architecture, it illustrates perfectly that a building with its own expression and order can contribute far more to a received collection of buildings than one which half copies them. Without Lasdun I would never have learnt how much you need to do, and how far you have to go, in order to design and construct a building that you can respect yourself for having done.

I worked from Monday to Thursday each week with Denys; on the other days I conducted a tiny private practice, which included two houses; in Camden Mews and at Bartholomew Villas. The former was built by myself, my wife Rosalind, by friends (especially Rob Howard), and members of our families, during two years of Sundays between 1962 and 1964. We moved in with our three children in 1964 and spent much more time finishing it.

At that time the assumption was that a house on a site like this would be a two-storey rectangular block set between parti walls and set back ten feet (three metres) from the mews and an equal distance from the back boundary, making a little yard in front and another at the back. Instead we built a parti wall right along the north boundary, which shrank in thickness floor by floor: 3.3 metres south of the wall a line of concrete posts supports a long beam of Canadian Hemlock. The roof spans from the parti wall across the beam, and was made and waterproofed very early in the process, so that a site that was normally in operation for one day in the week was thereby made secure and dry for the protection of tools, materials and possessions. Most of the rest of the house was made of bolted softwood, dangled down from the completed roof and then glazed. The house faces almost south and I had learnt by then that in our latitude you need overhangs to gain from the low winter sun and exclude a lot of it in the summer; the house has them at every 'dangled' detail, which also protects the softwood from rotting in the rain. To the south of the house, a brick and concrete workshop forms an extension of a southern parti wall, the top of which makes a terrace. 'Indoors' is contained by sticks and glass, and 'outdoors' exists within the frame of the solid ground and two solid parti walls.

I think it a shame that most young DIY architects in Britain are only able to undertake the grizzly chemical business of stripping and renewing the interiors of old houses for themselves. Building whole new ones to your own radical programme is more outdoors, more varied, easier (if you design it to be), and more fun, as you rise from the dark glutinous depths of foundations in London clay to the swift, clean, dry construction of roofs.

In the summer of 1964, when down a hole making foundations for the garage and workshop at Camden Mews, I heard the well-honed voice of Michael Brawne from way above me. He was offering me a job, teaching at Cambridge in the second year. I took it, I have taught architecture ever since, and in many places: it is one way of learning.

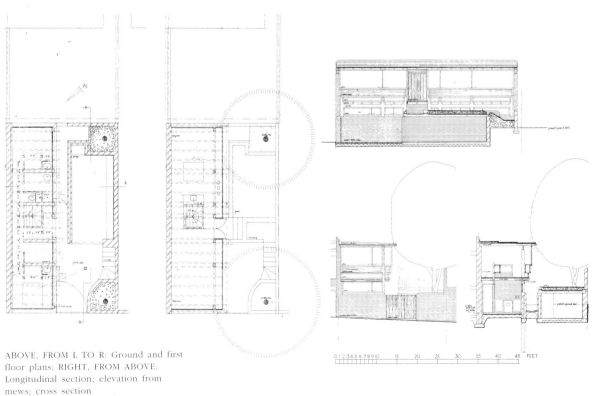

ABOVE, FROM L TO R: Ground and first
floor plans; RIGHT, FROM ABOVE:
Longitudinal section; elevation from
mews; cross section

0 1 2 3 4 5 6 7 8 9 10   15   20   25   30   35   40   45 FEET

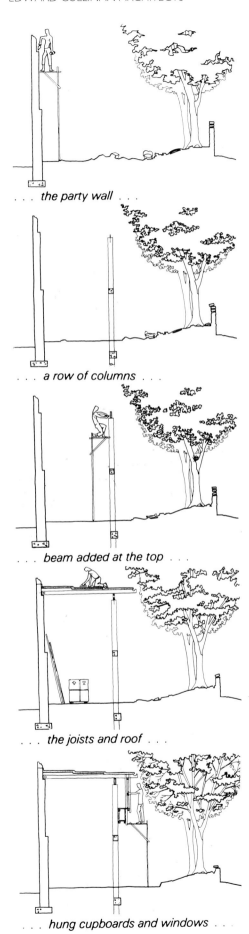

. . . *the party wall* . . .

. . . *a row of columns* . . .

. . . *beam added at the top* . . .

. . . *the joists and roof* . . .

. . . *hung cupboards and windows* . . .

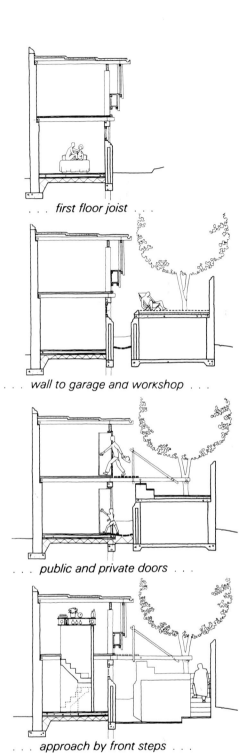

. . . *first floor joist* . . .

. . . *wall to garage and workshop* . . .

. . . *public and private doors* . . .

. . . *approach by front steps* . . .

BARTHOLOMEW VILLAS
1964-65

This house was designed for a devoted musician and his wife. The site was to be leased for ninety-nine years; for a peppercorn in the first year, and in subsequent years for an amount that could be raised from the rent paid by a ground floor flat. Living and sleeping accommodation were located on the middle floor, with a gallery above for chamber music, and a flat and two garages below.

It was a perfect package for a man with very little money; but when we opened the tenders (for under £6,000) my client declared that he was 'in flight through life' and could not be anchored by a house: he was right, and the house was built for Adam Kawecki, who worked with me for Lasdun. The house is a 'lean to', which completes the bombed-off south half of the last of a row of mid-nineteenth-century, double-fronted villas. Facing south, the house reduces the scale which introduces you to the first of a row of smaller, later villas which are on a curve.

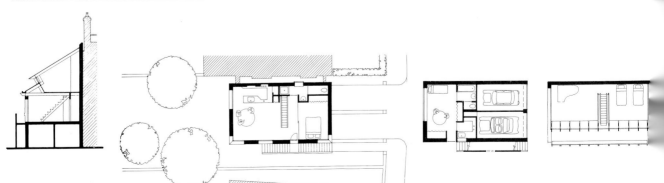

THE GARRETT HOUSE
1966

This project on the edge of south London has the same kind of plan and section as Camden Mews: compact, compartmented, soundproof and of heavy construction for bedrooms below; open, lightweight, barely divided for shared living areas above; a gallery. It is an urban development of my earliest experiments with composing combinations of very closed and very open places. Its contribution to setting derives from Bartholomew Villas, though in this case, the setting is suburban rather than urban.

A garage with a sloping roof is added to the last of a seemingly endless row of early twentieth-century villas, and forms the north slope of a valley whose south slope is the roof of the house itself, completing the endless row of villas with a high vertical wall.

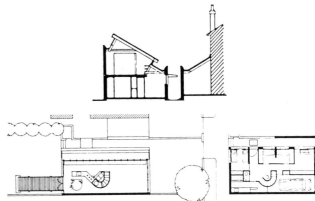

THE LAW HOUSE
1966-68

The Law House in Hampshire is a comfortable, fairly large house notched into a south-facing slope of the South Downs, with fabulous views.

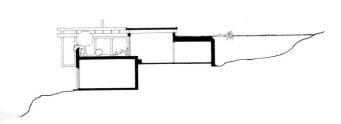

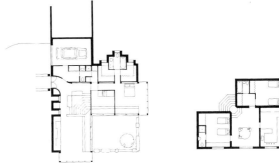

OPPOSITE: Bartholomew Villas, cross section and floor plans; FROM ABOVE: Garrett and Law Houses, cross sections and floor plans

MINSTER LOVELL MILL
1967-76

It was here that I was first involved in a recognised holy place: it seems to me that we are rapidly returning to the Dianic cult which preceded Christianity in these islands – the worship of nature and our ancestors – the cult that does not trust the present, but loves only what we receive from the past, or things that grow in a manner which is assumed to be natural or according to the laws of nature. An old miller's house, a barn, a long dry-stone wall, a malthouse, the ruins of a mill, and lovely gardens lying beside and across the River Windrush, right on the edge of the Cotswolds, all made of glowing Cotswold stone would seem to constitute a holy place for us today.

Since Minster Lovell, the practice has completed many buildings and schemes in holy places: Oxford, Cambridge, Winchester College, Edinburgh, Barnes Village, the London green belt, bordering St Paul's, Fountains Abbey and Covent Garden, largely because of this first project. All of them were agonisingly difficult to do, because of the power of the lobby that would like to copy or half-copy the past by lifting features from the old buildings, or by reproducing them more or less whole. Instead, we have always tried to study and respect the formal quality of the shared places between old buildings and our new ones so that they may be enriched by the differences between the old and the new buildings which frame them: it is a hard idea to get across; pastiche is easier.

Minster Lovell was designed to be a residential study place, specifically a 'Centre for Advanced Study in the Developmental Sciences'. It was the enlightened brainchild of Tony Ambrose, who had inherited the buildings and the garden from his father. He gathered together a formidable building committee, including Kit Ounsted who ran the Park Hospital for autistic children in Oxford. After a few fruitless looks at Minster Lovell as a diagram, we started to look at it for what it was; a collection of buildings along a dry-stone wall on the north side of a river. We looked at those buildings with our clients and we agreed that the L-shaped house would make offices and common rooms with a dining gallery above, the malthouse would become a library, and the barn would make an excellent upper level conference chamber with smaller ones below.

So we designed the alterations to these buildings and used the study bedrooms together with connecting covered ways to connect the old buildings to one another. As a finale, further study bedrooms are grouped around a double level foyer which introduces people to the upper level conference chamber in the old barn; and there are two or more ways to almost everywhere.

The barn roofs were extended downwards and outwards, giving a key to the large, floating stone roofs over the new accommodation. These new roofs, or large canopies, are supported on a dry construction of bolted and connected wood, which in turn rests on modular concrete masonry.

The dry-built, calculated, elemental twentieth-century construction is loosely clothed with Cotswold stone walls and roofs.

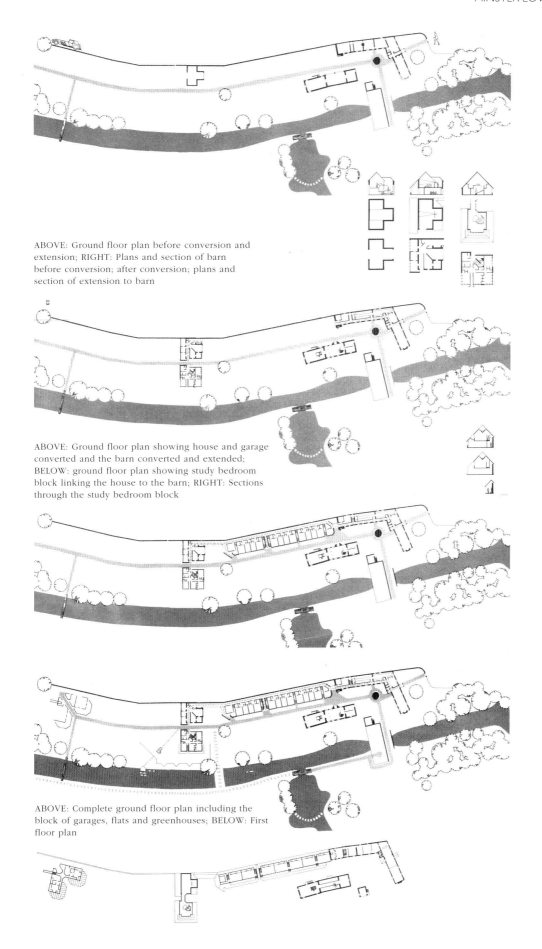

ABOVE: Ground floor plan before conversion and
extension; RIGHT: Plans and section of barn
before conversion; after conversion; plans and
section of extension to barn

ABOVE: Ground floor plan showing house and garage
converted and the barn converted and extended;
BELOW: ground floor plan showing study bedroom
block linking the house to the barn; RIGHT: Sections
through the study bedroom block

ABOVE: Complete ground floor plan including the
block of garages, flats and greenhouses; BELOW: First
floor plan

OLIVETTI
1970-72

In 1969 Olivetti's most inspired manager, Carlo Alhadeff, came from Japan to Olivetti in Britain, as he later did in the United States and China. The idea we have of culture seems to me too often confined to writing, but for Alhadeff and many other Italians, it most surely includes architecture. He studied it for his degree, he understood its history and the powerful way in which architectural form both informs and inspires us. He positively wanted to create buildings which would advance the company and to underline its commitment to the art of architecture and design. In Japan he used Kenzo Tange, in Britain he chose Jim Stirling, and in the USA, Richard Meier.

Olivetti bought Branksome Hilders, a big, red-brick and tile late nineteenth-century mansion, between Hindhead and Haslemere in the sandy, brackened Surrey hills. Alongside it Jim Stirling designed his only fibreglass (and glass) building, which contained the lecture halls and teaching rooms of Olivetti's training centre.

When Julyan Wickham brought the news that Stirling and Alhadeff wanted us to remodel the house, I was in St Bartholomew's Hospital with a skull fracture, after skiing into a pine tree in Austria: it was curative news. The house itself was to be the residential part of the training centre, with three sides facing outwards, forming a U-shaped back service yard. We inverted it so that the yard became a combined atrium, entrance foyer, bar and ground-floor circulation space, with stairs and galleries leading from it to the upper levels. A connecting atrium led out from its flank to the teaching building. By creating new horizontal and vertical connections, all the good spaces in the house were released for use.

From Branksome Hilders we moved to designing branch offices for Olivetti in Belfast, Carlisle, Derby and Dundee. I would travel with Mr Bertolino, Olivetti's facilities manager, on damp diesel rail cars, looking for suitable sites on various hopeful industrial estates. We would choose them there and then, and start work immediately. The site at Dundee for example, was chosen for its hilltop view over on to the roof of the National Cash Register factory, which tickled Bertolino pink.

The four sites were diverse in shape and size, something which was also true of later sites. As a result of this we designed a system of U-shaped buildings, the long sides of which made whole elevations to the street; two 'tails' followed the sides of the sites as far as the required accommodation allowed them to, creating an open courtyard. The ends of the tails were temporary, from which the building could grow to use the whole site, thereby creating a closed courtyard. They were painted the colour of dried blood like a dismembered limb, as if to remind Olivetti to allow the building future growth. All the working accommodation was at first-floor level, entered at one front corner via the front entrance and 'social' space; at the other by a workshop entrance. Beneath the working floor were service rooms and covered spaces for the salesmen's and mechanics' cars which nosed in around the edge. So in those days you saw the tails of Lotus Cortinas and Mini Coopers like bicoloured piglets round a sow.

The buildings were single-storey, on basements of *in situ* construction; their upper floors were prefabricated from plywood and metal, with demountable partitions.

The building at Carlisle became a Chinese restaurant, then a night club; the Dundee building is occupied by zippy designers – such are the vicissitudes of commerce and the demands of flexibility.

Roof plans of Olivetti branches in Dundee, Belfast, Carlisle and Derby

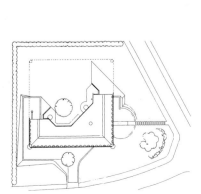 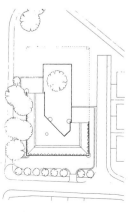 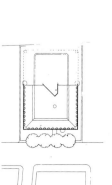 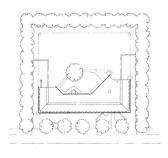

HIGHGROVE
1972-77

Coming home is coming home; it has little to do with any real understanding or feeling for what home is like. When amazed Californians asked me in the early 1960s why I was going back to England, I would sometimes earnestly tell them that I wanted to design groups of houses for many people rather than single ones for a few. Highgrove offered that chance.

My friend and favourite quantity surveyor, Bert Stern, had shown Minster Lovell to Thurston Williams who was Architect to the London borough of Hillingdon. Hillingdon stretches from London Airport to the Northwood Hills on the northwest fringe of London; from tightly-knit suburbia to 'loose' fashionable suburbia, almost country-side. It had a Labour administration which was determined to build 1,000 houses a year; to this end they had increased the permitted densities in some of the more elegant northern areas, thereby raising values and tempting home owners to sell to developers. They were further helped by the developers running into trouble, due to the effects of the oil crisis and thus forced to sell sites on to the council. One of these sites was an eight-acre field which had been attached to a house called Highgrove, on the very edge of the former village of Ruislip.

It later transpired that Alderman Bartlett, the leader of the council, had asked his architect to find other designers who could build 'traditional' houses, anticipating Prince Charles by more than a decade. The Minster Lovell project convinced Williams that Edward Cullinan Architects would fit the bill (a misunderstanding, for Minster Lovell was an existing building, whereas Highgrove required new houses on a greenfield site to be imagined and invented). Despite this, we received nothing but the most energetic, ingenious and creative support from Williams throughout, right through to our combined public presentation of the final built result in the lecture hall of the RIBA.

During the twenty-five years since the Second World War the bureaucrats who sanctioned loans (or not) for local authority housing, had become incredibly rigid about procedure, and fixed in their ideas about what was possible in terms of building and what was not.

The received wisdom at the Department of the Environment was that to achieve the desired low costs, houses needed to be built in terraces of eight to 12, each house measuring 12 feet (3.8 metres) wide. Being so narrow they could reasonably have about 20 feet of front garden and 30 feet at the rear, before they became ridiculously long. At 70 people to the acre, this allocation of private space left you with a vast area of public open space, POS no less, which nobody liked, and which the local authority disliked having to maintain. Therefore at Highgrove we devised a way of making wide-fronted houses in groups of four, wherein each house had a kitchen, dining and living space, all opening onto a large garden, thereby fully possessing the landscape. As the drawings show (pages 75 and 77), the site plan has paths and mews at right angles to the two roads, lead to front and garage doors. As the detailed plans and sections show, there are many different kinds of houses and flats, but in each one the solid spine walls and floors are clothed in a kind of light-weight umbrella, in which the windows support lightweight, prefabricated, insulated roofs: in cross section there are no external walls.

By these radical moves we achieved a more genuinely suburban division of land than 'traditional' terraces would have done; people no longer had to travel to their allotments – the allotments came to the houses.

To avoid tedious descriptions of endless meetings in the offices of the Department of the Environment in their dull towers in Marsham Street, there follows a talk which gave in 1978 to a students' colloquium that had the general title, *A Question of Style*. The first imaginary documents will amuse, while the fourth gives a flavour of how it was at Marsham Street in the early 1970s.

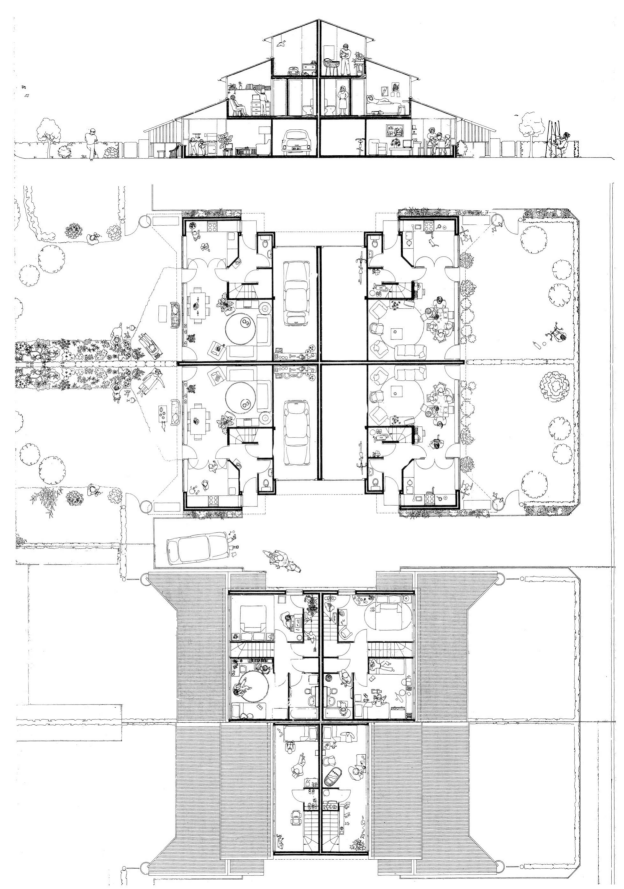

FROM ABOVE: Section, ground and first floor plans for type A housing

A QUESTION OF STYLE

Architecture has suffered more than most arts in recent years from the twentieth-century disease that attempts to quantify rather than to describe quality. It has tended not to be regarded as an art in itself, with its own inspiration and disciplines, but thought of more in terms of, for example, Sociology, Building Science, Management Technique, Engineering, Computer Technology, Environmental Control, Functionalism, Geometry, Stylistic Revival or Politics.

It seems to me that we should now begin to look at our shared subject primarily as an art of its own that requires intelligence, insight, inspiration and inventiveness, and quite deliberately sets out to propose an environment that is felt to be enjoyable or *stylish* or, in the words of Pirsig, in that marvellous piece of pop philosophy, *Zen and the Art of Motorcycle Maintenance*, possess its own *quality*.

I use the word *stylish* rather than *style* because *style* seems reminiscent of a 'battle of the styles' scene such as existed in the nineteenth century, and in some circles exists again today as various particular aspects of the early Modern Movement are deliberately revived to set against the weedy products of the neo-vernacular and other cop-outs. By *stylish* I mean the deliberate attempt to create within a proposed building an atmosphere and an order; by understanding and feeling the nature and quality of the whole as it is made of ordered solid and void, sticks and skin, junction to ground and sky, straight parts and corners, repetitive elements and unique parts. Deliberate composition leads to a certain ambience beyond the necessary one created by usefulness.

Which is to say that the degree to which a building has style, a determined quality or is stylish, is not a matter that can be added later but is contained irrevocably in the first intention at the very start of the design process. This should be embraced, welcomed, enjoyed and included in one's development of the place and never regarded with embarrassment, or as beside the point of the main grim issue of getting it designed and built.

I hope to illustrate the proposition that the style or quality of a future building is written deeply into it at the very start of the design process, by reading four imaginary letters or fables to you, concerning buildings about to be built, and I think that you will quickly receive a vivid picture of the ambience of each as it will be when it is carried out.

July 6th, 1948
The Chairman
Much Wentworth War Damage, Slum Clearance,
Town Planning and Building Committee

Dear Roger Stonebridge,

Thank you for your optimistic and supportive letter of July 1st and for giving me this opportunity to enlarge on the philosophy that lies behind our scheme for the renewal of the inner area of Much Wentworth, known as Shotover Fields.

As you know from the excellent History of the Town written by Hugh Kenworthy Smythe in 1926, Shotover Fields was developed as an industrial village in the 1840s around the two large iron and steelworks, the railway marshalling yards and warehouses, and beside the main cattle yards on steeply rising ground on either bank of the now polluted river Went. The existing houses are in closely-packed back to back terraces: only one in ten has an integral bathroom. The fumes and the smoke from the various industries in the area and from the coal burning fires in the houses themselves have caused much deterioration in the fabric of the houses during the years since they were built, and this deteriorating situation has now been hastened by the fact that twenty-five per cent of the existing stock was destroyed or rendered structurally unsound during the bombing raids from which Much Wentworth suffered so heavily during the recent war.

It is to take advantage of this situation, and the proposed closing of the marshalling yard, the electrification of the railway and the smoke control orders that you are proposing to apply throughout the town, that we are now proposing that a start be made for the progressive renewal of the whole of the housing stock in the Shotover Fields area of Much Wentworth.

You have asked us to start with a scheme for forty units and we are proposing to place these on the high ground at Shotover Crag, the tower having four two-storey maisonettes (a new type recently developed by the MHLG) at each level, thereby reaching a height of twenty storeys. This tower will not only provide a visual point of reference in a rather derelict area and lend impetus to the progressive renewal of the whole downtown area, but it will also release much ground around it for landscape parkland, play areas, crèches, nursery schools and other community activities while symbolising an energetic post-war spirit and the rapid economic recovery of Much Wentworth in the second half of the twentieth century.

Of equal importance is the effect that it will have on the occupants who will enjoy distant views, clean air, freedom from traffic and noise, convenient access to community services, easily managed patios in the air as well as warm and dry dwellings with fitted bathrooms and kitchens for the first time in the history of the town.

Finally, let me stress again that this first tower is only a beginning: that as other towers replace the present derelict areas of Much Wentworth, so the system of parkland and vehicle/pedestrian separation will grow across the town bringing with it not only trees, flowers and birds, but linking paths to schools, shops and places of work.

Do let me know if there is any further information that you need.

Yours sincerely,

Gray Bloomfield Jones
High Wycombe, Bucks

Conversation in a North Californian Forest, 1965
Man one: Hey man! How do you like this stuff? It causes you to voyage into worlds unknown, to travel far without the encumbrance of your body, to dream dreams, to wander in the paths of nirvana, mirrored in the mirror of your own reflection, striding over moons and hunting celestial joy in honour of the supreme sun; son of man, summary of wholeness, tripped-out in easygoing nothingness, onwards outwards, far outwards, warding off the ifs and buts...

Man two: Fuck it baby, do you ever dry up! you dry me out you do, but speaking of bats I rolled this noo one which you should now by all means possible get lit and stuck between your super-mobile lips lest they spout out so much my hearing ear gets bent flat to my head, man; and where did you score?

Man one: Let me unravel myself sufficiently from this bed of pine needles, and raise my shaggy head from the barky surface of this Californian stringy dry barked redwood log to tell you my old friend that I scored this stuff over on the other side of the hill down the unpaved path, path of a trail from those bums who are newly liberated from the San Francisco rat-run most of them at all times now, for ever man, and some hanging into this liberation for the weekends only, some in shacks, some in covered trucks – Jesus man it went out, roll me a new one for love – as I think I may have been saying unto thee some in shacks, some in covered trucks, some in tents, some on the ground (ground hogs ground bread out of flowers among which they sleep! Shit I lost it). Now I feel it again, now I must tell you that some have it now got it together to start in on making themselves homes on their four-acre plots of which there are forty in this forest and I am most certainly told that some have drawn nigh unto completion – it knocks me out, completion – its unbearably beautiful. I lost it again. I'm losing it, it's gone, oh fuck, it's out again. The lights are going out all over the world oh mother!

Man two: Now may I stir your head with my thoughts sufficiently to say to you my brother that I too, one day when and if I have lain long enough in this forest on my four acres of true domain to feel the motherly vibrations that will say to me how to do so gently, will take from my gunnysack my grandfather's Diston saw, my hammer being twenty-four ounces and nails nils like Jesus nails man and I will make me a home to which I shall ask a by then hopefully liberated Barbara and their holiness our holy children to share our lives together liberated, freed on wholemeal, oh whole meals man! How will that be; our bodies warmed by sun, our souls alone, and cooled by rain. Oh man the rain how beautiful; the fire's gone out I feel the heavy dampness of my old sleeping bag, clinging wetly, beautifully, blissfully to my legs in Levis, toes in leather boots, stomach wet naked: tomorrow I start my house.

Man one: Oh dear lovely wet sleeping bag oh beautiful itchy pine cones all inside the bed with me to o o o m u c h zzzzzzzzzzzz

Man two: building, bubbling, budding, babbling, baubling, building of house for Barbara bara barabarabara zzzzzzz ZZZ zzzzzzzzzz

Her Grace the Duchess of Much Wentworth
Much Wentworth Castle
Much Wentworth
Wentworthshire

Your Grace,
I am this day sending your Grace by the hand of one

Roberto Venturi who often has cause to pass Wentworth whilst journeying from Cambridge to Oxford, drawings of the elevations and an aerial view of the almshouses for the forty deserving parishioners of the parish of Much Wentworth and surrounding villages that you have graciously desired me to undertake on your behalf.

Had the said Roberto Venturi been passing thither at an earlier time, your Grace would have had the drawings presented to you the sooner; though much has transpired in London during the past year or so as to interfere with the speedy execution of this undertaking on your Grace's behalf.

The plans of the disposition of rooms in the separate apartments your Grace has already seen, and indeed, they are of small concern being similar to those erected on other parts of your domain and much suited to occupation by the elderly poor.

Therefore let me say that the pictures now sent are designed to show your Grace that the almshouses being to one side of the parterre which lies on the central axis of the newly finished castle, will not obtrude themselves on the prospect from the main rooms of the castle but will instead show only the top of the entrance gate tower above the trees to the west of the parterre or promenade. From a position further south on the parterre however, by the fountain erected in honour of your late and revered Lord, the greater part of the principal elevation of the almshouses will be visible to those who elect to stroll so far as to enjoy the serenity of the prospect across the lake. Being executed in a humbler manner of antiquity than the castle itself, the almshouses will nevertheless have a nobility of appearance such as to create a most soothing impression on the onlooker as he beholds the edifice itself, and below its reflection in the lake. At the same time the edifice is far enough removed from the promenades adjacent to the castle as to avoid the annoyance that the daily events of the humbler way of life contained therein might cause to those whose home or place of rest is more suitable lodged within the wall of your Grace's castle.

And as to this last matter, your Grace will also notice that entry and departure from the almshouses will always be by the main gate, which opens onto the town square of Much Wentworth, under the watchful eye of your Grace's second bailiff; and that this gateway is on the side of courtyard round which the almshouses are gathered that is furthest from the castle.

I shall attend your Grace in the company of master mason, Robert Adam, on the twenty-sixth day of the next month to discuss this and any other matters pertaining to the ornamentation and the layout of the parkland around the castle, and in the meantime I await your instructions as to the speedy execution of this undertaking, and I beg to remain,

Your most obedient servant,

Quinlan Terry
Lincoln's Inn Chambers
October 1714

Report Accompanying Submission of Scheme Design (RIBA Stage D) for the Development of Housing Site 264, known as Shaggy Brow 3 to the Development Sub-Committee of the Much Wentworth Expanding Town (Mark 2A) Development Corporation:

Site 264 is bounded to the north by Road R6, to the south by Arterial Road AR2, to the east by Local Road LR23 and to the west by Local Road LR24. The area of the site for DoE HCY1 purposes is 1.0111 has (hectares) and the units have been placed on the site in accordance with the recommendations contained in MWDC 32 (Access to dwellings for fire engines and refuse collection purposes) in the proportions set out in MWDC 84/ds which yields 2 No 7-p (bedspace) units (5% of total), 4 No 6-p units (10%), 22 No 5-p units (55%), 4 No 4-p units (10%), 2 No 3-p units (5%), 3 No 2-p units (7.5%) and 3 No 2-p APDs (Aged Persons Dwellings).

This mix produces 14 No bs's (bedspaces) in 7-p units, 24 No bs's in 6-p units, 110 bs's in 5-p units, 16 bs's in 4-p units, 6 bs's in 3-p units, 6bs's in 2-p units and 6 bs's in 2-p APD units; a total of 182 bs's in 40 units which is the permitted 180 bs's per ha on the HCY1 site area of 1.0111111 ha's.

For planning purposes however, the site area measured to the CLs (centreline) of LR23 and LR24 but to CLs of the slip road off R6 and AR2 is 1.04 ha's and the permitted density is 150 hr's (habitable rooms) per ha.

As all the dwelling units have been signed according to MWDC/AP6/76 (Approved Plans for dwelling units in Expanding Areas), the two 7-p units have 12 hrs, the four 6-p units 20 hrs, the twenty-two 5-p units have 88 hrs, the four 4-p units have 16 hrs, the two 3-p units have 6 hrs, the three 2-p units have 6 hrs and the three 2-p APD units have 6 hrs, giving a total of 154 hrs or 148.077 hrs per ha which is within the permitted 150 hrs per ha and which includes the designated 14M Amenity Strip beside 1R2 and the required 25% of POS (public open space) and achieves a PR (plot ratio) of 0.4 as predicted in the earlier report.

Car parking at the rate of 65% of 7-p, 6-p, 5-p, 4-p and 3-p units has been provided in hardstandings for 22 cars (being 65% of 34 units) and 45% of 2-p and 2-p APD units, being 3 cars (45% of 6 units) and an area has been reserved to bring future parking up to 100% of all units, a further 13 cars (40 minus 27). In addition to this, a further hardstanding has been provided for parking at the rate of one visitor's car to every four dwellings which results in 10 further parking spaces.

The scheme has received HCY1 approval from the DoE and the issue of Design Relative to Setting has been resolved, as well as an agreement concerning allowable Ad Hocs. So that it now only remains to produce production drawings to proceed to DoE 80/76 form A, and TA/HSG to be followed by TC1 and TC2.

Lecture given in 1978 and subsequently published in Spazio e Societa *Number 15/16, September-December 1981, GC Sansoni Editore Nuova SpA, Firenze, Italy.*

WESTMORELAND ROAD
1974-79

Here too, the developers could not afford to maintain their sites; the Solon Housing Association came into possession of this lovely south-sloping site just north of the North Downs in leafy suburban of Bromley. Solon was an inner London housing association, many of whose members were black, and obtaining planning permission from Bromley proved difficult.

It was finally agreed that a single volume on the north edge of the site would be acceptable, and the building is a development of this requirement. The front doors to all the maisonettes and apartments in this six-storey building, open from three levels of pavement which overlook the north forecourt. All six different kinds of flat and maisonette have indented balconies which overlook and thereby possess the shared garden, which slopes away southwards.

BELOW, L TO R: Cross sections of houses; planometrics

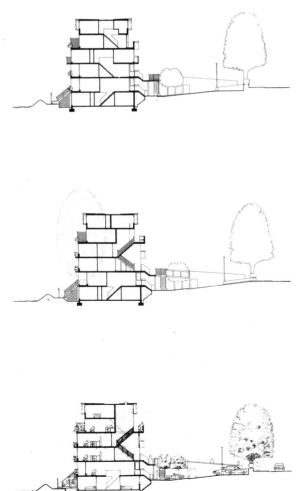

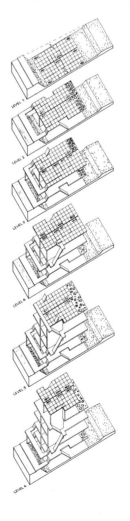

LEIGHTON CRESCENT
1974-79

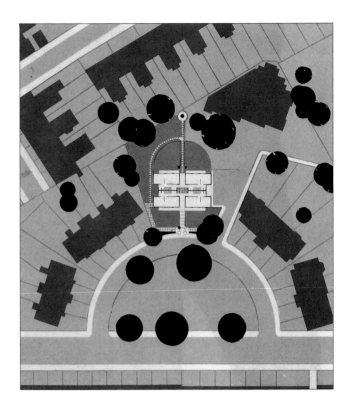

Leighton Crescent finally brought together housing and the historic. It is not in essence a very profound historic setting but becomes one when seen through the eyes of present-day nostalgia. Our building of local authority housing was to replace the ruined centrepiece of a nineteenth-century crescent in north London. Here the Highgrove scheme of things was used to make 16 apartments on split-level floors, side by side and back to back, over four two-storey houses with their own gardens. The apartments and houses, being wide-fronted, could be divided as the users wished; and their wide-frontedness allowed us to compose elevations which had a large, broad, balconied scale which was sufficient for making a proper centrepiece to the large-scaled Victorian crescent.

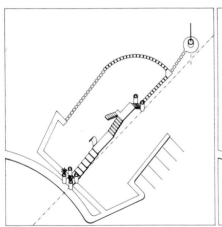

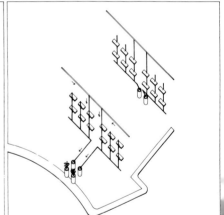

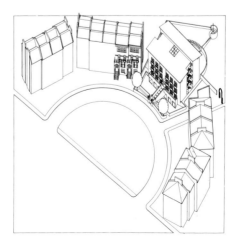

FROM ABOVE: Site plan; axonometric diagram of routes, rooms and balconies; axonometric of site plan

As this building had deliberately composed elevations which attempted a certain sophistication, it seems right to include here my contribution to the issue of a Japanese magazine *A Decade of British Housing, '70s*, edited by my friend Edward Jones. This will also serve to summarise our efforts to make 'housing' as opposed to houses during that decade. It was called 'House, Architecture, the Cocktail and the Dry-Stone Wall' which in Japanese looks like this:

住宅 建築 カクテル
そして
ドライストーン・ウォール

and it went as follows:

HOUSE, ARCHITECTURE, THE COCKTAIL AND THE DRY-STONE WALL

The cocktail is a ritual melange of delectable ingredients; the juices of many cultures, gathered worldwide, blended to taste with considerable skill, served with a cocktail of food in prettily-arranged, deliberately artificial air-conditioned surroundings; to a background of light conversation, chink of glasses, rattle of ice, sound of live music: smart, suave, profligate, surplus, elegant, stylish and in some ways sophisticated. I will use it here to characterise, though not to describe, those aspects of twentieth-century architecture that celebrate the luxury of choice, deliberate self-expression and the pleasures of artificiality: the Dusenberg, Scott Fitzgerald, and the foyer, ramps and terraces of the Villa Savoie.

For centuries, dry-stone walls have formed the boundaries to fields on the higher stonier ground of the north and west of Britain; the stonier the ground, the smaller the fields, since clearing the ground and making the boundary are both parts of the same process. The large scale of the hilly landscape is ordered and grained by the boundaries within it. All stones and *only* stones are used; megaliths as gate posts and ends, large stones at the bottom and as through stones, polygonal ones to make the two pretty faces that are rendered an integral part of the structural system by the small stones that support and divide them in the middle and by the flat ones laid sideways as soldiers along the top to stabilise, weigh down on and terminate the completed structure.

To the twentieth-century eye the walls are no longer the simple art of necessity that they were; they are invested with a notion of purity and honesty, and thought of as honourable and morally good, natural, linked with a purer past and a possible future, even fatuously as a lost art vaguely connected with ley lines and the wisdom of the ancients. I am using the dry-stone wall to characterise those aspects of twentieth-century architecture that enjoy limited means and hope for honesty, truth to materials, creating architecture as a democratic experience: the lightweight bike, the Chaplin film, the hedges, paths and houses of the garden suburb.

In late nineteenth-century Britain, over ninety per cent of families lived in houses rented from private landlords, companies or great estates, often squalid. Eighty years later as a result of ordinary social pressure and deliberate policy, over half own their houses and just under half rent them from local authorities. Nearly all the houses and apartments built by those local authorities were designed by architects in public or private practice, and they are largely responsible for what they are like: for although the Government may set cost limits and minimum standards, architects are the enablers and their insight and 'shove' will determine the quality of the place that results – it requires shove since Government tends to be ponderous, opaque, dogmatic, conservative and full of bureaucratic verbiage – to Polly Adler[1] the celebrated madam, 'a house is not a home'. To the Department of the Environment a house is not even a house, it's a dwelling unit lived in by Ps who occupy bedspaces – there is a knee-deep river of jargon to wade through on the way to the deeper waters where many a scheme has sunk: cost yardstick, 'HCY1s' Ps per ha and Bs per ha, ad hocs, Parker Morris, Planning and so on.

Good work has come through this process but mostly good in the sense characterised by the honest, honourable dry-stone wall. Letchworth, Hampstead Garden Suburb, Port Sunlight, Welwyn, the LCC cottage estates between the wars, the Swedish influenced 'Contemporary' style (modern was a dangerously luxurious word) estates and new towns of the 1940s and 50s – all of these are examples of the system of design sometimes known as 'people's detailing' or in the 1970s as that which is loosely called the neo-vernacular/pseudo-vernacular. In the 1970s schemes became smaller, therefore more influenced by their surroundings, inherently more traditional.

Through this whole eighty-year-long trend, the influences that I lightly characterise by the sophisticated cocktail (but which include such modern notions as the asymmetrical interpenetration of spaces and planes, both vertically and horizontally, the pleasure of sunshine, and light, the integration of inside and out, the use of tops of buildings and of plate glass and plastic materials), aiming towards social and spatial liberation, have largely been absent. Absent too, our current reinvestigation of the city street, the square, the park, and the contributions that the composition of the collective elevations of houses and other buildings make to those shared places.

This is not surprising. Throughout the period and throughout the world; despite their protestations to the contrary, architects have been able to respond to their private clients with a certain luxury of spatial imagination which is absent from what has variously been known as housing, housing estate, council housing, workers' housing or mass housing. To me much of the quality of 1970s housing lies in the extent to which it redresses this absence. In our work for the London Borough of Hillingdon at Highgrove, we attempted to carry suburbia beyond the sum of its separate parts, and to introduce a larger-scale pattern of houses and hedges and to give those houses a wide frontage flexibility of division in their family rooms and much interconnection between their insides and their own hedge bounded gardens and terraces. In Clive Plumb and Company's work at Langdon Hills for Basildon New Town, double-height family rooms, overlooked by galleries with stairs that rise to them below the sloping roof line, make the spatial interconnection while preserving the degrees of separateness and togetherness required by families in houses. At Branch Hill by Benson and Forsyth with the London Borough of Camden, the hill is exploited and formalised into layered terraces for the houses that open onto them. At Alexandra Road by Neave Brown also for Camden, houses upon houses open and close their plans and sections to make the connections and divisions that houses need, and they open Southwards on to terrace upon terrace. At Westmoreland Road and Leighton Crescent, we developed a language of solid wall and openings around the apartments, with a further layer of lightweight posts, sticks and mesh to carry those apartments beyond their enclosed selves on to balconies and terraces that also make a formal presentation to the old parts of the city in which they sit.

In Hodgkinson's Foundling Estate in Bloomsbury, houses with territory indoors and out in sun and light make the sides and tops at once to the larger shops, cinemas and other city buildings below them.

These are a few examples from many: there is work in Britain that is well beyond utility and out of sight of the usually timid and derivative work of the private sector.

Whilst appreciating the pleasure of eating oysters in boxing gloves,[2] my predeliction is for building dry-stone walls while having cocktails.

1 Polly Adler *A House is not a Home*, Heinemann, 1954
2 Oma, *Architectural Design*, May 1977

Previously published in The Toshi-Jutaku, Urban Housing, *no 156, October 1980, Tokyo.*

ST MARY'S, BARNES
1978-84

St Mary's, Barnes and the Lambeth Community Care Centre were designed and built during a time of heated debate about 'community architecture'. They were both repeatedly presented to various interested groups, at large vociferous public meetings. Both might be described as a kind of community architecture. But what kind?

One form of community architecture poses no difficulties for anyone: you simply gather together a public meeting of interested parties and ask them to decide or vote for a list of 'features' which the building or buildings should contain. Then by a wonderful act of suppression of ego, the architect proceeds to cobble those features together; which nearly always turn out to be nostalgic; dormers, gables, chimney pots, half-timbering, arches and so on. The sad results are visible all over our land, just as when Ford designed the Edsell in 1955, (following the largest feature by feature consumer survey ever conducted), and it flopped.

We tried to practise a different kind of community architecture, more suitably called community engagement. This involved understanding that the biggest limitation on the quality of a building is the architects' ability to conceive and to realise a suitable, elegant and necessary response to the situation which is presented to them. So from the very first meeting, to each and every one with two, ten, twenty or 300 people, we took illustrations and models that we could use to imagine a total and detailed composition for the building. This was of course a hairy process, since a great deal of 'self' has to go into making each proposal which is then publicly put at risk.

On occasion whole parts of imaginary schemes were questioned, and we would have to imagine again – at other times what we proposed enabled people to explain to us more clearly what they wanted. At all times the architects need to hang on firmly to what they can truly and genuinely imagine composing – never to cobble pieces together. It can work; it has to work: people are becoming more and more interested in having power over their surroundings, and somehow we need to find a way that satisfies that longing inventively and truthfully.

The Parish Church of St Mary's in Barnes, south London had all the qualities most likely to inspire nostalgia. Some parts were medieval, for example, the bell tower, with a vast Georgian rectory beside it. It was close to the village green which had a duck pond with weeping willows, a lich-gate and yew trees – it was and is a vital part of the collection of pieces which allows the population of this Victorian London suburb to refer to it as The Village or Barnes Village. It was and is an icon.

Burnt to the ground in 1978, only the church walls remained standing; walls which dated from the twelfth to the early twentieth centuries. These enclosed a small

medieval church and tower which had become the south aisle of a large early twentieth-century nave and north aisle. All parties were agreed on a careful restoration of the medieval church. However, controversy rampaged through Barnes and far beyond between two groups. The first, not trusting the architecture of the late twentieth century to rise to the occasion, wished to rebuild the whole church as it had been, though rather smoother. The second, led by the Church Council who represented most of the regular churchgoers, wanted to make a church more suited to their present needs, and wanted Edward Cullinan Architects to do it. It is impossible to describe the heat that was raised round this particular parish pump – it was very hot and frequently painful – but the second group were very tenacious, very brave and mostly had their way. Now nearly everybody I meet in Barnes claims to be of this view.

These pages show the church before the fire, the medieval tower, nave and chancel (by the south aisle and Lady Chapel), the early twentieth-century nave and north aisle side by side. Axonometric sketches show the reconstruction of elements of St Mary's past, retained and developed.

Also shown are a small round stair turret and the vestry, together with the geometric and constructional system, to re-roof and extend the medieval church to the north, to a new crossing, and thence west and east to the existing round stair turret and vestry. Two trusses of multi-coloured steel and wood cross the old nave and become dual ridge trusses for a new and wider nave extending north to a new high wall.

The altar is free-standing; secondary ridge trusses form transepts that terminate the round turret and the old vestry. From the trusses, the roofs fold down to the eaves, hipped and valleyed to form a continuous canopy over old and new work. Inside, the medieval church reads as a whole nave, chancel, and altar for small congregations, or as the narthex to a much larger church, with a wide nave and transepts that place the congregation in front of or around the altar.

Barnes church takes a complicated built history and powerful local feeling as inspiration, not as encouragement to nostalgia or pastiche. Immediately after its completion, while the bruises were still healing, I wrote the following piece:

TRADITION AND NOSTALGIA

On behalf of *The Architectural Review* Penny McGuire is about to see me. She has agreed to ask me and a number of other architects if we think if there is such a thing as an English tradition in architecture and if so, whether it is in a recognisable shape today. A question for the 1980s and, I assume, related to the 150th anniversary of the RIBA. My answers to the two questions are, in essence; 'Yes, probably' to the first and 'No' to the second.

I want to take tradition in architecture to mean a shared and continuous development of a way of doing things towards practical artistic and social ends. I do not want it to mean in the estate agent's sense, 'old-fashioned'. So when architects respond to the recurrent waves of nostalgia for the past that surge over our land, by making old-fashioned-looking housing estates and supermarkets, they are not being traditional, they are being no more than old-fashioned or nostalgic. In doing this they accurately reflect the fear of the present that many feel, due in

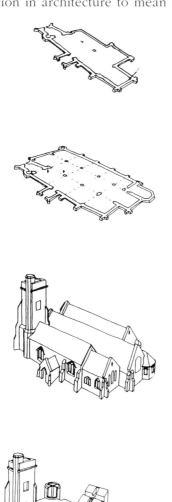

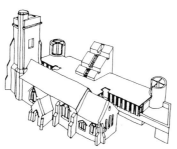

Transformation of St. Mary's, Barnes; LEFT, FROM ABOVE: plans and axonometric before the fire; axonometric of scheme 1; RIGHT, FROM ABOVE: Axonometrics of scheme 2, old elements, new elements and as built

part to the world that we have created and fear of the inventions that we have let out of the laboratory cupboard to menace it. Nostalgia is escapist.

On the other hand, if one looks at the period during which a 'tradition' of domestic architecture developed and grew in England and then elsewhere, it is to see a very different process that concerned itself quite largely with making better futures, and was hopeful of them. It is the period of the development of the bourgeois house as an object in its own right, not as a small scale imitation of the aristocrat's house, as it had been before then.

William Morris (whose 150th anniversary it is) and Philip Webb thought they were devising a way of thinking of and making for everyman, but even now that great day is still to come; for the great English freestyle houses were built for the rapidly rising middle class of Victorian England. Nonetheless a large part of the inspiration for those houses was to do with trying to make a better, more liberated world for the future, and we can see it in the work of Webb, Shaw, Voysey, Mackintosh, early Lutyens and in Europe; then, most especially, down the route of the Shingle style to Wright and early Prairie houses.

From the Red House (1859) which itself derived from the domestic tradition of the earlier village schools and vicarages of the early gothicists like Street and Butterfield; and from the realisation of Wright's first 'pure' Prairie house, Ward Willits (of 1902), one can see in the work of this tradition the development of a domestic architecture that was deliberately asymmetrical, composed in three dimensions, and tending towards lowness and wideness, thus creating outside spaces rather than elevational backdrops and inside and outside spaces that interpenetrate one with another. Though the earlier work tends to justify itself by looking back to an ideal medieval past and the later, especially in, America, looking forward to modernism, it is all informed by a broad idea of a new kind of life for a new kind of people, and rejection of the old hierarchy of the rich man in his castle, the poor man at his gate. Architecture was thought of as liberating.

The period of the early 1900s seems to me a fairly certain time for this tradition to run out of steam. It was a period of quite shattering invention and consequent ideas; of electricity, radio, movies and motor cars and flight; of Einstein's proposal of the first

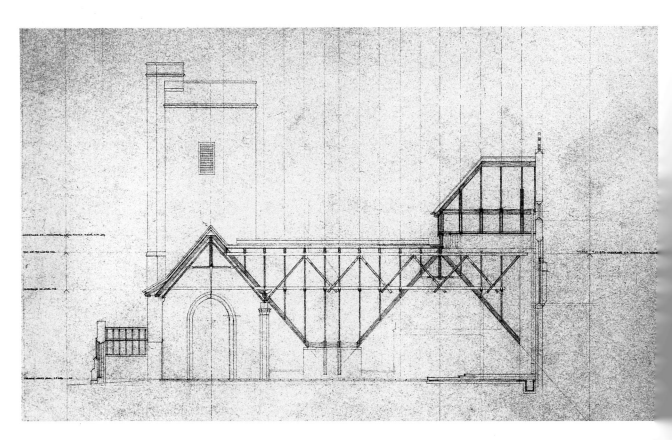

St Mary's, cross section

theory of relativity and most powerfully in our own art, the idea of cubism and the idea of the machine age allied to the existing idea of architecture as liberator. And it is at this time that England, lost perhaps in dreams of imperial glory soon to be shattered, faltered and lost its domestic architectural tradition in the developing and inventive sense, and started to see it only nostalgically. Europe had already borrowed the tradition through Muthesius' book *Das Englisches Haus* and others, while only Mackintosh had a live connection with European thinking. It was the beginning of our period of architectural and artistic sleep, the period during which Lutyens' formidable formal talents were turned away from ideas of inventive domesticity, towards the Viceroy's palace in Delhi; the period of the development of the modern tradition in Europe, represented here only in the work of Lubetkin and a handful of others. It was the period when the Academy continuously railed against what was known derisively as 'modern art', which culminated in the 1945 Picasso and Matisse exhibition at the Victoria and Albert Museum that caused shock and horror forty years after what John Berger calls 'The Moment of Cubism'. It ended in the

1950s when England, through the Smithsons and others, was reconnected to an international tradition and to an architecture of hopeful invention.

So for now I must say that although there have been fairly significant English contributions to architecture in the last thirty years, New Brutalism, Archigram, Stirling, Situationism, High Tech and so on, England is now part of a large scene; and though one can trace a number of peculiarly local reactions in the design of buildings, none could be said to constitute a live and particularly English tradition. Not at least, if by tradition, one means a shared and continuous development of a way of doing things to achieve practical, artistic and social ends.

For the strange thing about a living tradition in architecture is that it needs to be inventive and energetic, to be liberating, to respond to the present, to create futures; the opposite to the debased use of the word traditional to mean nostalgic.

In a way it is like Gertrude Stein saying that America is the oldest country in the world since it has lived in the present for the longest.

Speech given at the 1984 RIBA Conference, York.

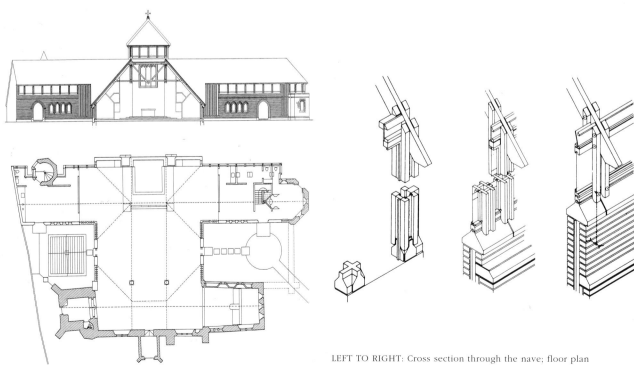

LEFT TO RIGHT: Cross section through the nave; floor plan

LAMBETH COMMUNITY CARE CENTRE
1980-85

The Community Care Centre in Lambeth (a rather derelict area of inner London) was nurtured in a simpler, less tortured manner than the church at Barnes. For years Sue Thorne, chairperson of the Community Health Council, together with Roger Higgs and other local doctors, had been trying to build a community hospital on part of the site of the derelict Lambeth General Hospital. This site had previously been used to represent the South Bronx in the film *Death Wish II*, starring Charles Bronson on a motorbike. Despite allowing for the even worse conditions in the real Bronx, the site was definitely derelict and definitely unprepossessing. On one part they wanted to build a hospital for fifty day patients, with twenty beds, in which GPs could care for their own cases.

The practice was selected in part for the excellent reason that we had never designed a hospital before, and therefore could not have developed bad habits or know the short-cuts. It was a while before the health authority accepted this reasoning but at that time there were riots in the streets of Liverpool, and an anxious government looked for inner-city projects to which it could contribute; the Lambeth project had been prepared on faith, and it was built.

A long thin building, the care centre has an entrance forecourt on the north side and creates a garden oasis on the south. The ground floor has consulting rooms overlooking the forecourt, and large dayrooms open southwards into the garden. Upstairs small wards and bedrooms open on to a terrace: all parts are connected by corridors which widen and narrow to make various meeting or sitting places, and window seats – the two levels are jointed by a stairway conservatory with a water garden.

The Lambeth Community Care Centre was designed by the process I have described: the practice put forward models of how it might appear, to a series of meetings, large and small – we listened and drew what we could truly imagine.

The gardens were developed during a series of community 'plant-ins', and are maintained in the same way. When the Prince and Princess of Wales came together to open it, they too brought their own tree to a terrific local party, and planted it to wild applause. I was teaching at the Massachusetts Institute of Technology at that time and I had to get back to give a lecture there the next morning. Here is the letter about the return journey which I wrote the next day to Claire Herniman, my partner and our practice manager.

BELOW: Ground and upper floor plans

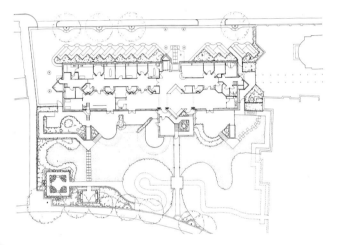

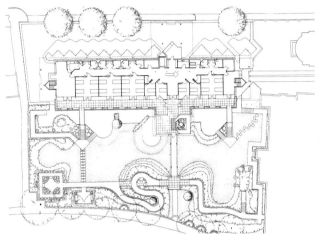

A LETTER TO CLAIRE

Dearest Claire,

The most important matter is that I promised you a description of my journey over there which you organised *so beautifully* in spite of the travel agents!

In the general mêlée towards the end of that truly wonderful occasion at Lambeth, with, as it turned out, a quite unnecessary degree of anxiety, I sought with diffidence the permission of Jack Stenhouse to depart in advance of their Royal Nibs, who by then were completely hemmed in by their adoring subjects: to the extent of having to hold their cups of china tea above breast-level. Stenhouse – stressed by then – gave his blessing to my disappearance and I fled through the crowds in the street, steel band and all, who shouted 'When, when, when oh when are *they* coming?'. 'Soon, soon,' I cried and ran round to the getaway car that already contained Ros and Max. Then began (by eagerly charging up two or three blind alleys and screaming back out of them) by far the most dangerous and terrifying part of the entire journey. Theories as to the quickest route were exchanged with passion between the three intrepid 2CV travellers – leading to a passage through many strange streets down the Kangaroo Valley end of town that would not have immediately occurred to the average motorist or even taxi driver. There also seemed to be a large need for police cars, security vans and fire-fighting equipment to storm through the rush hour that day in aid of various distressed citizens. I must say that it can only have been the presence of St Christopher in the 2CV with us that ensured that Max, in his uncontrollable excitement did no more than distress the twenty or thirty-odd citizens who we stopped within inches of, or who were brushed by the bumpers or wings, or had to display their fitness at leaping aside, or were addressed with verbal vigour or dazzled by Max's repeated attempts to prove that 2CVs are only half as wide as other cars. But we got there and I am proud to say that I was only once frightened beyond speech and we followed the Concorde signs and we parked insolently, as we felt we should, not in the park but with three limos in front of the door, and meandered into the sleazy luxury of the Concorde/first-class check-in. There we found a pop star and his moll, a movie mogul, a number of rather self-conscious, high society English executives of all ages, some quite regular Americans out for the trip, and three secretaries with ten tickets each, and piles of bags to check in. In front of me was an American couple who had arrived on spec to be given the devastating news that the 'thing' was full and that they would have to travel 'regular' first class instead: I sympathised greatly with their little boy, who they said would be extremely disappointed. Max and Ros and I were also a bit selfconscious but consoled by the fact that if you feel up to the effort, you are allowed to carry your bags into the cabin with you. So by now we were checked in and horribly early – only twenty past six: so I hopped it into the gents and changed into jeans and we all had coffee and sticky buns with the lower orders: before kissing goodbye and me ambling down to the Concorde lounge which was full of Movie Moguls, Captains of Industry, Pop Stars, Ordinary Americans out for the trip, and me – all having the first free goodies (exotic cocktails and a lot of special messages for Mr So & So and Mr So & So, quietly and seductively whispered on an upper class sound system). With five minutes to go we were joined by a substantial number of even more superior persons who had their check-in done for them in the manner already described. Then we all upped and ambled into the craft at a whispered suggestion over the PA. Now I have an important revelation to make to you who have previously and mistakenly thought that 'Flying the Tube' meant the underground railway: for I know now that I am a member of the supersonic underground, that 'the tube' actually refers to Concorde.

It has twenty-five rows of double seats down each side which makes fifty seats down each side which is 100 seats altogether and the cross section is like the Northern Line, but squeezed. But the whole thing actually has a rather delicious 'early days of modern travel' flavour to it, all grey and smooth and designer and anthropometric and minimal and efficient but posh with it, with such things as neat little roll-front wardrobes every eight rows for coats on coat hangers, with the luggage of those who'd the energy to carry it on below them.

So then came a message on the quietly modulated

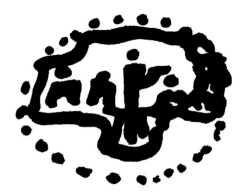

sound system which was addressed primarily to those (a pathetic minority of course) who had not flown on Concorde before: it was to warn us that a severe change of note would take place halfway through take-off when the 'afterburners' switched off, and not to take fright or try to clamber out through the windows – the size of the windows is shown below.

Then denouements of denouements: Heathrow being what it is we had to wait while three or four jumbos heaved their proletarian carcasses into the sky before, shrugging the fifth to one side, we set off down the runway with acceleration well in excess of the Beedle BMW, and without much apparent effort beyond a thunderous roar achieved an angle of forty-five degrees and proceeded up into the sky, followed quite soon by the heretofore mentioned afterburner cut-out which produces an eerie silence. This silence was broken by two astounding events. The first was the voice of our Captain, not only on the sophisticated and reassuring speaker

system but was the most 'educated' voice of any captain in the whole of British Airways. He told us that we were rising, that in ten minutes we would be over the Bristol Channel, that we would then rise again to 58,000 feet and that he expected we'd land at Kennedy in three hours and twenty minutes time. The second astounding event was the return of Princess Di: for it so happened that BA had chosen for the service of our section of the craft, none other than herself: pretty, gregarious and with exactly the same hair style. It was a clear night, so my eyes were glued to the mini-aperture right up to the Bristol Channel, when rising into the stratosphere was rapid and, combined with Di's offer of cocktails and the menu, unglued me. There is also nothing to see but the moon and stars and black night in the stratosphere. And that's interesting too, because the effect is pure 2001 but without the space music and silence, only the accompaniment of quite a bad roaring noise, reminiscent of a 1950 American V8 cruising steadily through a silent desert at about eighty mph: obtrusive but nostalgic. The choice on the menu was steak, slimmers' salad or partridge with numerous befores and afters: I chose partridge for the sheer thrill of seeing such a bird, dead though it was, flying at 58,000 feet. My neighbour, in the aisle seat chose nothing, since he was being met by his daughter in New York and being taken off to a decent meal there – he was the movie mogul. He kept offering me bits and pieces of the free handouts that were poured upon us by Di in case I wanted them: but I, with great dignity turned them down – all of them – actually all but this box of Concorde chocs which with mine we guzzled today with Denis Pieperz and Greta Jones.

So we had our four courses and our fine wines and our Remy Martin: all served by Di and boyfriend with such style, grace and aplomb as was musterable in the small cross section of the craft, and my friend took delivery of a box of fine Havanas and smoked one: whilst all the time I sorted your excellent Corbu slides into separate categories, on the two inches of spare seat beside me, in the crevice between my thighs and on the one-and-a-half inches on my fold-out table to the left of the dinner tray – and I went through Alan's acetates in the air in front of me, making mental notes about the forthcoming talk, since the above-mentioned sortings had occupied the whole of my bit of the stratosphere, leaving no space for writing in it. And the next thing you know – you're coming down again! As Mark said, like a falling leaf, brilliantly: like from space: it feels more like vertical decent than horizontal movement: down through the clouds from 58,000 feet, with our captain apologising for the fact that it has taken three hours and twenty-two minutes instead of twenty, but boasting that we averaged 1,000 mph from start to finish and got up to 58,000 feet and 1,350 mph. And when it lands it does that lovely thing of first touching down on its rear wheels and then being tipped forward on to its front one. So we arrived: there were of course a lot of vital messages for Messrs So & So and So & So: and proceeded to the immigration procedure. Now here is another message, for all those of you who have spent hours in immigration at Kennedy after alighting from Virgin or People's or other regular flights: fly Concorde – they are terrifically nice to you and I had one who was particularly interested in Bannister Fletcher – oh! oh! I've just seen the point: it might have been a test of my credentials as an architect: might it have been? So I got out to the NY helicopter bus and checked in at the NY helicopter place in the TWA Saarinen terminal and at 6.30 (left Heathrow 7.00pm: arrived JFK 5.22: left 6.30pm) took off across Manhattan,

via La Guardia to Newark: Manhattan towers all lit up in the early gloaming, us lower than the tops of the highest, engines roaring mightily, very very beautiful, very Italian

Futurist, now a proud Twentieth-Century person. Proud Twentieth-Century person landed in the new terminal at Newark and walked to the free bus (half a mile) to the People's Express concrete-block terminal a couple of miles away and began his descent towards ordinariness again. The PE craft had slightly larger but rather grubbier seats than the previous craft, and the drinks cost money – nearly everyone had cokes – I had my normal postprandial water; Perrier being unavailable. Thirty-five minutes later we landed at Logan and I walked nearly a mile to where we'd taken off four days before, the Pan Am counter, and opposite it I found the next source of my decline from the heights: the ghastly yellow and black outlines of the rip-seated, lock-jammed, wiper-rattling, Samis Dodge: which started, turned out to have cost forty dollars for its sojourn and took me, with a Concorde-like cruising note to 492 Putnam – and there, waiting in the headlights were – you'll never guess – Kiko and Monkey, the cats, wanting supper. I got there at 9.45pm and I wrote my talk till 1.30am and gave it the next morning. I think it went OK: at least I know that the excitement and the 'lag' suddenly disappeared about twenty minutes into it.

Thank you for your arrangements. It was a thrill to remember!

All fond wishes to you and to the rest of the mob,

With love from Ted.

WORCESTER COLLEGE
1980

Worcester College is the first of three buildings built around courtyards bordered by arcades, leading to rooms (and groups of rooms). Each strikes a balance between the requirements of privacy and community, but for three very different groups: dons, graduates and undergraduates at an Oxford college; delegates at a building society's conference and training centre; and one hundred single men in a hostel on the outskirts of Basingstoke. Worcester College is described here; the others follow.

Oxford colleges are usually walled-off from the city which enfolds them; elaborate gateways mark the openings in these walls.

At Worcester College we proposed such a gateway between city and college, with three floors of student rooms in a small guardian tower above it. Two similar gateways were to be built, one leading to the historic quadrangles of the college, the other to its playing fields. The three gates and the towers over them stake out three corners of a quadrangle: the fourth corner is marked by a rooftop belvedere which overlooks a banana-shaped lake. At the other end of this lake lie the historic quadrangles of Worcester College.

In addition to the rooms over the three gateways there are rooms for dons on two sides of the new quadrangle, below the grass-topped belvedere terrace. Future terraced houses were planned to form the remaining two sides. While overlooking the college quadrangle their front doors would open on to two mews (extensions of the city streets), so the houses themselves become an occupied 'wall'.

When I think back to my efforts with Sunand Prasad and Giles Oliver to find necessary expression for a residential building in this spot, I am reminded of a piece which I wrote in 1980 to be included in Norman Potter's book, *What is a Designer?*

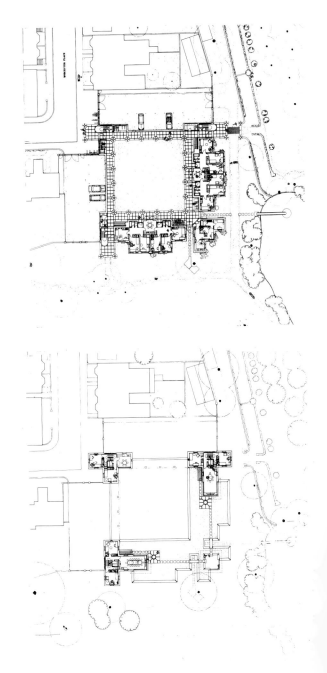

FROM ABOVE: ground and first floor plans

103

HANG-GLIDERS AND SAILING SURFBOARDS

As one struggles to design buildings and other artefacts that have a certain degree of leanness, grace and inevitability, one is also trying to unearth something beyond the 'cold programme' that comes with the project; a programme that is at the same time more demanding and poetic than the original.

For example, in house design the cold programme concerns numbers of units, areas, angles of light, cost, building regulations, ministry approvals, and planning requirements; so that the quality of space and place is almost entirely dependent on being inspired by a further programme of one's own discovery that lies beyond. Often this discovery that produces the completed design only occurs after repeated efforts to satisfy the demands of the cold programme.

It is with a certain envy that one looks at two products of the last ten years that have extremely demanding programmes, solved with pure, necessary poetry. Hang-gliders and sailing surfboards are toys which respond to, react to and extend the capacity of the human body and use no source of power other than that body in reaction to the elements of wind, air and water, via the toy itself. They both require skill and balance to achieve the reward they offer. Thus the medium of the toy itself makes its own demands; the dimension and mass of every strut, board, membrane and wire is critical, and both offer consummation to our longings to fly and to sail. Neither of these deceptively simple artefacts could have happened without having gone through the cold programmes of the development of powered flight and commercial and sporting sailing. The reduction to the graceful poetic minimum only comes after many secrets have been unearthed through passing more cumbersomely through air, wind and water.

Previously published in What is a Designer?*, Norman Potter, Hyphen Press, Reading, 1980.*

UPLANDS CONFERENCE CENTRE
1982-84

The second of the three quadrangles, this site already contained a late nineteenth-century house; and a great deal more: rotting back additions to the house, for example sheds, decrepit tennis courts, 1950s accommodation. All this was stripped away, leaving only the pseudo-Gothic house as the mainspring or pivot to a new composition. Beyond and to the north of the modest front hall, two great stairs rise on either side of a 'valley' of space, leading past the doors to first-floor conference rooms and bridge back into the upper 'seminar' rooms in the house itself. Beyond the valley lie ground-floor dining rooms, and to the east and west arcades stretch out round the edges of study bedroom quadrangles.

Georgina Livingston designed the precisely detailed planting of the study bedroom balconies, the landscape (which gives a particular quality to each quadrangle and court), and the broader landscape of the grounds beyond, as a seamless part of the expanding composition.

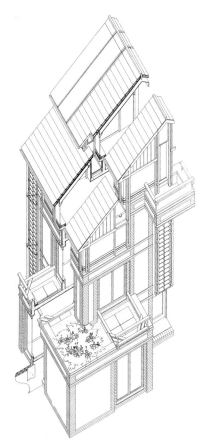

Sectional isometric of pavilion; BELOW: Site plan

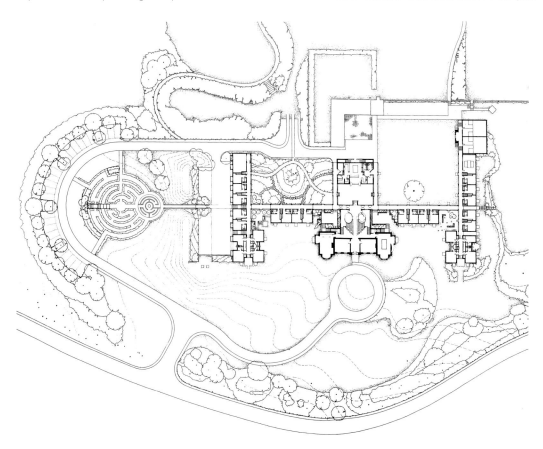

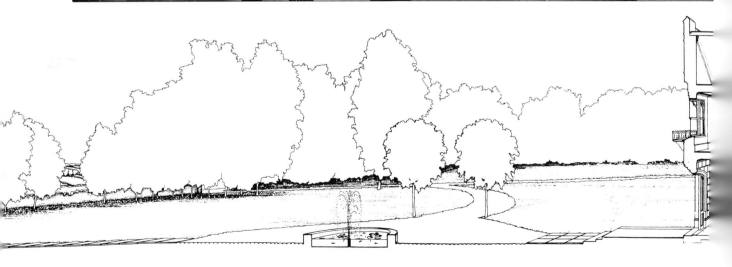

Sectional perspective

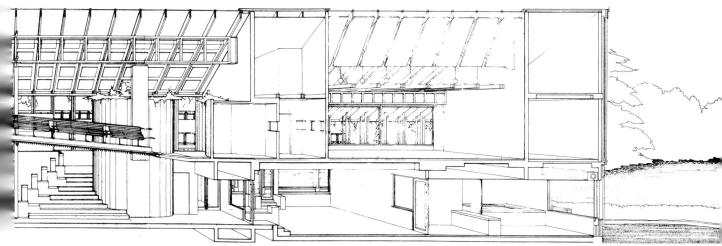

BEECHWOOD LODGE
1983-87

The last of the three quadrangles is in Basingstoke, a small Hampshire town expanded in the 1960s with a mix of ringways and roundabouts, pedestrian shopping decks, corporate buildings, manufacturing/retail sheds and housing estates, to become a largish new town today. This required a large workforce, many of whom were housed in the disused prefabricated wards of a prefabricated hostel for construction workers called Nelson Lodge.

A determined group of councillors wanted to replace this dismal accommodation with something better on a new site. The site lay between the noisy Caribbean (night) Club and the noisy Basingstoke to Aldermaston road, well below the highway at the foot of a steep embankment. So here, as at Oxford, the quadrangle is a sheltering device. A five-storey building on the north side contains bedrooms above common rooms and cafe, protecting the court from road noise; two-storey buildings on the remaining three sides are designed like houses with six rooms each, and screen out other local noises. Here the upstairs rooms differ from each other, according to orientation, and differ again from downstairs rooms; corner houses have different rooms to straight houses and end rooms are different again. In the five-storey building there are regular rooms, end rooms, disabled people's rooms, rooms and end rooms under the roof, with still further rooms below an upper roof. Approximately 100 people, staying for anything between one night and permanently, live in about twenty different kinds of rooms. Considering the different particular locations for each kind of room gives a real sense of place and belonging for each person.

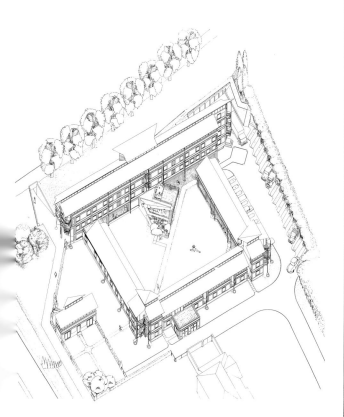

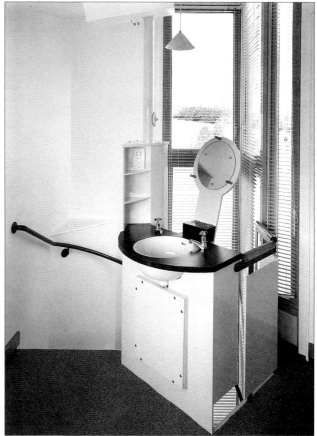

FIVE IDEAS

The sixteen coloured pictures which follow are grouped into five broad and overlapping sections:

Simple south-facing buildings which border their locations and achieve passive solar gain:
Horder House, Hampshire
Media Building, Cheltenham
Farnborough Grange Junior School, Hampshire

Drawings:
University of North Carolina at Charlotte, USA; master plan
RMC International Headquarters, Surrey; drawing of chess piece ventilators
Tama Forest Study, Japan; on site studies of old stations and new greenwood station at Kawai with details

Additions to historic buildings and buildings in historic settings:
Fountains Abbey, Yorkshire; the abbey tower from the Visitor Centre
RMC International Headquarters, Surrey; new courtyard for seventeenth-century house
St John's College, Cambridge; library porch

Details:
Fountains Abbey Visitor Centre, Yorkshire; demountable services ceiling
St John's College, Cambridge; the ventilating lantern
Media Building, Cheltenham; overlapping 'skinny' detail

Interiors:
St Mary's Church, Barnes, south London; from twelfth to twentieth century
Media Building, Cheltenham; working environment
St John's College, Cambridge; working environment

COVENT GARDEN
1984

We spent a substantial part of 1984 responding to the various stages of a selection procedure for the redevelopment of the Opera House in Covent Garden and the site next door to it. It was an enthralling business, like musical chairs but more lethal.

This was a four-stage competition, moving from an initial write-in by some 120 entrants, to a demonstration of ideas by four practices, then to a far more detailed presentation. The groups remaining at this stage were: Jeremy Dixon (who had allied himself with Building Design Partnership by then), Richard Rogers, Jack Diamond from Canada and Edward Cullinan Architects.

By this stage we had developed a technique for presentation which involved building up a cardboard model in front of the selectors showing; first the site today, then the establishment of a direct escalator link from car parks, and the underground railway to the Opera House foyer, the building of a new opera backstage area, then the building of new steel arcades round part of two sides of Covent Garden Market. Others showed the re-erection of the glass facade of the nineteenth-century Floral Hall as a restaurant in Bow Street; the upper levels of dressing rooms and studios against the opera itself and commercial offices round a huge atrium beside it. Above that, models showed stepped levels of residential buildings like the Hanging Gardens of Babylon, and the fly-tower, which also had apartments above.

I gave an introduction, then, while my partners (Tony Peake, Robin Nicholson and Mark Beedle) constructed the model, I described the various stages of growth, drawing their emergence on an overhead projector until the whole composition was complete in both model and drawings. Tony Peake then gave an epilogue about 'buildability'; the areas of different uses and costs. An illustrated book which described the whole process again was left for their perusal; the pictures on these pages are taken from that book. It was the first of a series of syncopated presentations that we have made since.

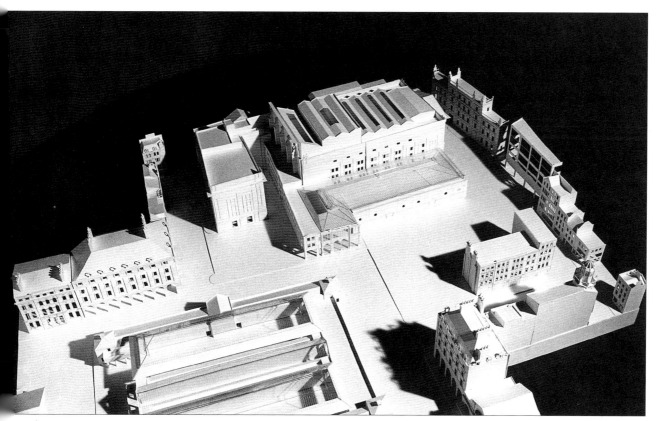

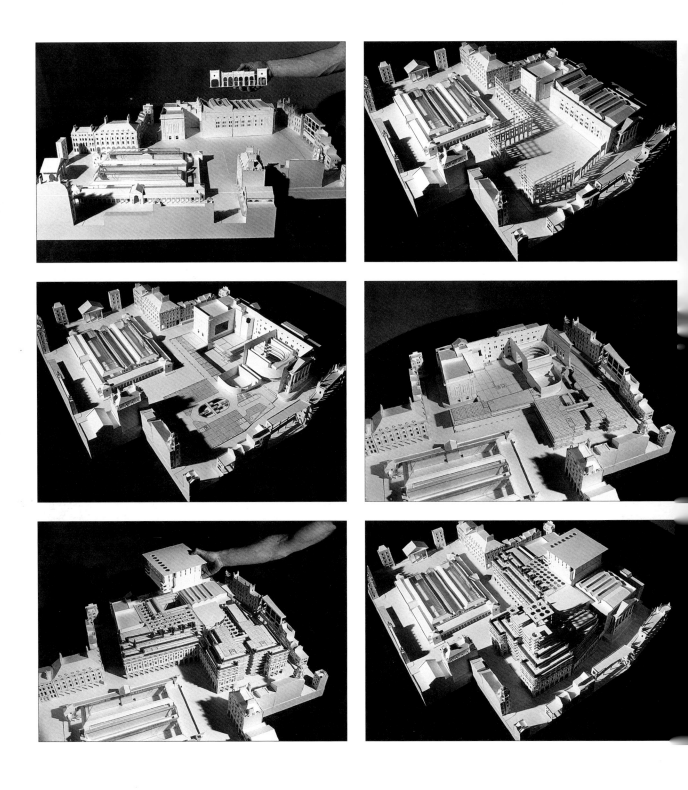

FLEET CALTHORPE
1981-83

Fleet Calthorpe was the first of five school projects built during the 1980s, which comprised two remodellings of 1960s system buildings, a remodelling of nineteenth-century buildings, buildings for children and adults with special needs, and a brand new building on an empty site. All are schools but their situations are very different.

Colin Stansfield Smith, as County Architect, brought into being a unique series of good, purpose-built schools in Hampshire. But the County had also inherited large numbers of schools, prefabricated in the 1960s under a system called SCOLA. This system expected far too much of painted softwood; the schools were poorly insulated, they leaked and were beginning to rot.

The common way to repair these schools was to strip them down to the frame and put up new fibreglass walls and new flat roofs; but at Fleet Calthorpe we saw a different way. We let it stand as it was, and simply repainted, double glazed it, and piled insulation onto the roof, then sheltered and shaded it. This was done by giving it a new 'umbrella' consisting of a metal roof and new plastic rain-water shedders (which are also solar shades at each level down the sides). The new bits of plywood building were sheltered and shaded in the same manner. This process had the effect of 'moving' the building to a warmer, drier, balmier climate, and proved most effective.

CROOKHAM JUNIOR
1984-87

At the Crookham Junior School we developed the idea of shading and sheltering by adding highly insulated shutters which closed at night, and many lovely, inventive, colourful touches contributed by David Linford. The Gurkha Regiment is camped nearby, they send their children there and they think it very Tibetan in atmosphere.

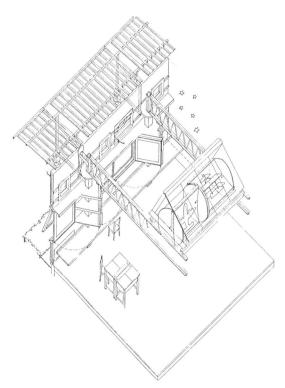

RIGHT: Internal study, axonometric projection

WINCHESTER COLLEGE
1982-84

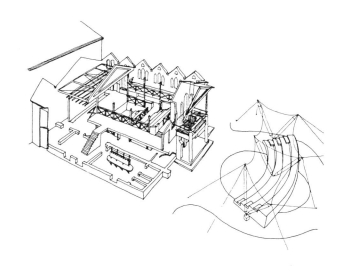

The Fleet schools were twenty years old, Winchester
1,000. Here the polychrome brick Victorian gym was
transformed into a theatre, with a porch added to the
gable end and a balcony above, so that actors can make
announcements, and give 'tasters' from the plays within.
A small picture gallery was placed between (connecting)
two blocks to convert their Victorian sanatorium into an
art school.

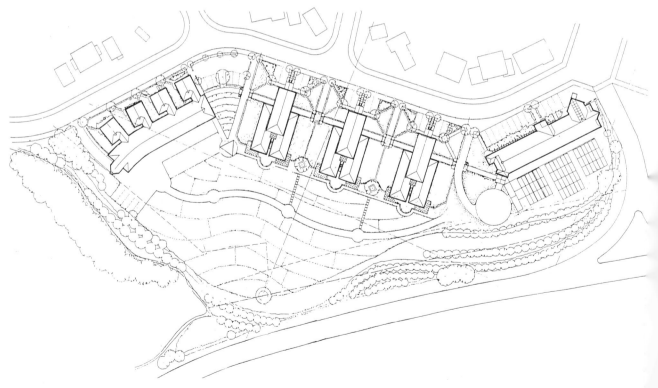

Great Holm master plan

MACINTYRE
1979-88

MacIntyre is an organisation which runs residential schools for children (and more recently adults) who have learning difficulties. They seek secure-feeling, gentle, house-like places, and this in part led us to experiment with the possibilities of roofs pitched at forty-five degrees. A new courtyard was attached to the original school, Westoning Manor. The project also included houses, meeting hall, weaving studio, greenhouses, bakery and plant shop at Great Holm in Milton Keynes. Here people live and work in local industry, making and selling bread, among other things, to the surrounding community.

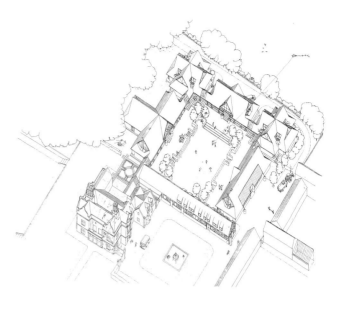

ABOVE: Westoning Manor, axonometric of site plan

FARNBOROUGH GRANGE
1987-90

This was to have been a further development of our ideas for refurbishing system-built Hampshire schools, but the existing junior school was found to be so rotten that it was pulled down and we started again.

The school is designed for passive solar gain. The main teaching areas face south, with two levels of shaded glass to let in winter sun and keep out summer sunshine. They overlook and possess a large green playfield, and are backed up to the north by much more solid rooms for

offices, music, cloaks, assembly, sport and so on. Up in the tower is a room for teachers to retreat to from the hurly burly of schooling.

After all the previous refurbishments and insertions, it was lovely to design a whole new school, with Sasha Bhavan. Building a new junior school was a stark contrast to the government's misguided efforts to close down architectural schools. What follows is a piece I delivered to a demonstration against education cuts in 1985.

Site plan

EDUCATION IN ARCHITECTURE

The first point is a general one; it concerns higher education as a whole. Our country is aiming to expand its capacity to design and to make things: for thereby we may both earn our living, and desire to unearth knowledge and understanding for the benefit of ourselves and our fellow beings all over the world. Therefore, in times of recession, rather than penny-pinching now, we should seek to enlarge and to spread a knowledge of science and art through higher education; to prepare to invent and to expand, to love knowledge and to deal with information.

We know also that we need more insight or 'know how' for our future, and somewhat less muscle: so again we know that education needs to grow, to offer more to more people, to guarantee our future and to fulfil the longings of most people: to satisfy our natural inquisitiveness and interest. So higher education, like all education, should not be cut back in size, but should rather improve in quality: and that requires money as well as much faith and commitment. This should come at the expense of some less useful things, at the expense above all of wasted speculation on nuclear weapons.

My second point concerns, more particularly, a higher education in architecture. The study of architecture is firstly the study of a subject that throughout our history, has been valued with literature and poetry, music, mathematics and science, painting, dance and drama, as a source of pleasure beyond the immediate necessity of eating to live and making money to eat, to live. And as such it has profound value as a study.

In Britain our culture is dominated by literature, music and science. Higher education concentrates on those aspects of our culture: architecture follows, rather belatedly, a little lower down the line. But in Italy for example, architecture is a normal course of higher education for those who will practise as architects, as well as for those who will do many other things: and that is to value the subject for its historic and present worth; for its profound effect on our daily lives and its ideas; to treat it as a subject for study.

The study of architecture is a bridge between science and art; one of the few remaining ones and therefore – at a time when we are learning to realise that science is not only 'dry' and burdened with fact but dependent on insight, and that art is not 'wet' but equally factual and dependent on insight – it seems to me a particularly valuable discipline to support.

I must argue that in these hard times (quite practically, and with an immediate view to the present, and with the 'cost benefit analysis' approach that is currently fashionable), if there was a surplus of architects, we would find substantial unemployment among them, as with many other occupations within the building industry. However, since there is little unemployment, there is unlikely to be a surplus.

Rather than close schools, we should seek to improve them until such time as young men and women vote with their feet and no longer want them. For to close schools now by saying that certain ones are currently too poor or that certain regions have too many schools, is an essentially arbitrary process that obfuscates the need to seek to raise the standards of our architecture. For architecture is the very being of the surroundings of our daily lives. It demands the teaching and learning of the science and the art of architecture, its history, its ideas, its achievements, its present and its future. *For it is the subject whose objects touch us all, most of all, most of the time.*

Speech delivered at a demonstration against education cuts, Tottenham Court Road, London, 1985.

WHERE DOES MY BAGGAGE COME FROM?

In 1985 I was writing about architecture as well as teaching it. At that time I gave a course on a history of modern architecture, in the architecture departments at the Technical University of Nova Scotia and the University of Toronto. It was *a* history, not *the* history; it was by no means inclusive, but stuck instead to a way of seeing modern architecture as a developing way of composing in an open form manner – as the development of Cubism and abstraction in architecture shows.

Here is a summary of that course, turned into a single lecture for the Royal Society of Arts in 1986. It was one of a series called *Architecture: a Local or a Universal Art*.

It may be that I am the last person who should be talking to you. For Charles McKean has eloquently placed the architecture that he described into its local or universal context, into its position in the cycle of revivals, into likenesses and dissimilarities. But I can do no such thing, for I neither know nor care much whether our architecture is more local or more universal. Though of course I'd be happy if critics or historians saw fit to place it anywhere: for one of the vital things that architecture thrives on is earnest discussion, especially discussion by those who do *not* do it! We need more of it.

Now I know, of course, that our architecture is bound to be affected by the local and the present situation, by:

- for example, our damp, moderate, windy climate;
- recurrent waves of nostalgia that assail the English;
- disappointment with the architecture of the recent past;
- the power of conservationism;
- the unadventurous, inhibiting power of aesthetic planning control.

And on a more positive note, by:

- a rising interest in environment and architecture;
- a rising demand for a say in its making;
- a palpable longing for harmonious places to be in, and by the all-pervading, lasting English dream of a sublime and sylvan past: a world of gardens!

But these local and present conditions are in no way a source of inspiration for the architecture that we make. Though they may modify it, and though critics and historians may choose to detect a certain 'Englishness' in the result, the architecture that we attempt to bring to our struggle within the practicalities of the English climate, the forces of nostalgia, the conservationists, those who are fed up with the architecture of the recent past, the planners and the public meetings full of people who long for an harmonious environment, comes from elsewhere as well as 'here and now'. It comes from our attempts to understand certain aspects of architecture, aided by ideas of the comparatively recent past (European, Oriental and American); honed by our own efforts to apply them and to cause them to grow, to adapt to today.

It is these ideas that I shall now attempt to describe and to illustrate to you in an attempt to show you that, however the results may be described, a responsive, inventive and suitable architecture needs all the inspiration it can find in the world; and far beyond the parish pump.

Although I can just imagine 'Scottishness' or 'Celticness' being a small part of the inspiration of Charles Rennie Mackintosh in the boom years of Glasgow in the 1890s, and though I can just imagine the great expansion of America across the prairie being a small part of the inspiration of Frank Lloyd Wright in the same period, I would need to be less interested in new things; less inquisitive about other people; more conservative than I am, to want to see inspiration from the idea of Englishness today. For though I like England enough, I like other places too, and I am put off by certain, rather frumpy parochial and nostalgic aspects of Englishness.

On a higher note, I must say that it seems easier for Charles McKean to revel in Scottishness or Celticness and the high dark romance of Claymore, bagpipe and the memories of howling Highland hordes, than for us to be similarly inspired by the present state of 'Englishness'. It is nicer for Romantics to be closer to the Middle Ages than to have experienced quite so many years of bourgeois history as we have in England:

If Architecture is to be
Profounder than we often see
The Englishness of English Art
Will play a rather minor part

That is all I shall say about localness or Englishness, and now I will try the hard part: a description of some wider ideas that affect our architecture – or in other words: 'where does my baggage come from?'

At this time we suffer horribly from the presence (and the past) of a kind of modern architecture that produces anonymous slabs and towers: an architecture that I prefer to refer to as *recent building* and not as *architecture* at all. It is a puritan architecture which takes from the modern idea only those parts of it that are to do with mass production, the idealisation of a standard solution, generalisation, and such necessary matters as the perfection of light angles and cross-ventilation: the cold douche of a stripped-down aesthetic. It is the architecture that results if you design only the overall shape of things, and then detail them with the overriding aim of hiding the joints, of achieving smoothness: it avoids detailed design. It is the architecture that results if you take a housing crisis and turn it into an aesthetic by mistake: a tragic confusion of medium and message! It is a repetitive and predictable architecture that was simple for governments and large corporations to administer in a centralist way. It could not and will never be a 'people's' architecture or a genuinely popular architecture, in the sense of being created through a popular process.

In the despair that we feel when we are assaulted by the presence of these buildings, and when we must listen to the people who have to live in them and among them, we could do one of two things. We could attempt to climb back into our own past, by raiding history for skimpy references (in the manner of certain American Posts); as in England by an umpteenth revival of so-called Georgian architecture; stuffy, symmetrical, polite, provincial, Palladian pastiche; and also by the universal 'in keeping' style which is beneath description. Or we could assuage the despair that we feel by remembering that we might belong to and prolong a great tradition in architecture; a tradition that is at least 120 years old, a tradition that concerns itself with particular conditions and particular situations; one that composes with asymmetry and balance; is open in form and is expressive, and through expressiveness is decorative; a

tradition that uses industrial production in the service of particularity as opposed to using its methods as a guide to an aesthetic of sameness and repetition. It is the tradition of which Aldo van Eyck's 'Great Gang' was a part, and it is the tradition that I propose to examine, sadly in a most cursory and fragmentary way; illustrating it with recognisable buildings, which are in approximate historical order, but which also contain many other links.

I am starting in 1859 where everybody used to start – from Muthesius to Pevsner – with the Red House; that by now rather 'suburban' looking house in Bexley Heath which at first glance makes us wonder what all the fuss was about. We go on wondering what all the fuss was about when we read the bald statements of many historians, that the house was merely concerned with the use of simple materials and integral handmade decoration, and that it was largely derived from contemporary school-houses and vicarages by Street and Butterfield.

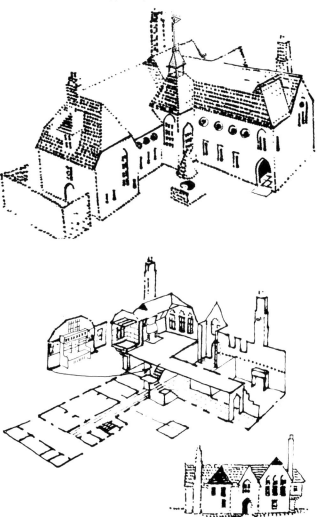

So I want to look at it in another way; in a way that will place it into the tradition that inspires me.

The largest series of three windows in the most substantial gable of the house lights the main salon. The entrance door is an aedicule or a model of the house; a hole and an invitation to enter, guarded by the pair of windows to the small room over it. This 'entry house', when viewed from inside the house, leads you into an arrival hall; a hall which contains Philip Webb's green-roofed cupboard-cum-seat, to leave things in, *another* little house.

Straight ahead is the stair, a signal that the upper gallery and the lower are of equal importance; it is both a pivot for the asymmetrical cross plan, and makes a corner turret to the garden court. The stair is a natural part of the paths through the house. To the right is the dining-room that contains the three-gabled sideboard, and to the left is the lower gallery – seen through a screen to make it slightly less available than the stair – which edges the garden court, leading past rooms to a door to that court.

At the top of the stair, the upper gallery runs above the lower at right angles to the hall, edging the garden court with the stair as the pivot. At the stair end of the gallery is the salon, and opposite, on the far side of the salon is a little bay to sit in and to see out sideways; another house within the house, a response, propped up there for the purpose.

The salon's embellished ceiling, sadly now less so, occupies roof space, and thereby exists within the canopy of the roof. It contains and is completed by the settle that you can climb to be within the roof canopy, which is in turn enhanced by Burne-Jones' frieze.

The house contains the garden court, edged by the two galleries above one another, and the kitchen wing. The stair turret is again the pivot, and the well is a dot contained by the surroundings.

So the Red House is organised asymmetrically, but in a balanced manner through the use of paths that pass through it and lead to places that contain embellishments which are responses to the movement through the house. The paths and places not only have their essential parts embellished but are further augmented by the objects that sit within them; which objects are both useful and responsive to the places and serve to highlight them.

The interior is so organised as to create the exterior, front and courtyard. The openings in the walls respond to the requirements of the rooms for light and scale, and to mean what they are doing to the composition of the exterior. It is a far cry from the formal, stuffy, stucco villas of the period in which it was built.

I should like to extend this discussion of openings to the concept of depth of a facade, the thickness of skins and the use of sticks or screens; a good example is the New Zealand Chambers, London (destroyed). Built in 1873, it was designed by Norman Shaw, who, like Webb and Morris, had learned much in the office of George Edmund Street.

The brick and stone front wall plane of the Chambers, on the back line of the pavement, flush with its neighbours, is so eroded that it almost amounts only to the substance that you would need in order to establish it as a plane.

The only holes cut out of this plane are, significantly, around the front door; the very point where you would expect to penetrate the wall of a building.

There is a hole for the doors, a round one for the guardian office beside it, and a small pair of lanterns engaged into the protective pediment above.

And lying three feet behind the front wall plane, another plane breaks forward only to support the bottom office windows.

The back wall plane is a supporting frame for the light stick and glass construction of the office windows,

bulging forward again and ordered according to their position in the facade; below, centre, above. As part of the white-stick construction of the windows, a top cornice springs from them, masters the front wall plane too, and projects over the street.

finally, above that cornice, the dormers cap and recapture the back plane from which spring the other windows: an upward springing and a final crown. Remember that this building, layered, responsive and particular in its parts, was a six-storey office block.

Now let us go from Shaw to Gaudi, who knew of his work. While discussing six-storey buildings and the depths of skins, thirty years later in Barcelona, is his Casa Batillo. Its plan is either a series of hollows

eroded from a solid or the spatial result of sinuous walling membranes, like drops of oil on water. Notice the rippling surface of its wall-skin, tiled, stretched and bobbly, including door and window openings.

The upper balconies, which need to be increasingly less protective, break up from the frames of the lower ones, become ever less. In turn they inform the crown of the building; its frame to the sky. On the thickness and the occupation of edges, I can do no more than to sum up with the market terrace at the Parc Guell, Barcelona. *Seat – protective parapet – edge – drain – overflow – elaboration – celebration!*

Mackintosh's Hill House (1902) spreads across the hollow of the door and makes a seat for the light and sticky window over: the negative of the library window crowned by the positive bulge of the window back to the bedroom above it. The bedroom itself, an

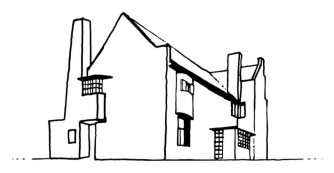

exquisitely detailed hollow, responds to and needs that window bulge. The little lightweight house beside the house makes the living-room bay; and above it the corner chimney rises between the two negatives of the re-entrant windows, to become its own whole self above the roof.

And look at the Glasgow School of Art; the building has a normal solid section, with lighter attic studios above: on the left the section is elaborated by the entrance and the stair, which is also a gallery which you rise up through and into. Finally, the section is elaborated by the many-storeyed library, a room and galleries, a place that contains furniture and which is itself a large piece of hollow, indirectly-lit furniture: an expressive totality of detailed design.

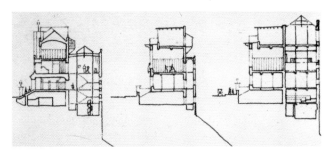

Expressive detailed design like the arched roof steels that sit, expressively capable of rocking, on the solid corbels of masonry at Berlage's Amsterdam Stock Exchange (1898-1903). Or the lattices that arch and stretch from the edges, through the galleries, across the top of Victor Horta's Maison du Peuple (1895-98); a celebration of necessity.

Or we might travel from Norman Shaw through the long, low, ever more open-sided sticks and canopies

of the American Shingle houses: to the time of Frank Lloyd Wright (Berlage's friend) to the making of the Ward Willits House in 1902. This is an astonishing development of the idea of interpenetrating space supported and embellished by detail: a development out of the Arts and Crafts, through a real understanding of Japanese design, on to the surface of the great American prairie.

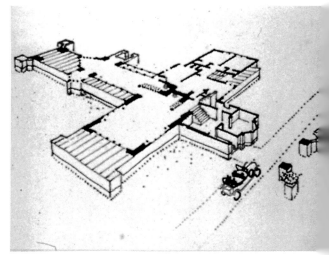

The Ward Willits House takes the surface of a rea prairie that has become an imaginary or suburba one, organising it into a platform, T-shaped about hearth; an enclosed piece of ground which is a approach or vestibule to the platform (as shown t the right of the platform) and a piece of ground (t the right of the vestibule) which is for arriving by ca or on foot, and which is delineated by two pos which support the roof canopy above.

The upper floor and the canopy of the roof flo above the platform and ground, leaving fully e closed space on the platform, open-air space c

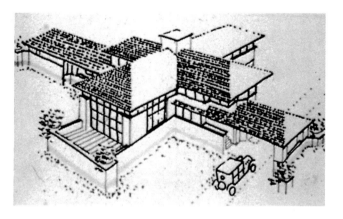

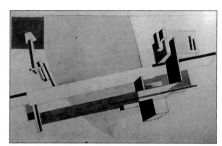

Which brings us to Rietveld's Schroeder House (1924) which has been – strangely, I think – compared by Colin Amery to the campus of the Illinois Institute of Technology.

the platform, open-air space on the platform, and covered but open-sided space both on and off the platform. Spaces of all kinds exist and are organised in a balanced, linked, asymmetrical way; generally between the two great planes of ground/platform and roof.

The construction, its details, and the details that further derive from, exist both for their own sakes and, as we have seen before, to highlight the nature of the places they create; a celebration of necessity, far beyond mere necessity.

One could say the same of the Gamble House by Greene & Greene of 1908, open-structured, open-sided, layered and deep, and with details that lighten the whole. Ashbee wrote 'I think Charles Sumner Greene's work is beautiful: like Lloyd Wright the spell of Japan is upon him, like Lloyd Wright he feels the beauty and makes magic out of the horizontal line.'[1]

Following that introduction to the idea of con-structed openness, and asymmetrical, balanced paths and places, heightened by detail, and layers and sticks, the same theme might be continued by follow-ng Wright's footsteps to Europe; to a way of design-ing architecture that is rather close to his work and partly derives from it and his visit to Europe in 1909. But it is a way of designing architecture which would be impossible without the idea of abstraction, the occurrence of Cubism around 1907.

The Greene brothers' Blacker House staircase of 1906 is a much loved collection of sticks and joints, which is loved for the love of them, moving towards abstraction. El Lissitzky's *Bridge* of 1919 is equally 'architectural' but becoming more abstract and using colour in place of materials and texture.

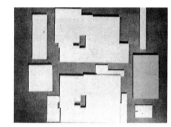
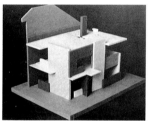

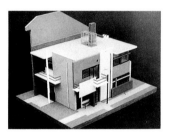
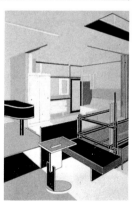

Images show the major and minor planes, balconies and so on, the major planes plus the sticks and win-dow frames from which the place is made.

Now, I want to read a part of the article on the New Architecture that Theo van Doesburg wrote before the Schroeder House was built:

The new architecture is anti-cubic (not cubist); that is it does not seek to fix the various space cells together within a closed cube, but throws the functional space cells away from the centre towards the outside, whereby height, width, depth plus time (fourth dimension), tend towards a wholly new plastic expression in open space. In this way architecture acquires a more or less floating aspect that, as it were, works against the gravitational forces of nature.

Now it seems to me that this piece of writing, which predated and predicted the Schroeder house, is a quite thrilling development of the ideas of an open form of architecture that I have been trying to describe. It is a quite opposite kind of architecture to the generalised, enclosing skins of the Mies boxes at the Illinois Institute of Technology. The architecture is an outward moving architecture of interpenetrating space, like the plan of Mies' brick villa of 1923 or the two great sanatoria; Duiker's in Holland in 1926 and Aalto's in Finland in 1929, partly derived from it.

How could I, as an architect, fail to respond to the ideas which were alive in the 1920s, ideas that form an integral part of the tradition to which we belong, and which I have been describing. It is the very speed of development of those ideas during the 1920s; their *impermanence* as a settled way of building, combined with their *permanent* contribution to the development of our architecture, that makes them so poignant.

And so we come to the Villa Savoie, which partly derives from two earlier steps of Le Corbusier's in the open organisation of spaces: the first in the Maison La Roche (1924), which sees a continuous series of upward path-like journeys through a succession of different interpenetrating spaces: the second, the eroded cube of Villa Stein at Garches.

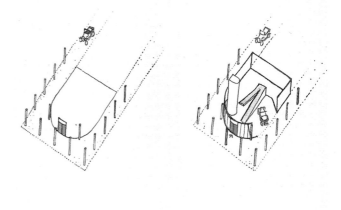

To the Villa Savoie! You arrive by car and pass under one side and halfway round the second side, where you find the main door: the car passes on and burrows into the flank of the house proper, into its garage. At the main entrance, you are presented with a ramp and a secondary stair: the ramp penetrates deep into the building and back again, taking you to the main floor of the house; living-room, kitchen, bedroom suite, an open and a covered terrace: an indoors, a roofless outdoors and a covered outdoors, all above ground.

Finally, an open-air returning ramp over the indoor ramp proceeds to the top roof. It is a ramp that is a path and is itself a roof: and, more importantly, is a revealer of many different aspects and spaces. At the top we come to a protected sitting and sunning place, and a window from which you see from the open-air indoors out over the open-air outdoors. What a powerful idea of interpenetrating space and movement: requiring, through its formal power, only the smallest amount of embellishment and highlight.

I would mention, to show you that I am not a purist or a hopeless fanatic, the Chrysler Building of the same year (1929), which has a much less ambitious plan and section, but equally elegant elevations embellished at the fortieth floor with triglyphs and metopes; abstracted Chrysler hub caps and radiator grilles, and near the top with vast versions of the American eagle that used to grace Chrysler bonnets.

And a kind of 'super-obvious' but elegant summary of the idea of paths and places, is Lubetkin an

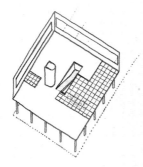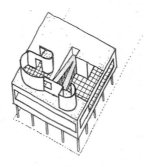

Tecton's Penguin Pool of 1934; illustrating movement contained by a taut, penetrated skin. And here the ground floor plan of Highpoint 1 reveals a device for capturing wanton ground and taking it to the feet of two lifts and two stairs:

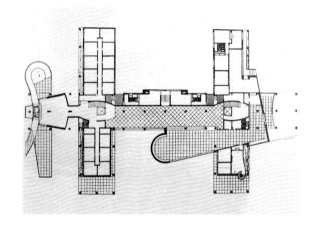

Below are two buildings by Lasdun, separated by thirty years, to show you the way towards an architecture that is expressive beyond simple need. The Hallfield Primary School, in which the low-ceilinged, protective, small-scaled quartet of birdlike rooms for infants, is guarded and protected by the more earnest line of classrooms for juniors.

And there is Scharoun's Berlin Philharmonic, an amazingly disciplined, asymmetrical series of graceful floating trays for sitting on in congregation: understanding both the acoustic advantages of broken asymmetry and the expressive possibilities of it, both for bringing people together and heightening the experience, in a formal manner.

In my last analysis I will attempt to tell you what I think of Le Corbusier's Chapel at Ronchamp, which is a pilgrimage chapel, a blip on a hilltop; the southernmost hilltop of the Vosges mountains in eastern France. It is an abstract, asymmetrically balanced, partly hollow-sided object from outside, and an abstract, asymmetrically balanced, lit space within.

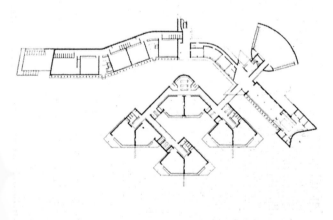

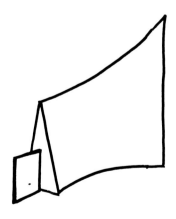

and the interior of the Olivier Theatre, like a formalised 'coomb' for sitting in, gathered together for shared performance.

If one starts with the great processional, occasionally used, enamelled pivoting door on the south side, one finds to the west a high tower, and on the eastern side, the low, stable, wide end of the south wall, which narrows its base and gains height as it moves eastwards. This is the means through which strong, joyful south light enters the interior, controlled in quality and colour by many glazed openings. This wall ends high, exactly vertical and thin, which is further enhanced by a slit between it and the east wall, which has statue, altar, choir lofts and pulpits on both its sides, inside and out, for small and large gatherings.

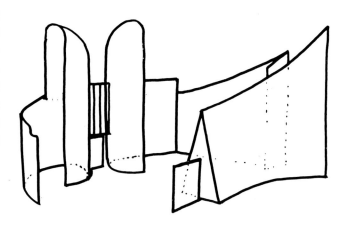

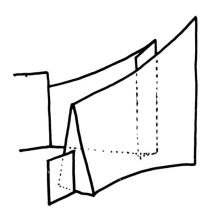

In turn the east wall diminishes in height towards its right-angled corner junction with the north wall, which is planar, until it turns 180 degrees into the building, and over itself to create a towered lighting device for a chapel within the curve.

From the second tower the enclosing wall follows a continuous, tense curve, from north through west to south. It drops to a low point where the roof water spouts off, then rises again to end by again bending through 180 degrees; rising above and over itself to create not only the largest of the three towers, but the largest side chapel within; and a west flank to signal the processional entrance, on the east side of which is the low, wide part of the south wall, which is where this description began.

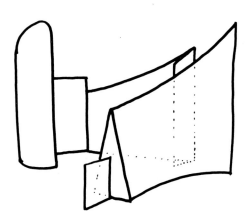

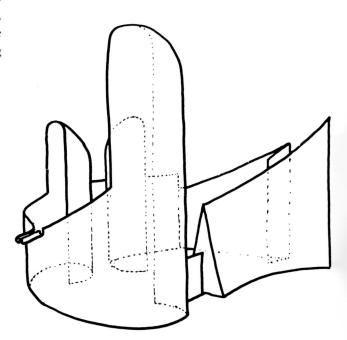

This stops, to start again with another, mirrored device of tower and chapel: so that the outer sides of the two curves, towers, lighting devices and chapels, create the main or unusual entrance to the place within.

All these walls exist between the detached canopy o the roof and the floor, which is level and sloping ir parts; in functional, palpable counterpoint to roo and walls. The roof overrides the vital south and east walls, but is held within the other walls and the three towers. The floor is all contained within. All the graceful details and pieces are scaled and ordered to create the most controlled, finite, abstract, multivalent, inventive and calming lit space that I know: a masterwork, created towards the end of a life of architecture.

And, inasmuch as architecture is to do with light space, you will enjoy this picture of the varied light coming through the many-sized, coloured holes of the south wall at Ronchamp, some in openings tapering from small to large from outside to in, some the other way round; all openings differently occupied but of a family of openings, and ordered as a whole.

Thus ends this abbreviated tour from the Red House to Ronchamp; from the idea of simplicity, of asymmetry, leanness and completeness: the ideal of the simple life: to its development into a mature architecture at the time of Mackintosh, Wright and Gaudi; and to the contribution which that mature architecture made to a new kind of architecture that attempts to come to terms with Cubism and abstraction: an understanding of sticks and planes and of interpenetrating space: an architecture of expression and colour and necessary embellishment, as op-posed to an architecture of repetition and system.

Having tried to show whence comes at least a part of my baggage, I will declare that to make our future we must surely understand our own recent past and our present, and seek in it (and in ourselves) an inspired, expressive and responsive architecture to offer vividness to the debate that we must have with the public: a public that in England today can very often be relied upon to provide only the timid and conservative part of that debate. For, whereas I am totally committed to making architecture *with* people and *for* people, I am convinced that if architects bring no understanding, no commitment, no ego even, and only their obedience to that discussion, there will never be any risk, *but neither will there ever be any architecture again.*

And as a final reminder of the starting point of this talk, I'll say that:

> With Englishness before the Art
> You get a horse without a cart.

1 Charles Robert Ashbee, from *CR Ashbee Journals*, from *CR Ashbee: Architect, Designer and Romantic Socialist*, p152, Alan Crawford, © Yale University, 1986.

Speech given at the Royal Society of Arts, 1986, and subsequently published in the RSA Journal, *No. 5366, Volume CXXXV, January 1987.*

CARSHALTON
1988-91

To follow the five schools and developing certain aspects of them, here is the built fragment for a large theatre and arts project in south London; an upstairs theatre workshop above shops, cafe and market within an old village hall, and a new scenery building and painting workshop whose section is derived from both the village hall itself and the need to hoist scenery for painting purposes. The main theatre, arts cinema, museum, and the rock barn are yet to be built.

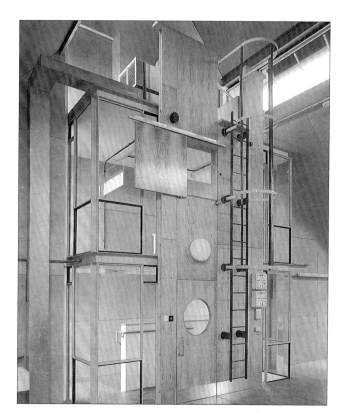

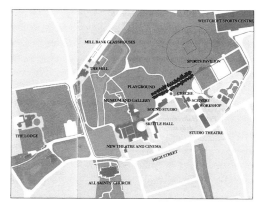

ABOVE: Master plan

LEEDS PLAYHOUSE
1985

The Leeds Playhouse was the first of three competitions that we entered for major buildings in major cities: Leeds, Edinburgh and London. It was an ordinary two-stage architectural competition; we reached the second stage, but we did not win it. Edinburgh was a developers' competition for 'a complete package' which we lost because the city did not think it looked profitable enough. Petershill was an invited competition in two stages, which we won; but it was never built, mostly due to the impact of the recession.

All three schemes aimed to locate modern buildings in important parts of inherited cities, in a manner which supported and improved the quality of those cities by understanding them.

Like many others, the city of Leeds has a high street: Westgate, The Headrow and Eastgate run consecutively down through the city centre from a huge traffic interchange at the western end to Quarry Hill in the east. Quarry Hill was the site of a Roman Camp, with other significant settings before and after, culminating in a vast 1930s housing scheme which was famous for its high level of servicing. Latterly it had become a car park.

In our proposal, the main theatre was placed on top of Quarry Hill and its fly-tower raised beyond necessity to make a beacon of it on the axis of Westgate, the Headrow and Eastgate; a beacon that would be visible from many parts of the city. Approaches to the theatre are threefold: straight up the hill; along a ramp from the

city bus station to the foyer via the restaurant; and finally from a setting-down point to the south at the foot of the hill. At this point an extinct square called Saint Peter's was re-created by placing the small theatre beside an existing warehouse. This theatre workshop has glass-sided access on three levels to make the movement of people inviting and exciting at this main entrance: thereafter you move up through the foyers, to the hilltop theatre. Many small details enliven this progress, for example, the foyer is designed to the precise dimensions that would accommodate 'two-swing' trapeze acts.

Francis Reid, the theatre consultant, wrote in the *Architects' Journal*, 'Ted Cullinan's exciting piece of rather dangerous living highlights the central point. If this competition has demonstrated anything, it is that the way to commission a theatre is still to have interviews between client and architects in search of a mutual rapport. This fact was appreciated by the Royal Opera House in Covent Garden: it devised a selection procedure, when searching for the designer of its new extension, which permitted detailed discussion of the brief with the competitors. Cullinan's design for Leeds is full of creative energy and risk-taking. His debate with the client might have produced a Playhouse that pointed the way ahead, rather than, as is the case, a series of essays in state-of-the-art, cost-effective professionalism which have resulted from this experiment in competitive design.'

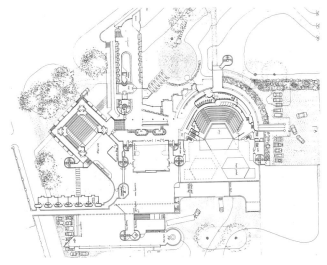
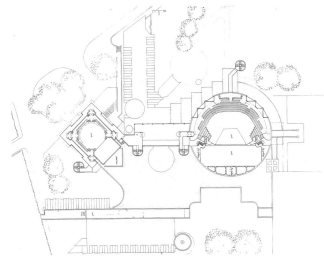

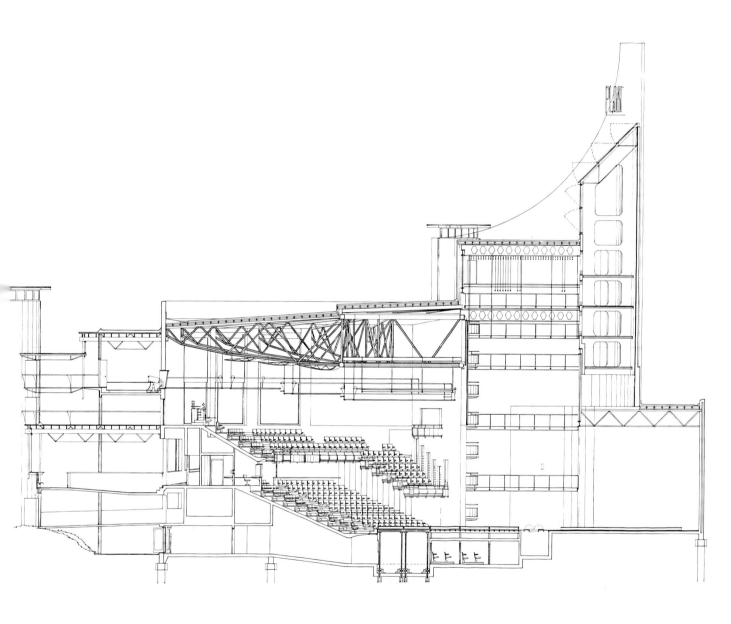

OPPOSITE, FROM L TO R: Ground floor plan; third gallery level; ABOVE: Large theatre section

MORRISON STREET
1987-89

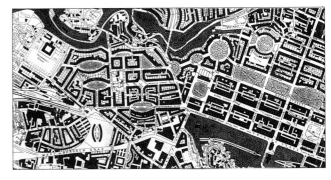

Looking down from the Castle at the Edinburgh New Town, or walking through it, you discover one of the finest series of connected places on earth; formal parkland, squares, circuses and crescents joined together by streets, roads, ginnels and boulevards. These connected places were built continuously between the late eighteenth and the late nineteenth century.

By the western entrance to the city lies a derelict piece of land upon which stood the Morrison Street Goods Yard; the only vestige of which is a relief road which follows (none too conveniently) the line of the old goods railway. The goods yard is now one of the twentieth century's most necessary and most meaningless places – a car park. It was the site chosen for this development, and the proposal consisted of six main attributes:

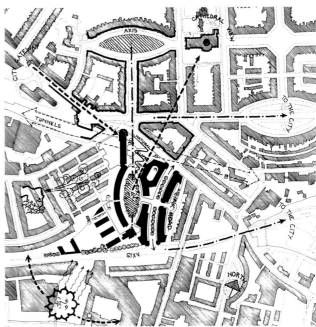

- it continues the series of connected places which run through the New Town, with a final crescent;
- it joins the new relief road with a new boulevard to Morrison Street and thereby into the city itself;
- it continues the nature of the spaces between the famous Edinburgh Colony Houses across the western part of the site;
- it thrusts a hotel northwards out to the edge of Morrison Street to make a gatepost by the gateway into the city;
- it mixes houses, apartments, offices and hotels for the purpose of framing the public places and they have the necessary scale to do so, and therefore,
- the architecture can be of a kind that we can imagine today and which is useful for our purposes; since issues of response to surroundings and to the city have already been covered under the first five attributes.

CENTRE: Site plan; OPPOSITE: View within the Circus

PETERSHILL
1989-91

To the south of Saint Paul's Cathedral, the Petershill Steps run down to the River Thames. This flight of steps forms a pathway, the upper end of which is the south transept of Saint Paul's with the dome above it. It is an unsatisfactory realisation of part of the Abercrombie plan for London which was drawn up during the Second World War: unsatisfactory, because it is built off the ground, above roads and car parking, and because it leads to nowhere at the riverside, and is therefore unpopulated. If the Bankside power station on the south side of the river is converted into the Tate Gallery of Modern Art, with a bridge connection, it will become more populated, but this will still leave the question of the sheer lack of quality of this pathway, this bleak flight of steps.

At the upper west Saint Paul's end of the Petershill

steps lies a conservation area containing buildings from the seventeenth to the twentieth centuries, engaged around the remains of a medieval street pattern. To the east this pattern was destroyed when new buildings were built in the 1950s and 60s, buildings that seem to have been thought of as objects dispersed about a plateau; objects whose trivial purposes and repetitive elevations leave them stupefied in the powerful presence of the object of Saint Paul's; cheeky objects which shatter space and destroy places because they cannot frame them.

The Petershill proposal is designed to rectify these matters by recapturing the historic street pattern (including the lanes which were destroyed when the Petershill Steps were made), and by creating buildings that frame space and provide oblique vistas, built along the old street lines.

Aerial sketch of St Paul's and surrounding area

FROM ABOVE: Isometrics; site plan

159

RMC
1986-90

The Romans established Londinium on the first substantial gravel banks as they sailed or rowed or floated on the tide up the River Thames. Further upstream, gravel and sand predominate over London clay, and here today are the established sand and gravel pits from which come the raw materials for the concrete that rebuilds the city. They are in turn filled in by demolished buildings *ad infinitum*. Recently, some of the these pits have been turned into recreational lakes, and the largest of these is a kind of inland seaside created by the Ready Mix Concrete Company at Thorpe Park in Surrey, only a few miles out of London. Discretely distant from the frivolities of the park the company had a site beside a lake whose banks are nibbled by old-fashioned (therefore educational) sheep and whose surface is only disturbed quite frequently by a re-created Mississippi stern wheeler. On this site there was a seventeenth-century classical house, its stable block, and a late nineteenth-century Arts and Crafts villa, all listed; and two listed garden walls and many trees, all scheduled for preservation. All the new accommodation is placed within this framework, received from the past; offices for 200, foyer and restaurant, dining rooms, squash courts, gym, swimming pool, teaching rooms, bedrooms, laboratories, meeting and board rooms, and service rooms.

The red-brick outside edge (framework) of houses and walls – itself an extension of the roadside walls in Thorpe Village – encompasses the site and is penetrated only by vital entry points. Within is a world made of fair-faced painted concrete, steel, hardwood and plate glass; gardens of grass, water, shrubs, trees and flowers; with gardens on top of and between the buildings as courtyards. All the buildings are naturally lit, naturally ventilated, highly insulated and heavily built for temperature retention; in these ways they predict a future of low-energy, ecological building.

Anthony Peake and Richard Gooden put their whole selves into these buildings and so did many others. But the construction took place in the early days of project managers, when they were thought to be heaven-sent, This led to a painful lack of communication between the us and our clients, but eventually we returned to the necessary, creative and productive relationship with the managers we needed to talk to, the infinitely patient Company Secretary, Tony Jessup and with the terminally outspoken Chairman, John Camden. But of course you would expect a certain energy and directness from the man who had built the company from almost nothing to the largest of its kind on earth. When receiving a prize in the Whitehall Banqueting Hall, John Camden let the world know that he thought that architects were like lawyers, an unfortunate necessity. I loved that, for we are utterly necessary.

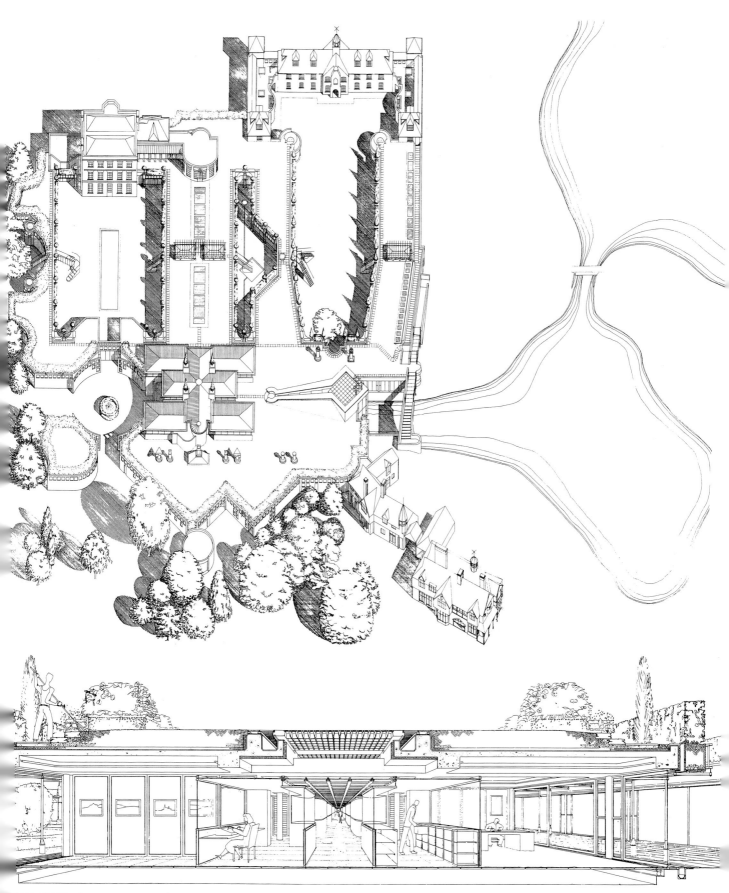

FROM ABOVE: Planometric; sectional perspective

CHILWORTH
1988-90

The RMC headquarters building possessed after all, real clients, with a precise set of requirements and a satisfyingly demanding location. Morrison Street in Edinburgh and Petershill in London both had a high proportion of speculative office space but they both had very demanding city-centre sites. Chilworth and the offices at Bedfont Lakes were both speculative office schemes on greenfield sites – in this situation the advice you receive from surveyors, letting agents and others is usually very generalised, conservative and safe. It therefore becomes important to search for usefulness, logic and grace in the general parts of a building; against which the heightened

quality of particular parts can be placed: and to discover which parts can usefully be particular. There is a truism which says, 'the typical parts of buildings predict their special moments'.

At Chilworth near Southampton, the naturally ventilated office buildings are engaged around a chalk stone ellipse on an axis. The front doors are placed where the corners of office buildings penetrate through the elliptical walls. Besides this highlighting of the front doors, much is made of the protective roof overhangs and the various ways of providing shade for the windows, whatever the aspect.

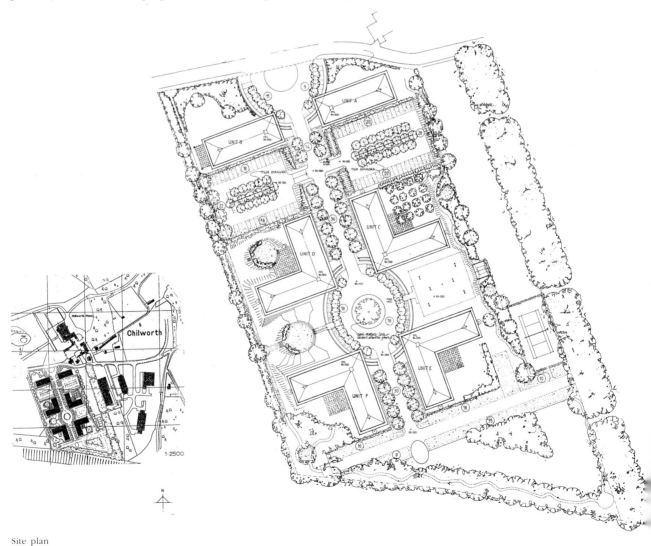

Site plan

BEDFONT LAKES
1989-92

New Square at Bedfont Lakes is an office development round a large rectangular space laid out by Michael Hopkins. The southern end of the square has buildings around it by him for IBM, whereas the northern end has speculative offices by our practice. Here the roof is overhanging and protective, but the base of the building is stock and engineering bricks to provide thickness and protection for proximate car parking. The entrance is highlighted from both square and car park below, and the way that the buildings end and respond to one another is emphasised at the corners, with staircase speaking to staircase across a gap.

New Square at Bedfont Lakes, Chilworth and the Petershill project near Saint Paul's were all commissioned by MEPC whose chairman at the time was Roger Squire, a fine client with a love of good architecture.

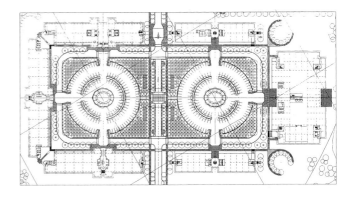

ABOVE: New Square master plan

FOUNTAINS ABBEY AND STUDLEY

SITE PLAN scale 1:
EDWARD CULLINAN ARCHITECTS Ltd

◆ •••••••• ◆ - WALK
◆ •••••••• ◆ - WALK
◆ •••••••• ◆ - WALK
◆ ◻◻◻◻◻◻◻ ◆ - WALK

FOUNTAINS ABBEY
1987-92

In the twelfth century a group of monks, disgusted by the luxury of Saint Mary's Abbey in York, moved twenty-five miles northeast to the valley of the River Skell. It was given to them by the Abbot of Ripon, and contained nothing but a Saxon water mill. They sent a deputation to Cîteaux, and were adopted by the Cistercian Order. In accordance with the demands of that order, they built a wonderfully simple, probably whitewashed, Romanesque abbey church with dormitory and refectory. During the next four centuries this abbey in turn grew rich and luxurious. By the mid-sixteenth century and Henry VIII's dissolution of the monasteries, the abbey had grown large and comfortable, including palatial abbot's lodgings and, (against the rules of the order which allowed no towers) a tower high enough to stand out above the valley, to be visible from all around. Fountains Abbey owned land from the Irish Sea to the North Sea and was said to run one of the three largest sheep businesses in the country. When dissolved, the buildings were razed for materials, at least in part to build an Elizabethan show-house called Fountains Hall just to the west.

In the early eighteenth century John Aislabie was banished to his Yorkshire estate of Studley Royal, next to the land on which Fountains Hall and the ruins of the abbey lay. Here he and (probably) Colen Campbell with others, and later his son, laid out the great gardens of Studley Royal; resulting in an avenue which leads from an obelisk at the west end, towards the west front of Ripon Cathedral – four miles to the east – and the great water gardens in the Skell valley. From an upper lake which curves round an artificial hill, two successive straight canals descend by waterfalls to a large lower lake which fills the valley floor. On either side of the canals, the old meanderings of the river – now cut off – are composed into formal and locally symmetrical settings of ponds and sculptures. Walking up from the large lake reveals a constant series of vistas and events which culminate in discovering the ruined abbey; half a kilometre away the curved lake passes round the artificial hill. But that is not all, for in addition to walking through the valley there are many look outs one hundred feet above the valley floor, with views across and down over the gardens; the final discovery is a distant view of the abbey from a small enclosed pavilion called Anne Boleyn's Seat. In the nineteenth century, at the end of the avenue, Burges' church of Saint Anne was added to this sublime composition, and in the twentieth century it was declared a world heritage site by UNESCO.

The visitor centre for Fountains Abbey and Studley Royal learns from Aislabie and applies the lessons for twentieth-century purposes. A new approach road on the axis of Burges' spire first sees it, loses it, then sees it again, but with the obelisk in front of it, then goes to the visitor centre along a new axis from that obelisk. As you enter the courtyard of the building you see across it the top of the abbey tower rising out of the valley half a mile away. You do what you will in the visitor centre; then enter a wood and lose the tower. Leaving the wood enables the rediscovery of a now larger, higher, apparently thinner tower; looking down over the valley edge reveals its full 160 feet. The walk along the valley edge via lookouts gradually reveals the whole vast abbey and the beginnings of the landscaped gardens. Finally, a rediscovered medieval road leads toward the layman's west front of the abbey church and into the landscaped valley itself.

The visitor centre is stitched into the exisiting landscape, and contributes a new one: it filters and enlightens the many thousands of people who wish to walk there today.

PPOSITE: Site plan

OPPOSITE: Perspective; RIGHT: ite plan as built; BELOW: ection looking east

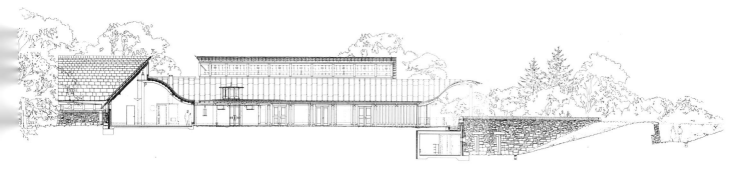

MEDIA CENTRE
1991-93

The Media Centre at Cheltenham is the first of a series of
three buildings specifically built for universities. The Art
School was built in the 1960s around three courtyards on
flat ground, which run in a row, north to south. Two are
open, but the central yard is roofed to make an art gallery
and a place of assembly. The composition is terminated
by a four-storey slab at the northern end, but the ground
falls steeply away to the south. Our additions to the Art
School, which house facilities for media studies, are therefore built around a fourth, enclosed court or atrium, which
steps down the hill. It has studios on either side, leading
to a high crescendo at the southern end; where student
rooms sit above editors' offices, which in turn reside
above huge film studios. Thus an existing building on the
flat – designed mostly in plan – when extended, responds
to the contours by becoming both plan and section at
once.

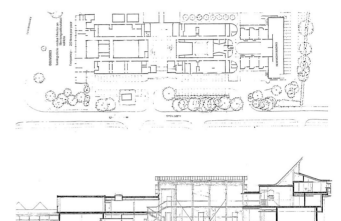

FROM ABOVE: Site plan; longitudinal section; BELOW, L TO R: Ground
and first floor plans

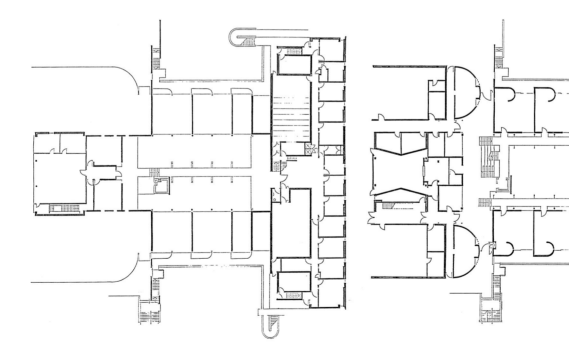

ST JOHN'S COLLEGE LIBRARY
1990-93

The western side of the third court at St John's College in
Cambridge, is formed by an intact sixteenth-century
library, complete with furniture and books. The ground
floor was gradually being destroyed in attempts to
interleaf modern library uses and books. This modern
section was also gradually and haphazardly spreading
through a nineteenth-century building in Chapel Court
next door. This, the Penrose Building, contained large
lecture halls, which had been so chopped up and butch-
ered over the years that its appearance was disliked. To
make the Penrose Building into a modern library, the
interior was cleared out, to reveal its original clarity, with
an entrance porch added in Chapel Court to provide
accommodation above it. To complete the project, a
closed apsidal building was built in the Master's Garden.
Natural ventilation and comfort were achieved by placing
a lantern with reversible fan over the resulting crossing.
The books are located in the centre, with reading places
like nests beside the windows, overlooking the courts
along the edges.

To follow is an after-dinner speech which I gave to the
Annual Dinner and celebration of the Cambridge Society
of Architects in 1993. Architects get very frustrated
sometimes, so it is a light-hearted attempt to lift their
spirits, and mine.

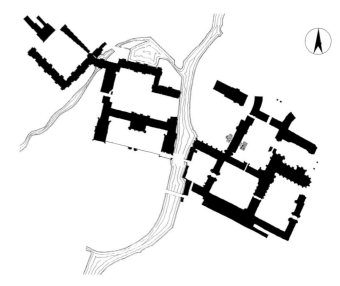

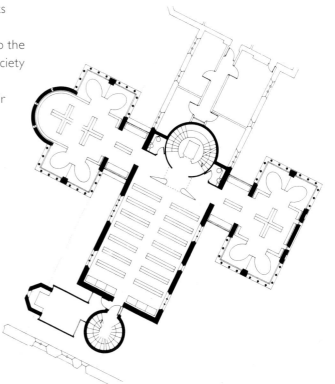

FROM ABOVE: College plan; first floor plan

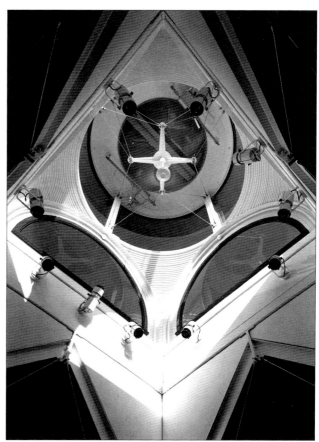

STICKING TOGETHER AND COMING TOGETHER

My dear sisters and brothers in the practice and the love of the art of architecture: architecture; the mother of the arts!

I want to repeat that little introduction, hippie though it was, for it will serve to introduce you to the three themes of my talk tonight. The three themes being:

1 Practising
2 Mothers
3 Arts

So, my dear sisters and brothers in the *practice* of and love of architecture, architecture the *mother* of the *arts*.

And let's start with practising. I love the word practice; the fact that we call our firms architectural practices, that we call what we do practising architecture or the practice of architecture: because practising means two absolutely brilliant things. Firstly, it means that we are always doing it and trying to learn and become better through doing it. Secondly, it means that we are always practising until the day we die, and that with all this practising we never get to the real thing (it's all training and no Olympics), and this is very good news indeed. For if practice makes perfection (and we all know that perfection is unachievable) then the ceaseless practice that leads towards perfection becomes the best and most continuous and most interesting, creative, inventive and stimulating thing to do. Also, this endless practising at trying to design building, introduces into one's life a highly stimulating mixture of excitement, conflict, passion and anxiety with small doses of real misery mixed in, which may explain why architects live to relatively ripe old ages. Artists are usually privileged to be allowed to be dirtier and smellier than other people. It's the ink, the paint, the copying machine, combined with long hours, and having to rush to get the jeans and T-shirt off and to put on the shirt, tie and the suit that you share with two or three others in the office, in order to go and see or to greet the important client or would be client. This combined with trying to clean up the pigsty of your board and the wasteland on the floor around it and to put his job on top of the other one on your board, does lead to slovenly habits. But it's all practice and that's good and it can lead to a ripe old age if that happens to be what you want.

Of course, I only mean a fairly ripe old age, not like ninety or more, because I think that very ripe old ages are only available to quite idle people – like the extremely eccentric, frightfully upper class mother of a friend of mine, who was the wife of the last man alive to be analysed by Freud and was an expert on witchcraft, who survived to a mighty age in the Jacobean pile her family had owned in Wiltshire for the last 700 years. On being asked for the secret of her longevity, she removed a Craven A cigarette wrapped in a rose petal from her lips and declared that the secret was 'my dear', to 'spend one's life doing practically nothing'. And I will positively declare that a very close second to doing practically nothing is to do everything practically possible which brings us back to the subject of practising.

Practising architecture does, of course, include getting yourself insured, working out fee tenders, dealing with contracts, learning the computer and the usual dutiful list of activities covered by that peculiar form of mental circuit training or weight training called Continuing Professional Development. It does include all these things, but by far the most valuable form of practice for all of us to take part in is the daily, hourly and minute by minute practising of the process of composing suitable, elegant, responsive, comfortable and expressive buildings, places and things. Flautists practise every day. Linford Christie practises every day, Lineker practises every day, my son's rock band practises every day, joiners practise every day: architecture needs to be practised every day; in this we are somewhat helped by the fact that most of the buildings we design are never built, so that particular and peculiarly frustrating source of disappointment is positively turned into a source of strength.

And to climax this, my first section called practising, I shall read you an extract from William Morris which is so good it will make you cry:

> Meanwhile, if these hours are dark, as indeed, in many ways they are, at least do not let us sit deedless, like fools and fine gentlemen, thinking the common toil not good enough for us, and beaten by the muddle, but rather let us work like good fellows trying by some dim candlelight to set out workshop ready against tomorrow's daylight – that tomorrow, when the civilised world, no longer greedy, strifeful and destructive, shall have a new art, a glorious art, made by the people and for the people, as a happiness to the maker and user.

William Morris, libertarian socialist and incurable optimist said this in a lecture called 'The Arts of the People' in 1879, in order to refute Marx's desperate theory that a revolutionary socialist should not try to make a better present because that might delay the coming of the revolution – as if better things needed no practising for – oh dismal theory!

So that's the end of practising and now we'll turn to mothers. For the buildings we make are our mothers on the inside, and in the manner of the inside and their gathering together around us on their outside, they are our fathers inasmuch as they stand apart, making their separate presence felt.

I am writing this in a courtyard in Salisbury, where I spend a lot of time these days, as we wrestle with the landscape and the setting of Stonehenge and its 430 neighbouring schedule tombs, tumuli, barrows, cursus, markings and mysteries – about which nearly everyone cares one hell of a lot, as we do too: there is one hell of a lot of disagreement and a million different opinions about the (now desecrated) landscape that attracts about a million visitors a year. (One day, by the way, I'll give you another talk on the mixture of excitement and anxiety engendered by working in the same 'tag team' as Jocelyn Stevens, now Chairman of English Heritage. It will be a very long, very bumpy lecture!).

But back to the courtyard in which I sit and write. Opposite me is a late medieval hall, added to and subtracted from over centuries: all gables and wobbles and organism. On either side of the hall, two sides of the courtyard are formed by fairly inventive Arts and Crafts eclectic buildings, which are quite good, but not a patch on Edward Prior (founder of the Cambridge School of Architecture). Behind me, making the fourth side, is one of those pathetic mid- to late twentieth-century semi-Georgian bland facade numbers, designed only to achieve a kind of universal in keeping that is in keeping with whatever you might name through being as close to nothing at all itself as is possible while still having a building at all. You can recognise it as Georgian because the windows have white divisions and they are in a red brick wall, but it's as though Palladio, father of the Georgian, had never articulated a doorway, had never composed bottoms, middles and tops, expressed a corner or modulated a series of interior spaces. It's the absolute tragedy of our time, the profound gloom of 'know-nothing nothingness', the misery of the lowest common denominator. For surely the courtyard in which I sit, the courtyard of all spaces, is an inherently composed and powerful containing mother of a space which should and can allow us to perform our only great task, which is to imagine – when adding to the collection of buildings we receive from our forefathers that form the other three sides of the court, made in our own way, from our own components – suitable, elegant, useful buildings of our time. As Kandinsky said, 'Every work of art is a child of its time'.

So to remind us to take our responsibility to our art most seriously, here is William Morris addressing the inaugural meeting of the Society of the Protection of Ancient Buildings in 1889:

> It cannot be, it has gone. They believe that we can do the same sort of work in the same spirit as our forefathers, whereas for good and for evil we are completely changed, and we cannot do the work they did. All continuity of history means is after all perpetual change, and it is not hard to see that we have changed with a vengeance, and thereby established our claim to be the continuers of history.

Old fogeys eat dust!
Young fogeys eat dust!
Fogeys eat dust!

William Morris was not the sweet old conservationist fart that some think him to have been! My chapter one was practising. My chapter two was mothers and now for my big chapter three, which is art: the art of architecture.

When you're next in a site hut being stitched up by an unholy alliance of project manager and/or contractor and quantity surveyor, none of whom loves or wants architecture, all appointed by the client as policeman to curb your imagination; remember that we share a secret, a great secret, the secret of which is obvious, clear and well known if we would but know it, and that secret is:

> That throughout history and prehistory, mankind's highest form of expression has been in the design, the deliberate, passionate, energetic and utterly committed design and composition of buildings and places, and so shall it continue and it is to that task that we are lashed and to the best of our ability is what we must do.

From Hopi Indian Circular Kiva to the Mosque at Cordoba, to Durham Cathedral to the total control of the total form of the object/container at Ronchamp and a hundred thousand other works of art that we possess.

When your boss sells your design down the river at a client meeting you're not at, remember the vast resource that you have within you to triumph in the end. When you think we live in uniquely ghastly and philistine times, remember Vanbrugh and the Duchess of Marlborough and struggle on. Here is Vanbrugh's letter to the Duchess which makes the point despite the fact that it is slightly confused by the fact that as well as designing Blenheim, he had attempted to arrange a marriage between her plainest granddaughter and his plainest friend, the Duke of Newcastle (typical architects do-gooding). The letter:

> But having since been shewn Mr Richards a large pack of building papers sent to him by your Grace, I find the reason was, that you had resolv'd to use me so ill in respect of Blenheim, as much make it impracticable to employ me in any other branch of your service. The papers, madam, are so full of far fetched Labour'd accusations, mistaken facts, wrong inferences, groundless jealousies and strain'd constructions: That I shou'd put a very great affront upon your understanding if I suppos'd it possible you cou'd mean anything in earnest by them; to put a stop to my troubling you any more. You have your end Madam, for I will never trouble you more unless the Duke of Marlborough recovers so far, to shelter me form such intolerable treatment. I

shall in the mean time have only this concern on his account (for whom I shall ever retain the greatest veneration) that your Grace having like the Queen thought fit to get rid of a faithful servant, the Torys will have the pleasure to see your glassmaker, Moor, make just such an end of the Dukes Building as her Minster Harvey did of his Victories for which it was erected.

> I am Your Graces most obedient Servant
> J Vanbrugh

And here is Nicholas Hawksmoor still involved, still loving, still trying many decades later on behalf of a deceased Vanburgh.

> Having always had the greatest affection and regard imaginable for the building ever since I had the honour to see the first stone laid and having spent so many days study upon that Fatbrick, I hope your Grace will excuse me if I still retain it in my memory as well as regard it with the best of my wishes ... that concern I have for that building is like a loving nurse that almost thinks the child her own.

Such is the commitment that we architects have to our sublime art; such is the commitment that Braque had when he wrote in 1912 concerning the nativity of Cubism: 'The things that Picasso and I said to one another will never be said again, and even if they were, no one would understand them any more. It was like being roped together on a mountain.'[1]

Remember such commitment when the planning officer tries to smother your dreams in plainness; remember our secret, that architecture is and always has been the mother of the arts. To finish this talk which I have tried to make most deliberately celebrational for a celebrational event, let me remind you what Alberti said in 1470: 'All arts were begot by chance and observation and nursed by use and experience and improved and perfected by reason and study.'

1 from *The Moment of Cubism and Other Essays*, John Berger Penguin, London, 1969, p133

After-dinner speech given to the Cambridge Association of Architects, 11 June, 1993.

MANUFACTURING CENTRE
1992-95

The University of Warwick has grown to its present size during the last thirty years, in accordance with a master plan drawn up by Yorke, Rosenberg and Mardell, as later developed by Shepheard, Epstein, and now Casson Condor. The International Manufacturing Centre consists of a large engineering shed, served by offices, lecture rooms, class-rooms and social rooms. The building illustrated is the first stage, about a quarter of the whole; the shed will expand northwestwards and the service rooms will grow along both sides of the shed. Warwick is mostly a university of white buildings, and we have enjoyed combining the white with black (or dark grey) to highlight the fact that the building completes and termi-nates the main boulevard through the university. The building is also connected back to the rest of the univer-sity by an upper-level bridge.

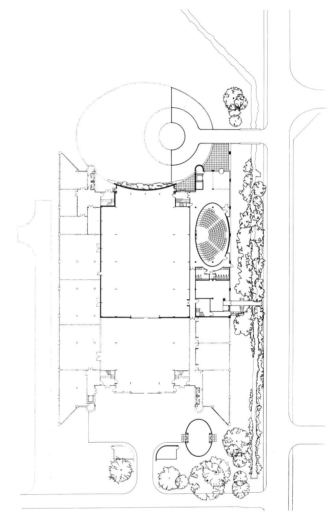

FROM ABOVE: Site plan; cross section; elevation

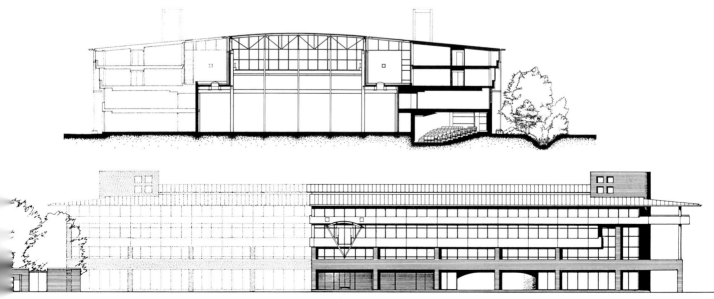

TAMA
1992-93

Our study and recommendations for the future of the Tama forest area near Tokyo, form the first of four proposals. All four could broadly be called master plans. Such town and country plans are often drawn from the overview alone, with no knowledge or consideration of the detailed pieces of building and landscape from which they will be composed. Hence the bleak disasters that so commonly result.

The earliest houses shown in this book were informed as much by their detailed system of design as by overall concept; in these four proposals we aim to show that this can remain true, even at the largest scale of project.

Two national parks, two areas of fine landscape, have more than twenty million visitors a year – the Peak District National Park in the middle of England, and Tama Forest are both under huge pressure. The practice was asked to put forward proposals for the Tama Forest development, as a result of its familiarity with the Peak Park and the work at Fountains. Here follow, at a detailed level, six sketches; a valley with side valleys, a developer's scheme for the valley, and our proposals. Also, at the overview level, Sasha Bhavan's section through the forest, from the highest mountains down to Tokyo City.

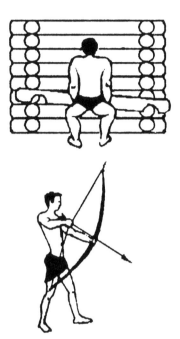

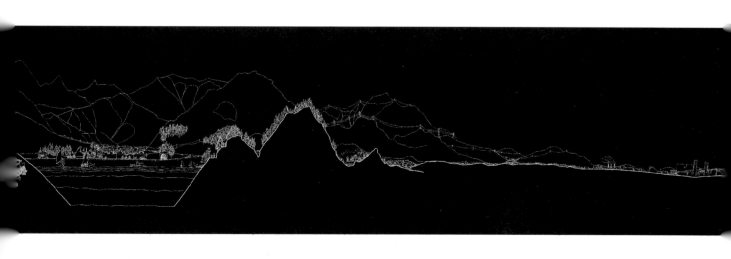

MILTON KEYNES
1991-93

Though the centre of the new city of Milton Keynes is coherent, the outlying industrial and commercial areas tend towards boxes swimming in a sea of cars. In this project, cars are removed to the edge so that a continuous series of buildings for many uses can extend coherently across the hillside for De Montfort University.

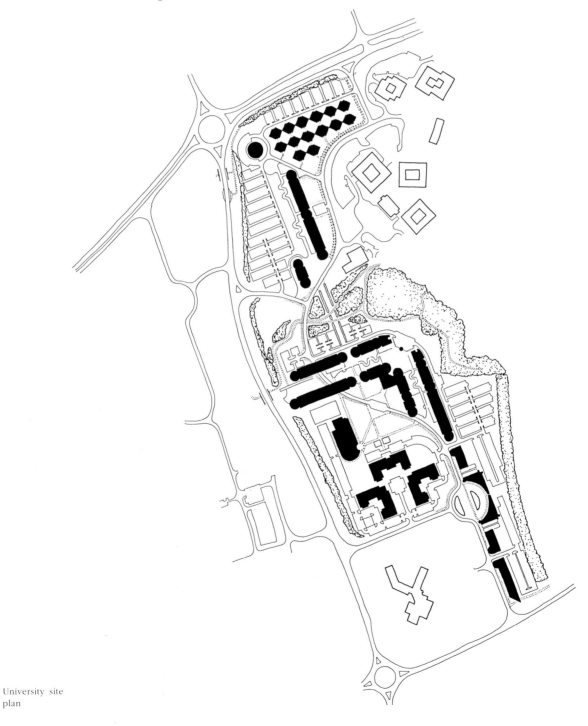

University site
plan

STONEHENGE
1992-

Late in 1992 Edward Cullinan Architects won a competition to provide facilities for visitors to Stonehenge and the myriad of related monuments in the surrounding area. Stonehenge is of vital concern to millions, so you would quite easily expect the debate and reaction which it creates. Here is an illustrated history of that debate and our reactions to it.

The drawings opposite are of the competition scheme on the site at Larkhill, a kilometre to the north of Stonehenge. They show the building particularly and the landscape in general, with the A344 road past the stones removed. Schemes were also planned on various sites for public consultation in June 1993. They are actual schemes on actual sites, not just chosen sites.

As a result of the Department of Transport's announcement that it was going to enlarge the A303 (the large trunk road past Stonehenge), followed by the English Heritage and National Trust's reaction to this, proposals were made for burying or moving the road. One recent proposal comprised a large service area for visitors just north of Amesbury, from which walks are available across miles of undisturbed archaeological parkland, and from which it is possible to go by tram, monorail or similar device, to a lookout and orientation point overlooking Stonehenge and the whole of the bowl in which it sits. Walks from here may be long or short – to the Henge and back, or perhaps around the bowl. The project is progressing towards realisation.

ROOF PLAN

SCALE 10   20   30mtrs

KEY
1. PROMENADE ON ROOF
2. CAR PARK
3. COACH PARK
4. THEATRE
5. TOILETS
6. OUTDOOR EXHIBITION TERRACE
7. VIEWING PLATFORM
8. TOWARDS STONEHENGE
9. ENTRANCE COURT BELOW

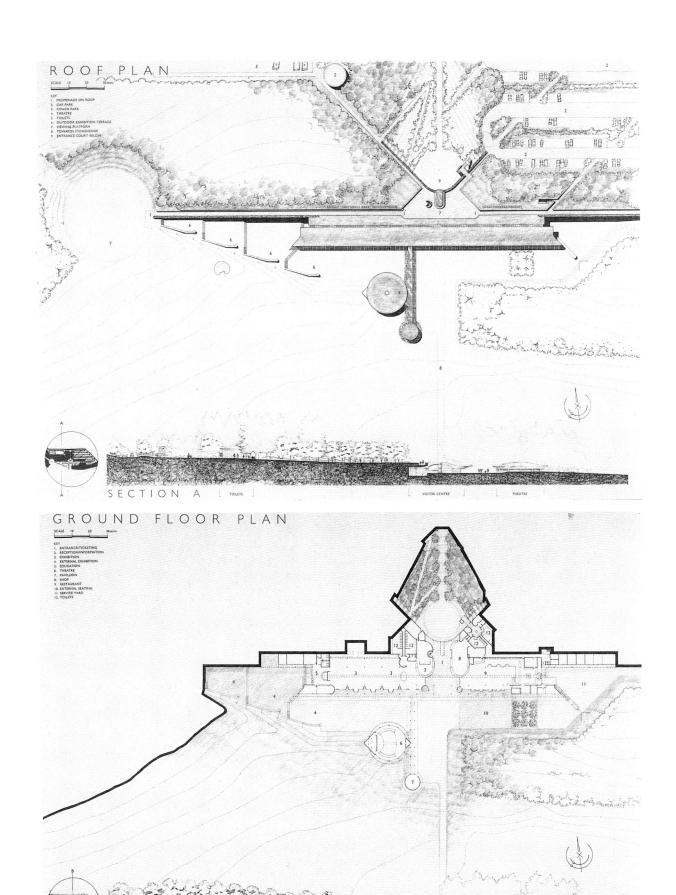

SECTION A   [TOILETS]   [VISITOR CENTRE]   [THEATRE]

GROUND FLOOR PLAN

SCALE 10   20   30mtrs

KEY
1. ENTRANCE/TICKETING
2. RECEPTION/INFORMATION
3. EXHIBITION
4. EXTERNAL EXHIBITION
5. EDUCATION
6. THEATRE
7. PAVILION
8. SHOP
9. RESTAURANT
10. EXTERNAL SEATING
11. SERVICE YARD
12. TOILETS

SECTION B   RAMPED APPROACH TO CENTRE   [GATHERING SPACE]   [VISITOR CENTRE]

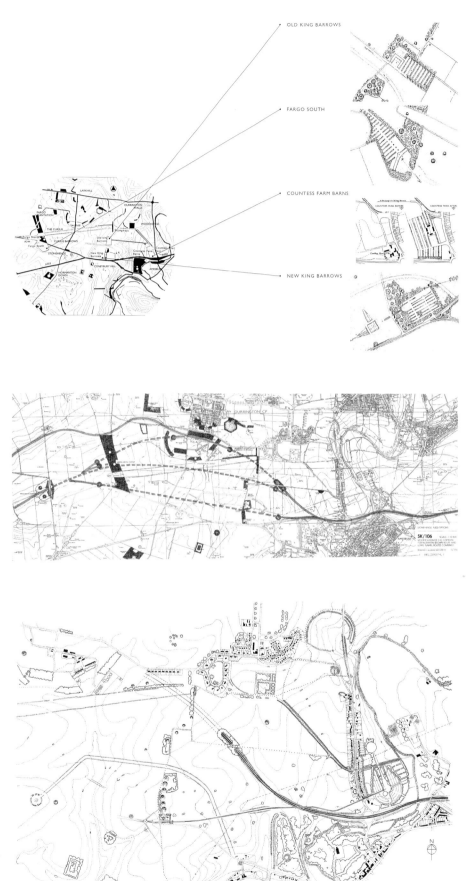

OLD KING BARROWS

FARGO SOUTH

COUNTESS FARM BARNS

NEW KING BARROWS

FROM ABOVE:
Stonehenge plans
showing alternative
sites; road options;
current scheme

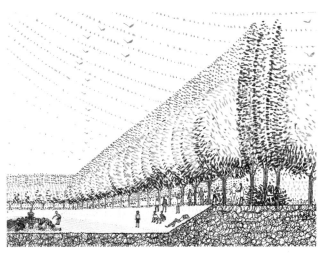

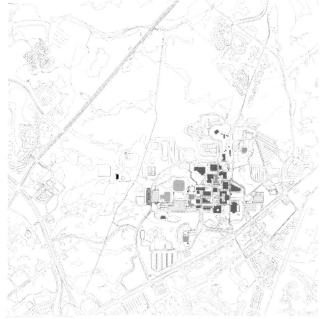

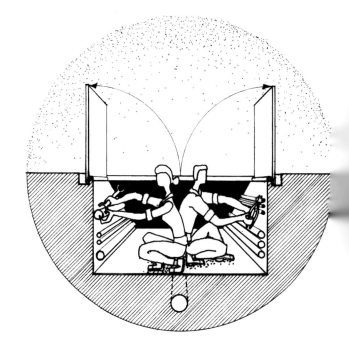

UNIVERSITY OF NORTH CAROLINA
1993-95

We are working with local architects, Lee Nichols Hepler to develop a master plan for the expansion of the university from 15,000 to 25,000 students in the next ten years (below left). With the Chancellor, Jim Woodward, we work alongside an active and perceptive task force, whose members represent various interests within the city and the university. The task force wrote a list of ten Visions and Values for the future university; each of them consisting of two opposite but balanced ideas. The picture to the right, 'Saint Jerome in his Study' by Antonio da Messina (1418) is on the cover of our report and makes clear the value of such opposites. Alone in his study, he is at the same time a part of the great public world outside and beyond the windows behind him. When working with the task force we first draw examples of various ways of solving the detailed design of the different components; housing, academic, commercial, social, roads, paths, bike tracks, utilities, landscape, sports fields and so on. With our clients we work out the best and most inventive solutions to these detailed pieces, while keeping an eye on the growing master plan that evolves (below right).

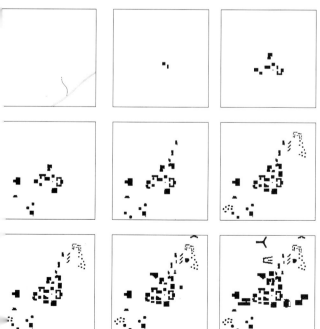

LUDGATE HILL
1994-

To underline the value of working together at the large and the small scale – macrocosm and microcosm – the following pages show the detailed and overall design of buildings the practice is working on at Ludgate Hill in the City of London, and the development of a series of small houses made from forest thinnings, for John Makepeace at Hooke Park in Dorset.

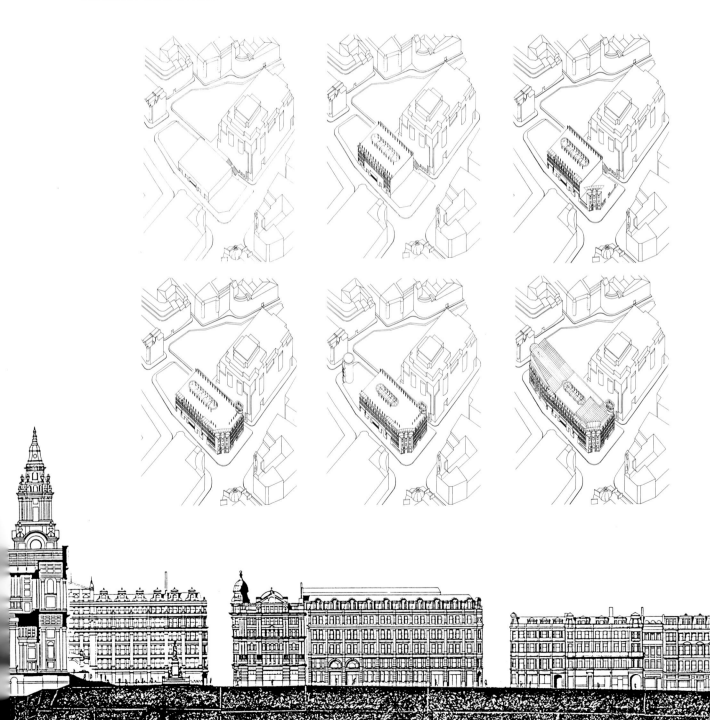

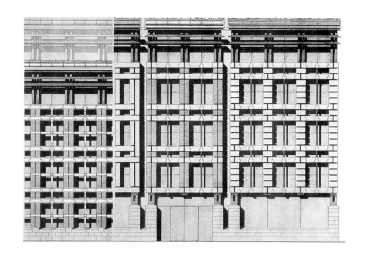

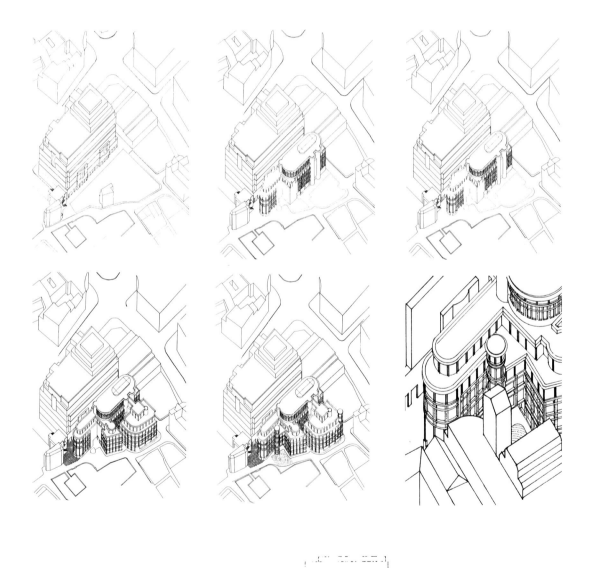

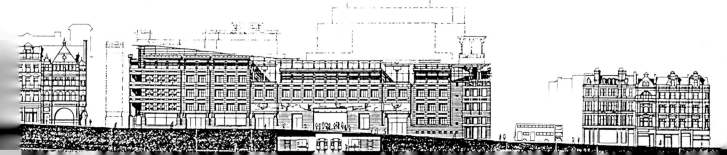

HOOKE PARK
1994-

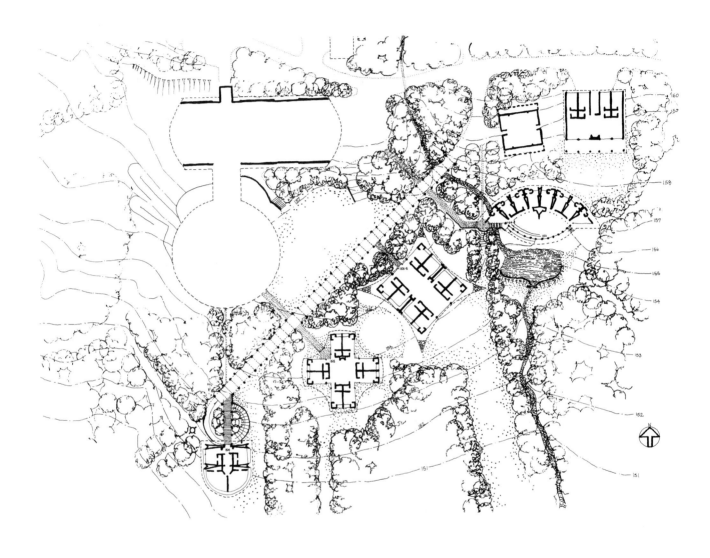

Site plan; BELOW: House types

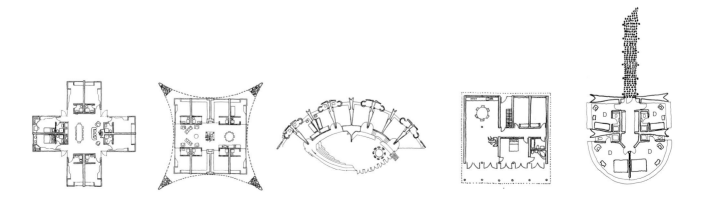

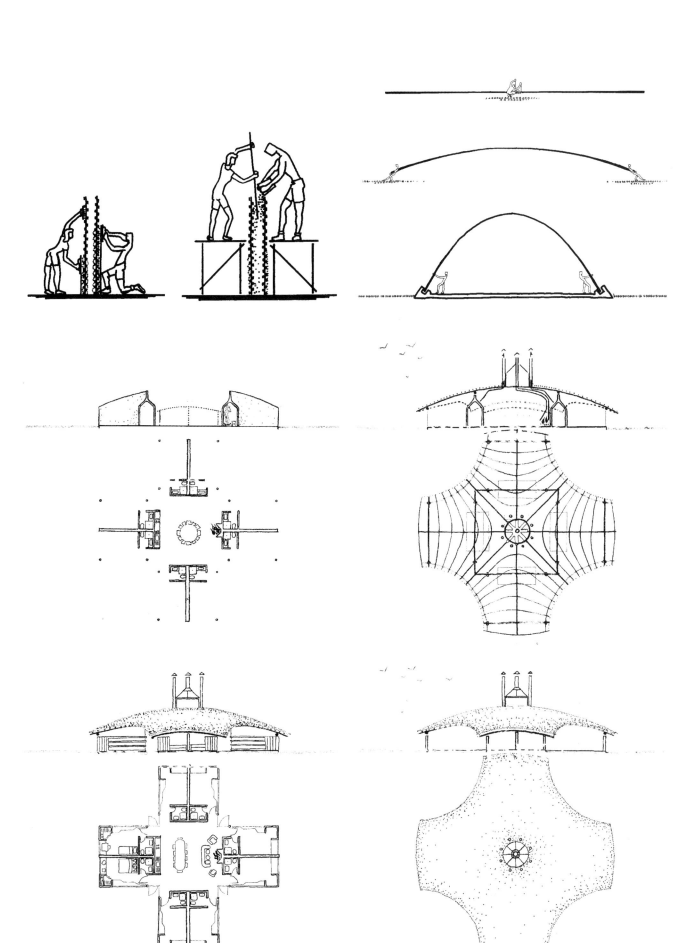

TAILPIECE

Here follows a piece about the recent history of design-ing, written as an introduction to a conference called Designing for People with Mental Disabilities, *in 1993.*

I am going to make a general introduction to this part of the session as you are going to see buildings and slides of buildings and hear from architects and their clients and about the uses of the buildings.

The subject of the session is *Designing for People with Mental Disabilities.* As soon as you get that mouthful of words into your head, you start to think about what disability actually consists of. This in turn leads you to consider what 'ability' (without the 'dis' part) actually is; and to realise that all our various abilities are very limited and very finite and largely controlled by the situations in which we find our-selves, and more importantly by the permissions that we imagine control our capacity to think and imag-ine. It has often been said that designers and archi-tects and people that make things, actually only make what they feel they have permission to do; and it is that kind of permit in life that is the disability or inability that we all have. So surely all of us should think of ourselves as more or less unable or disabled, rather than being really able, and this is mostly especially the case when it comes to the matter of designing buildings. To design buildings that are both elegant and suitable to purpose is an extremely difficult process, in the practice of which we are all of us more or less disabled or unable, and hence, in part, the title of my introduction 'The Normality of Disability'.

I will see if I can describe what I mean by talking a little about how I was taught architecture during the socially optimistic post-war period in the 1950s, when that optimism and hopefulness led to an idea that you could learn subjects with considerable certainty and achieve results through a system.

In the first year of architecture school, we de-signed a single house. Usually the tutors pulled out of a drawer the same brief for the project each year. In my case, it was a house for an author, built at the bottom of his garden, and it always resulted in a kind of 'dingle dell' architecture, which in the case of many students at the school of architecture in those days was the best building they ever designed, be-cause they learnt too much afterwards.

In the second year, during these hopeful times, a primary school was designed. Those usually turned out more or less like a Hertfordshire school, or latterly, after the Smithsons had arrived on the scene, a 'Hunstanton' school in style. But whichever it was, it served to introduce us to what was considered the all-important matter in those days; the circulation diagram. The circulation diagram was always a tree, always having an entrance here with some kink of control, and then it passed through all the subsidiary parts of the building (like heating, for example) and it finished with a whole array of twigs, which were the bedrooms out at the furthermost reaches of the building. In other words it went from the most public to the most private in a very steep and continuous one-directional line.

In the third year we studied commercial buildings, because commerce was admitted to exist in those days. There were factories, railway stations, ware-houses and even a disgraceful office block, but sadly nobody ever designed picture palaces or gas sta-tions. No, this earnest tendency had still be to chal-lenged by Cedric Price and Joan Littlewood's pro-vocatively named 'fun palace'. That is the great idea, which we tend to share, of a building whose func-tion is only being the building.

The fourth year was spent doing housing; not houses, but housing. This seldom owed anything to the exotic discoveries that students had made doing single houses at the bottom of the garden for authors – for peculiar people in odd places. The housing was much more earnest than that and suffered from it.

We finished in the fifth year by re-planning signifi-cant parts of the world, a process which had the only advantage (and it is not altogether a disadvantage) of injecting sufficient hubris into the infant architects as to allow them to survive into the world to come –

outside the walls of academia. The final-year scheme was a flight of fancy of one's own choice, and some spectacular flights resulted, nearly all of them along the lines of what Leonard Manasseh so prettily describes as 'a scheme for a cluster of ecumenical cathedrals on a lonely rocky promontory'.

I describe all this so as to illustrate a point that the teaching of the period (with brilliant exceptions) tended to try to establish that different buildings were only different types of buildings and that each type defined by its use could be designed by making a convenient plan, a circulation diagram, and then adding some sections and elevations that should ideally be a logical extension of what was called the type plan. I guess it goes without saying that almost everything that happens to you as an architect thereafter tends to disprove that thesis and to support the idea that buildings are not types but something more like 'possibilities' which need examining rather fully, often randomly, and despite one's inabilities.

Here is an example. During the latter part of the 1960s, I was designing a building which proposed to expand a Cotswold house (its disconnected barn, malthouse and mill building), to make a residential conference centre for eighty or more guests and delegates. While wrestling with the hopeless problem of rendering the disconnected collections of buildings received from history into a coherent tree diagram, which began with its reception at its root and ended with the furthermost bedrooms as its twiglets, I was taken away for the day by a wonderful man, Kit Ounsted, who was on the building committee.

Kit had a team of builders at the Park Hospital which used to try building rooms of different shapes for the children. Square rooms had made the children violent, they were slightly happier in oblong rooms because they could get away from the mêlée; they were no longer in a static space. The final solution was oblong rooms with alcoves off them which made for peace, since of course you could go to an alcove alone or in small numbers, and choose to venture into the oblong for more elaborate contact or for showing off when you were ready. That is just simply imagining for yourself a square space and trying to do something either alone or together in it. Aloneness and togetherness are actually two quite simple extremes. We can imagine ourselves trying to do it in a square static space but find it easier to do in an elongated space, since there is more choice in relationship. It is easier still if there are some places to go and retreat. Lesson one from Kit Ounsted: the circulation of children is random and willed, and thus form must precede function.

He had used the abilities of those with disabilities as a more demonstrative, less inhibited reaction to the nature of places to teach us a thing or two. He then proceeded to blow apart the tree diagram along with the classic notion of 'discreet places' (which was another great architectural phrase from the period) by telling me that, in his view, a conference centre or any place where people gather, should have two vital characteristics. The first is that from any room or place in the plan you should be able to move away in at least two, preferably more, directions; the second is that from each room or place it would be extremely good to be able to see to some extent where other people were going in either or any of those directions, both indoors and out, so as to be able to arrange to bump into them by choice in order to have a conversation, or to avoid them without seeming churlish.

These are absolutely lovely thoughts and they blow apart all those linear diagrams that one used to have in one's head. Kit learned all this from children with mental disabilities. His shattering of my own certainties led to the usual architect's bout of paranoia, and then opened for me the wonderful door onto a world in which one's greatest duty is to imagine good places for oneself to be in. Where better to do so than from people who are said to have disabilities (or are in some way unable), who often because of those disabilities have the most acute feelings about their surroundings. We are left with having to listen and learn from the experience of our clients and users; the simple and very difficult task of making places that are comfortable, elegant, useful, reassuring and understandable.

WORKS AND THEIR AUTHORS

(UNBUILT IN ITALICS)

1955-56
Bell Tout Lighthouse conversion for Dr and Mrs Cullinan at Birling Gap, East Sussex. Edward Cullinan

1958-60
New house for Mervyn Horder at Ashford Chace, Petersfield, Hampshire. Edward Cullinan

New house for Stephen and Mariah Marvin at Stinson Beach, California (destroyed). Edward Cullinan

1963-64
New house for Ted and Ros Cullinan at Camden Mews, London NW1. Edward Cullinan

Knox House 1, Nayland, Suffolk. Edward Cullinan

1964-65
New house for Adam Kawecki at Bartholomew Villas, London NW5. Edward Cullinan

1965
St Teresa's Church, Ashford, Kent for the Diocese of Southwark. Edward Cullinan

1965-66
Surgery, Ashford, Kent for Dr Cullinan. Edward Cullinan

1966-67
Filling station, Nayland, Suffolk for Mr Thompson (dismantled and reconstructed in Portugal). Edward Cullinan

New house for John and Wendy Garrett, Eltham, London. Edward Cullinan, Ian Pickering, Julyan Wickham

1966-68
New house for Peter and Ann Law, Sussex. Edward Cullinan, Alice Milo, Julyan Wickham

1967
Runcorn new town housing (competition). Edward Cullinan, Tchaik Chassay, Julyan Wickham

1967-68
Warehouse and print shop, Witham, Essex for Social Service Supplies. Edward Cullinan, Julyan Wickham

1967-74
Conference and study centre for Dr Tony Ambrose at Minster Lovell Mill, Minster Lovell, Oxfordshire. Edward

Cullinan, Julyan Wickham, Julian Bicknell

1968-69
Two barns and a farmworker's cottage, Aylesbury, Buckinghamshire for Robert Monteith. Edward Cullinan, Julyan Wickham

1969-71
Knox House 2, Nayland, Suffolk. Edward Cullinan, Julyan Wickham

Residential wing of training college for British Olivetti, Haslemere, Surrey. Edward Cullinan, Julyan Wickham, Julian Bicknell, Anthony Peake

1970
Office/workshop, Edinburgh for British Olivetti Ltd. Edward Cullinan, Tchaik Chassay, Julyan Wickham

1970-72
Four new branches for British Olivetti at Belfast, Carlisle, Derby and Dundee. Edward Cullinan, Julyan Wickham, Tchaik Chassay, Giles Oliver, Julian Bicknell

1971
North End Road development offices/ houses, London W14 for Semine Properties Ltd. Edward Cullinan, Tchaik Chassay, Jasper Vaughan

1972-73
Hockney Flat 1, London W11. Edward Cullinan, Tchaik Chassay, Julyan Wickham

Montpelier Housing Estate, London for the London Borough of Camden. Edward Cullinan, Anthony Peake

Houses at Hunters Hill, Wilmslow, Cheshire. Edward Cullinan, Philip Tabor, Anthony Peake

1972-74
Office conversions for Olivetti at Cardiff, Coventry, Thornton Heath, Hove, Bootle and Bristol. Edward Cullinan, Tchaik Chassay, Julyan Wickham, Julian Bicknell, Giles Oliver, Philip Tabor, Anthony Peake, Ron Smith

1972-77
113 houses and playgroup building for the London Borough of Hillingdon, at Eastcote Road, Ruislip, Middlesex. Edward Cullinan, Tchaik Chassay, Mark

Beedle, Brendan Woods, Anthony Peake, Philip Tabor

1972-
Gib Torr Farm, Buxton, Staffordshire for Ted and Ros Cullinan. Edward Cullinan

1973
House at Trebetherick, Cornwall for Rupert and Candida Lycett-Green. Edward Cullinan, Tchaik Chassay, Philip Tabor

1973-74
Dingwalls dance hall, London NW1 for Northside Developments Ltd. Edward Cullinan, Julyan Wickham, Tchaik Chassay

1973-75
Village hall, Mildenhall, Wiltshire (destroyed). Edward Cullinan, Mark Beedle, Glenn Shriver

1974-76
Berla House, London SW10. Edward Cullinan, Philip Tabor, Glenn Shriver

Factory and office at Chesterfield for Trojan Dynapower Ltd. Edward Cullinan, Tchaik Chassay, Charlie Wickham

Greer House, London W10. Edward Cullinan, Tchaik Chassay, Brendan Woods

Six old people's apartments, Northwood, Middlesex for the London borough of Hillingdon. Edward Cullinan, Philip Tabor

1974-79
16 apartments for the London Borough of Camden at 14 Leighton Crescent, London NW5. Edward Cullinan, Philip Tabor, Tchaik Chassay, Mark Beedle

36 apartments for Solon Housing Association at 36 Westmoreland Road, Bromley, Kent. Edward Cullinan, Brendan Woods, Sunand Prasad

1975-76
Six houses at Nassington Road, London NW3 for Adrian Barbieri. Edward Cullinan, Tchaik Chassay, Philip Tabor

1975-77
Hockney Flat 2, London W11. Tchaik Chassay

1976-78
Four maisonettes in London SE25 for Solon Housing Association. Edward Cullinan, Anthony Peake

80 new houses and 12 house conversions, Northwood, Middlesex for the London Borough of Hillingdon. Edward Cullinan, Anthony Peake, Tchaik Chassay, John Money-Kyrle, Susan Ford

1978
The Cathedral of St John the Divine, New York. Edward Cullinan, Tchaik Chassay

1978-79
Observatory/conservatory at Wilton House for the Earl of Pembroke. Tchaik Chassay, Edward Cullinan

Coates wine bar, London EC2 for Corney & Barrow. Tchaik Chassay, Mark Beedle

1978-84
The Parish Church of St Mary's, Barnes for the Barnes Parochial Church Council, Barnes, London SW13. Edward Cullinan, Mark Beedle, Alan Short

1979
Three houses at Ringmer, Sussex for Douglas Pollard. Edward Cullinan, Tchaik Chassay, Sunand Prasad

Basingstoke Labour Club. Edward Cullinan, Robin Nicholson, Sunand Prasad

1979-81
Workshop for MacIntyre Schools at Westoning Manor, Bedfordshire. Edward Cullinan, Tchaik Chassay, Robin Nicholson

158 houses for Milton Keynes Development Corporation at Bradwell Common 2, Central Milton Keynes. Edward Cullinan, Anthony Peake, Giles Oliver, Tchaik Chassay, Sunand Prasad

1980
Conversion and extension of 150 Goswell Road, London EC1 for Skoda (GB) Ltd. Edward Cullinan, Robin Nicholson

New residential quadrangle at Worcester College, Oxford (competition).

Edward Cullinan, Giles Oliver, Sunand Prasad

1980-81
Office conversion for Wolff Olins, London WC1. Edward Cullinan, Tchaik Chassay, Victoria Manser

1980-82
Charlie Chaplin adventure playground, London SE11 for the Handicapped Adventure Playground Association. Edward Cullinan, Sunand Prasad, Mungo Smith

1980-84
Theatre workshop and arts centre for Winchester College, Hampshire. Edward Cullinan, Anthony Peake, Alan Short

Conference centre for Nationwide Building Society at Uplands, Hughenden Valley, High Wycombe, Buckinghamshire. Edward Cullinan, Anthony Peake, Mark Beedle, Alan Short, Sunand Prasad, Tchaik Chassay, Ros Cullinan, Elizabeth Shapiro, Dennis Pieperz, Tony Belcher

1980-85
Lambeth community care centre for the West Lambeth Health Authority at Monkton Street, London SE11. Edward Cullinan, Robin Nicholson, Mungo Smith, Tchaik Chassay, Victoria Manser, Dominic Cullinan

1981
Nine houses at Brecon Mews, Enfield, Middlesex for Nicholas Holdings Ltd. Tchaik Chassay, Alan Short

Bedford Swan Hotel, Bedford for Paten & Co Ltd. Edward Cullinan, Tchaik Chassay, Sunand Prasad, Robin Nicholson, Anne Brandon-Jones

1981-83
Calthorpe Park School for Hampshire County Architects at Fleet, Hampshire. Edward Cullinan, Anthony Peake, Alan Short, Gregory Penoyre, Alexandra Freemantle

1981-87
100-bed hostel for the homeless for Stonham Housing Association at Beechwood Lodge, Basingstoke, Hampshire. Edward Cullinan, Sunand Prasad, Gregory Penoyre, Frances Holliss, Mary-Lou Arscott, Giles Oliver, Julia Wilson-Jones, Anthony Peake, Robin Nicholson

1982-83
House in Murray Street, London NW1 for Joy Cullinan. Edward Cullinan, John Money-Kyrle, Dominic Cullinan

1982-84
Residences for MacIntyre Schools at Westoning Manor, Bedfordshire.

Edward Cullinan, Robin Nicholson, Tchaik Chassay, Gregory Penoyre, Dominic Cullinan

1982-89
15-bed hostel for the homeless, Maidstone, Kent for Stonham Housing Association. Edward Cullinan, Mark Beedle, Peter Kirkham, Seán Harrington, Gregory Penoyre, Elizabeth Adams

1983
East London Water Users Forum for the London Docklands Development Corporation. Edward Cullinan, Anthony Peake, Gregory Penoyre

1983-85
Day-care centre for the elderly, Streatham, South London, joint project for the Mercers' Company and the West Lambeth Health Authority. Edward Cullinan, Robin Nicholson, Mungo Smith

1984
Redevelopment of the Royal Opera House, Covent Garden (competition). Edward Cullinan, Anthony Peake, Robin Nicholson, Mark Beedle, Sunand Prasad, Gregory Penoyre, Mungo Smith, Alan Short, Dominic Cullinan

1984-87
Crookham Junior School for Hampshire County Architects at Church Crookham, Hampshire. Edward Cullinan, David Linford, Richard Gooden, Anthony Peake, Alan Short

1984-88
12 houses at Great Holm, Milton Keynes for Habinteg Housing Association and Community Hall, bakery and weaving studio at Great Holm, Milton Keynes for MacIntyre. Edward Cullinan, Mark Beedle, Jeremy Stacey, Seán Harrington, Frances Holliss

1984-89
29 flats for the elderly for Cecil Houses at Chesterton Court, Ealing, West London. Edward Cullinan, David Linford, Wen Quek, John Romer, Mark Beedle, Alan Short

1985
Leeds Playhouse (competition). Edward Cullinan, Anthony Peake, Alan Short, Gregory Penoyre

Offices at King's Worthy, Hampshire for Sherfield Investments Ltd. Edward Cullinan, Anthony Peake, Alan Short

Social centre for Surrey Docks for Time and Talents. Edward Cullinan, Robin Nicholson

1985-86
Kitchen Pavilion at Wingrave for

MacIntyre. Edward Cullinan, Alan Short, John Money-Kyrle

Three houses at Downhead Park, Milton Keynes for Llewellyn Construction Ltd. Edward Cullinan, Anthony Peake, Alexandra Freemantle

1985-89
Purcell School of Music, Harrow on the Hill, Middlesex for the Samuel Gardner Memorial Trust. Edward Cullinan, Sasha Bhavan, Richard Gooden, Robin Nicholson, Richard Owers, Tom Cullinan

1986
Children's Museum, London (Competition). Edward Cullinan, Gregory Penoyre, Robin Nicholson, David Linford, Sasha Bhavan

Copped Hall offices, Essex for Sherfield Investments Ltd. Edward Cullinan, Anthony Peake, Sasha Bhavan, Peter Bernamont, with Georgina Livingston, landscape architect

Pembroke College, Oxford (competition). Edward Cullinan, Peter Bernamont

1986-88
Winery at Eversley, Hampshire for RMC Group. Edward Cullinan, Sasha Bhavan, Gregory Penoyre

Community Support Unit, London SW8 for the West Lambeth Health Authority. Edward Cullinan, Robin Nicholson, Peter Bernamont, John Romer, Elizabeth Adams

1986-90
Headquarters for the RMC Group at Egham, Surrey. Edward Cullinan, Richard Gooden, Alec Gillies, Miriam Fitzpatrick, Tom Fitzsimmons, Colin Rice, Helen Abadie, Gerry Adler, Mark Beedle, Sasha Bhavan, Anthony Peake, Gregory Penoyre, John Romer, Jeremy Stacey, Johnny Winter, Ian Goss, Ruth Parish

1987
Fountains Abbey Visitors Centre (scheme 1) for the National Trust. Edward Cullinan, Peter Bernamont

Social housing in Spitalfields, London E1 for the Spitalfields Development Group. Edward Cullinan, Robin Nicholson, Sasha Bhavan

1987-89
Mixed development of hotel, commercial and residential accommodation at Morrison Street Goods Yard, Edinburgh with Argent Estates (competition). Edward Cullinan, Robin Nicholson, Roddy Langmuir, John Cadell, David Linford, Sasha Bhavan, Peter Bernamont, Wen Quek, Peter Kirkham, Richard Owers

1987-90
Chilworth Park phase 2 for MEPC/ University of Southampton at Chilworth Manor, Southampton. Edward Cullinan, Mark Beedle, Roddy Langmuir, Mary-Lou Arscott, Brian O'Brien

Farnborough Grange junior school for Hampshire County Architects at Wren Way, Farnborough, Hampshire. Edward Cullinan, Sasha Bhavan, John Romer, Seán Harrington, Matthew Letts

1987-92
Redevelopment of Wingrave Manor, Buckinghamshire, for MacIntyre, leading to construction of seven new houses. Edward Cullinan, Robin Nicholson, David Linford, Wen Quek, John Cadell, Alec Gillies, Jonathan Hale

1988
Master plan and new main entrance for Kew Gardens (competition). Edward Cullinan, Robin Nicholson

Ambassador's residence, Moscow (competition). Edward Cullinan, Richard Gooden, Roddy Langmuir, Peter Bernamont, Richard Owers, Michael Haslam, Johnny Winter

Kilroy House, Oakley, Bedfordshire. Edward Cullinan, Sasha Bhavan, Miriam Fitzpatrick, Peter Bernamont

1988-89
Training annexe at Uplands Conference Centre, High Wycombe, Buckinghamshire for Nationwide Building Society. Mark Beedle, Mary-Lou Arscott, Sasha Bhavan

Redevelopment of Petershill House in the City of London for MEPC Developments (competition). Edward Cullinan, Johnny Winter, Alec Gillies, Roddy Langmuir, Peter Kirkham, Mark Beedle, Richard Owers, Tom Fitzsimmons

1988-90
Community care centre, Wembley, Middlesex for Parkside Health Authority. Edward Cullinan, Robin Nicholson, Peter Kirkham, John Cadell, John Romer, Richard Owers

1988-91
Charles Cryer Theatre and arts workshop for the London Borough of Sutton, High Street, Carshalton, Surrey. Edward Cullinan, Mary-Lou Arscott, Roddy Langmuir, John Cadell, Peter Kirkham, Mark Beedle, Anne Brandon-Jones, John Romer, Miriam Fitzpatrick, Michael Haslam

1988-92
Fountains Abbey visitor centre for The National Trust at Fountains Abbey and Studley Royal Estate,

Ripon, Yorkshire. Edward Cullinan, Alec Gillies, Jonathan Hale, Carol Costello, Jeremy Stacey, Tom Fitzsimmons, Louise Potter

1989
Theatre for Cumbria Theatre Trust (competition). Edward Cullinan, Peter Kirkham, Dinah Bornat

1989-91
Offices at Petershill, the City of London for MEPC and proposals for St Paul's Churchyard. Edward Cullinan, Robin Nicholson, Tom Fitzsimmons, Simon Knox, Peter Kirkham, Rebecca Hobbs, Joe Navin, Nick Turzyniski

Hotel and leisure facility, Danesfield House, Buckinghamshire for Danesfield Ltd. Edward Cullinan, Seán Harrington, Alec Gillies, Matthew Letts

1989-92
New office development for MEPC/IBM at 1-4 New Square, Bedfont Lakes, Middlesex. Edward Cullinan, Johnny Winter, Michael McGrath, Colin Rice, Robin Nicholson, Ben Chamberlain, Jonathan Hale, Seán Harrington, Steve Johnson, Catherine Peake, John Romer, Jeremy Stacey, Diana Timbrell, Peter Bernamont, Ian Birkstead, Axel Dorner, Boyanna Elks, Simon Knox, Margaret McCafferty, Jerome Partington, Deepak Rajani

1990
Installation for 'Contemporary Visions' Exhibition, the Director's Washroom, Glasgow School of Art. Edward Cullinan, John Cadell, Roddy Langmuir, Dinah Bornat, with Gareth Hoskins

A proposal for Spaghetti Junction for The Late Show BBC2. Edward Cullinan, Roddy Langmuir, Peter Kirkham, John Cadell

1990-91
Minster Lovell conference centre, Oxfordshire, Conversion for Danesfield Ltd. Edward Cullinan, Tom Fitzsimmons, Seán Harrington, Nicola Foot, Simon Knox, Miriam Fitzpatrick, Boyanna Elks

Eye clinic at Mnazi Mmoja Hospital, Zanzibar for Help the Aged. John Romer

The Institute of Child Health, Bristol for the University of Bristol. Edward Cullinan, Richard Gooden, Peter Kirkham

Master plan for Osterley Park Estate, Middlesex for MEPC Ltd. Mark Beedle, Sasha Bhavan, Peter Kirkham, Rebecca Hobbs with Georgina Livingston, landscape architect

1990-93
St John's College Library for the master and fellows of St John's College Cambridge. Edward Cullinan, Mark Beedle, Colin Rice, Simon Knox, Jonathan Hale, Joe Navin, Miriam Fitzpatrick, Louise Clayton

1991
New Library for Royal Horticultural Society and Wisley (competition). Sasha Bhavan, Robin Nicholson, Peter Kirkham

Museum of Scotland (competition). Edward Cullinan, John Cadell, Tom Fitzsimmons, Roddy Langmuir

Offices at Spitalfields, London E1 for the Spitalfields Develop-ment Group. Edward Cullinan, Sasha Bhavan, Robin Nicholson, John Cadell

School of Journalism and halls of residence, Cardiff, for the University of Wales. Edward Cullinan, Sasha Bhavan, John Romer

Jesus College Library, Cambridge (competition). Edward Cullinan, Johnny Winter, Mark Beedle, Sasha Bhavan

1991-92
International group learning centre in Berkshire for BP. Edward Cullinan, Roddy Langmuir, Tom Fitzsimmons, Robin Nicholson, Joe Navin, John Romer, Nick Turzyniski, with Georgina Livingston, landscape architect

1991-93
Master plan for De Montfort University, Milton Keynes. Edward Cullinan, Robin Nicholson, Peter Kirkham, Colin Rice, John Cadell, Joe Navin, Nick Turzyniski, with Georgina Livingston, landscape architect

Media centre for the Cheltenham & Gloucester College of Higher Education, Pittville Campus, Cheltenham. Edward Cullinan, Mary-Lou Arscott, Seán Harrington, Richard Gooden, Carol Costello, Peter Kirkham, Elizabeth Devas

Langmuir House, Avielochan, Scotland for Eric Langmuir. Roddy Langmuir, John Romer

1992
Arts centre, Welshpool, Wales for the Mid-Wales Centre for the Arts. Edward Cullinan, Robin Nicholson, Sasha Bhavan, Roddy Langmuir

Balliol College, Oxford (competition). Edward Cullinan, Richard Gooden, Jonathan Hale, Michael McGrath, Alec Gillies, Joe Navin, Nick Turzyniski, Peter Kirkham

D'Hautree secondary school, Jersey (competition). Edward Cullinan, Johnny Winter, Alec Gillies, Roddy Langmuir,

Michael McGrath, Joe Navin, Tom Fitzsimmons

Halls of residence, Goldney Hall, Bristol University (competition). Edward Cullinan, Colin Rice, Peter Kirkham, Robin Nicholson, Carol Costello, Michael McGrath

Technical high school, Lagny, France (competition). Edward Cullinan, Mark Beedle, Johnny Winter, Michael McGrath, Simon Knox, Tom Fitzsimmons, Joe Navin, Jonathan Hale, Miriam Fitzpatrick, Nick Turzyniski

Visitor facilities at Stonehenge (competition). Edward Cullinan, Robin Nicholson, Mary-Lou Arscott, Roddy Langmuir, Carol Costello, Nick Turzyniski, Miriam Fitzpatrick, Michael McGrath, Johnny Winter

1992-95
Manufacturing Centre for the University of Warwick. Edward Cullinan, Sasha Bhavan, Michael McGrath, Robin Nicholson, Seán Harrington, Alec Gillies, Peter Bernamont, John Cadell, Dennis Ho, Anna Joynt, Steve Johnson, Colin Rice

1993
Master plan and academy at Rostock, Germany for Grieger Mallinson. Edward Cullinan, Mary-Lou Arscott, Seán Harrington

Tama Forest National Park study, Tokyo, Japan for the CSK Institute. Edward Cullinan, Sasha Bhavan, Michael McGrath, Joe Navin, Jonathan Hale

Shimane regional study, Shimane, Japan for the CSK Institute. Edward Cullinan, Michael McGrath

Health and Physical Recreation Centre and re-design of Tyndall Avenue for the University of Bristol. Edward Cullinan, Johnny Winter, Joe Navin

1993-
Visitor facilities at Stonehenge for English Heritage. Edward Cullinan, Roddy Langmuir

1994
Cardiff Bay Opera House (competition). Edward Cullinan, Mary-Lou Arscott, Roddy Langmuir, Seán Harrington, Joe Navin

Offices at Brindley Place, Birmingham for Argent Estates. Edward Cullinan, Robin Nicholson, Colin Rice, Seán Harrington

1994-
Offices and shops for the Corpora-tion of London at Ludgate Hill, City of London. Edward Cullinan, Johnny Winter, Robin Nicholson, John

Romer, Joe Navin, Niall Gault, Philip Naylor, John Cadell, Parul Rewal

Five experimental greenwood houses for the Parnham Trust at Hooke Park, Dorset. Edward Cullinan, Sasha Bhavan, Mary-Lou Arscott, John Romer

Electronic further education college for Halton College in Runcorn. Edward Cullinan, Robin Nicholson, Roddy Langmuir, Michael McGrath, Seán Harrington, Karen Hughes

Master plan for the University of North Carolina at Charlotte, USA. Edward Cullinan, Robin Nicholson, Johnny Winter, Joe Navin, Tim Bradley with Lee Nichols Hepler Architecture

New visitor facilities at Oyne, Aberdeenshire for the Archaeolink Trust. Edward Cullinan, Roddy Langmuir, John Cadell

New student residences for the Cheltenham & Gloucester College of Higher Education at Pittville Campus, Cheltenham. Edward Cullinan, Colin Rice, Carol Costello, Tim Bradley

1995-
New Divinity School for the University of Cambridge. Edward Cullinan, Colin Rice, Johnny Winter

Master plan for Trondheim Hospital, Norway (competition). Edward Cullinan, Robin Nicholson, Carol Costello, with Ann Noble and Arkitektengruppen Cubus, Bergen

Ambulatory Care and Diagnostic Centre for the Central Middlesex Hospital (competition). Johnny Winter, Robin Nicholson, Mungo Smith

Master plan for the development of West Cambridge for the University of Cambridge (competition). Edward Cullinan, Robin Nicholson, Roddy Langmuir

Headquarters and offices for ICL at Old Windsor (competition). Edward Cullinan, Robin Nicholson, Johnny Winter, Michael McGrath

Note
This chronicle is not necessarily exhaustive, and has been compiled from available records.

PUBLICATIONS

General
'British Architecture', *Architectural Design*, Sept/Oct 1977
'Cullinan's Co-op' (Selhurst Road), *Architects' Journal*, 19 October 1977
'Edward Cullinan Architects 1959-1977', *Architectural Design*, Sept/Oct 1977
'Unbuilt Britain', *A & U*, Tokyo, October 1977
'A Decade of British Housing '70s' *The Toshi-Jutaku*, Tokyo, October 1980 (features Bradwell Common 2, Highgrove, Westmoreland Road and Leighton Crescent)
'The Cullinan Phenomenon – The Act and Art of Building', *The Architectural Review*, September 1983
'The Cullinan Collection' (Heinz Gallery Exhibition), *Architects' Journal*, 12 September 1984
'Cullinan Concepts' (Heinz Gallery Exhibition and Review of Work), *Building Design*, 14 September 1984
Reflections on Cullinan (Heinz Gallery Exhibition), *Architects' Journal*, September 1984
Edward Cullinan Architects, RIBA Publications Ltd, December 1984
'Rotfast Modernisme', Byggekunst, *The Norwegian Review of Architecture*, No. 7 1987 (features Cullinan House, St Mary's, Barnes, Uplands Conference Centre, Lambeth Community Care Centre, Whittington centre, Beechwood Lodge)
'Serving a Crowded World' The Royal Academy Magazine, Profile of Edward Cullinan by Jan Berney, Spring 1990
'Architects Today, Edward Cullinan Architects', Estates Gazette, 14 April 1990
'Edward Cullinan' (miscellaneous), *Controspazio*, Architettura Urbanistica, February 1992
'Edward Cullinan', Space Design (Japanese) special issue *London Avant-Garde*, February 1992
'Edward the Impresser', Kenneth Powell, *Perspectives on Architecture*, June 1995

Competitions
'Worcester College, Oxford, *Architects' Journal*, May 1980
'Royal Opera House', *Architects' Journal*, July 1984
'Curtain Call' (Leeds Playhouse Competition), *Architects' Journal*, April 1985
'Finals at Oxford: Pembroke College Competition', *Architects' Journal*, 11 June 1986

'The Architecture of Diplomacy' (British Ambassador's Residence in Moscow Competition), *Architects' Journal*, 14 December 1988

Avielochan (Clach Mhor)
'House in Avielochan, Scotland' RIBA Journal, September 1994
'Open House' – Clach Mhor for Eric Langmuir by Roddy Langmuir, Style Supplement of *The Sunday Times*, 13 November 1994

Bedfont Lakes
'Complimentary Co-Existence', Jeremy Melvin BD, Supplement on Business Parks, July 1990
'Business Parks' (Bedfont Lakes and Chilworth Park), *The Architectural Review*, March 1991, Vol CLXXXIX No. 1129
'Urban Fragments: Cullinan at New Square', *Architecture Today*, July 1992 No. 30
'Bedfont Duality', *The Architectural Review*, October 1992, No. 1148
'Flights of Fancy', Case Study Stairs, Lifts & Escalators, *AJ Focus*, February 1993

Beechwood Lodge
'RIBA Variety Show – Hostel at Basingstoke', *Architects' Journal*, October 1983
'Hostel at Basingstoke', *The Architectural Review* (preview issue), January 1984
'Reception Desk, Hostel at Basingstoke', *Designers' Journal*, January 1987
'Hostel In Basingstoke – Reception Desk' and 'Kindergarten Crookham Junior', *Detail*, Munich, May/June 1987
'Cullinans: Home Making as an Art', Building Study, *Architects' Journal*, 21 October 1987
'Rotfast Modernisme' Byggekunst, *The Norwegian Review of Architecture*, No. 7 1987

BP Inholmes
'The Hills are Alive' (University of North Carolina, Tama and Shimane and BP Inholmes), *Building Design*, 3 June 1994

Bradwell Common 2
'MK Two Housing' *Building*, March 1980
'A Decade of British Housing '70s' *The Toshi-Jutaku*, Tokyo, October 1980

Carshalton Arts Centre
'Dramatic Effect', *Architects' Journal*, 22 April 1992 No. 16 Volume 195
'Sound Roof Detailing', *AJ Focus*, No. 5, Volume 6, May 1992

Charlie Chaplin Adventure Playground
'Two Projects by Edward Cullinan Architects' (Workshop at Westoning and Charlie Chaplin Playground), *Architects' Journal*, June 1982
'Adventure Playground in London' and 'Workshops for the Handicapped at Westoning', Baumeister, Munich, August 1983

Cheltenham & Gloucester – Media Building
'Visual display', *The Architectural Review*, April 1994.
'Restructuration et Extension du Campus du College d'Art, Cheltenham, Grande-Bretagne', *Archicrée*, Paris, June 1994
'Material Gains in Academia', *Architects' Journal*, 27 October 1994

Chesterton Court
'Cullinan in Ealing: a palazzo for the people' (29 flats for the elderly), *Architecture Today*, April 1990
'Buildings Update: Sheltered Housing' (Cecil Houses), Case Study, *Architects' Journal*, 23 January 1991

Chilworth
'The Well-Tempered Window' (Bedfont Lakes), Case Study, *AJ Focus*, theme; windows, blinds and lintels, October 1990
'Business Parks' (Bedfont Lakes and Chilworth Park), *The Architectural Review*, March 1991, Volume CLXXXIX, No. 1129

Cullinan House
'Rotfast Modernisme' Byggekunst, *The Norwegian Review of Architecture*, No. 7 1987

Fountains Abbey Visitor Centre
'Cullinan: Harrow' and 'Cullinan: Fountains', *The Architectural Review*, February 1988
British Architecture Now: 'Cullinans at Fountains Abbey', Marcus Binney, *Architectural Design*, Volume 59 No. 3/4 1989
'Tea & Sympathy', *Building Design*, 4 September 1992
'Landscape of Ideas', *Architecture Today*, October 1992, No. 32

'The Abbey Habit', *The Architectural Review*, November 1992, No. 1149
'Liebeserklärung an has Handwerk', *Architektur Aktuell*, Vienna, February 1993
'Besucherzentrum', *Moebel Interior Design*, Germany, February 1993
'Fountain of Youth – A Contemporary Classic', *Roofing Magazine*, March 1993 Volume 42, No. 313
'The Extent of Time', Patrick Hodgkinson, *Spazio e Societa*, Milan, April-June 1993

Great Holm, Milton Keynes
'MK Creativity – Workshop & Housing (Great Holm), Milton Keynes', *The Architectural Review*, June 1988
'Case Study – Weaving Studio (Great Holm), Milton Keynes', *AJ Focus*, Timber, Joinery and Finishes, June 1988
'Moot Hall, Great Holm, Milton Keynes' *Building Design* Timber Supplement, June 1988
'Building Study – Caring in the Community, MacIntyre, Milton Keynes', *Architects' Journal*, 9 August 1989
'External Walls – Meeting Hall' (MacIntyre, Milton Keynes), *Architects' Journal*, 9 August 1989
'Einrichtuungen fur Behinderte Great Holm in Milton Keynes', *Detail*, Review of Architecture, June-July 1991

Hampshire Schools
'The Cullinan Collection' (Fleet School), *Architects' Journal*, September 1984
'Two School Refurbishments in Hampshire' (Winchester College and Fleet School), *The Architectural Review*, February 1985
'Une transformation à Winchester College, Hampshire' and 'Transformation d'une école a Fleet, Hampshire', *Architecture-Mouvement-Continuite*, Paris, October 1985
'Hostel In Basingstoke – Reception Desk' and 'Kindergarten Crookham Junior', *Detail*, Munich, May/June 1987
'Crookham Junior School', Editions Anthony Krafft, Switzerland, Volume 9 1987/88
'Building Study: A New School Outfit (Crookham Junior School), *Architects' Journal*, 9 March 1988
'County Class' (Farnborough Grange Junior School), *The Architectural Review*, September 1991, No. 1135

Highgrove

'Pick of the Projects – Highgrove', *Architectural Design*, May 1974
'Hillingdon Blues', *Building Design*, 27 May 1977
'Building Study – Highgrove Housing', *Architects' Journal*, 27 July 1977
'Cullinan and Hillingdon', RIBA Journal, February 1978
'A Decade of British Housing '70s' *The Toshi-Jutaku*, Tokyo, October 1980

Horder House

'A Studio near Petersfield', *House & Garden*, May 1963

Lambeth Community Care Centre

'Cullinan's Latest: Community Care Centre in Lambeth', *Architects' Journal*, 10 July 1985
'Lambeth Community Care Centre', Building Dossier, 13 September 1985
'Special Issue: Lambeth Community Care Centre', *Architects' Journal*, 16 October 1985
'District Nursing' (Lambeth Community Care Centre and the Whittington Centre), *Building Design*, 14 November 1986
'Rotfast Modernisme' Byggekunst, *The Norwegian Review of Architecture*, No. 7 1987
'Community Care Centre, Lambeth, GB', Editions Anthony Krafft, Switzerland, Volume 8, 1986/87
'St Mary Barnes' and 'Lambeth Hospital', Ediciones Atrium SA, 1987
'A Place Like Home' *A Radical Experiment in Health Care*, Gillian Wilce, 1988
'Buildings for the Health Service', Health Building Note 1, DHSS and The Welsh Office, 1988.
'Design Guide – the Design of Community Hospitals', NHS Estates, 1991
The Cottage Hospitals 1859-1990 by Dr Meyrick Emrys-Roberts, Tern Publications 1991
'Gesundheitszentrum Lambeth, London', Deutsche Bauzeitung, May 1992
'Better by design – Pursuit of Excellence in Healthcare Buildings', NHS Estates, 1994
'Environments for Quality Care – Health Buildings in the Community', NHS Estates, 28 November 1994
'Do You Need an Architect?' by Ana Selby and Robin Nicholson, *Management in General Practice*, Issue 4, December 1994

Leighton Crescent

'A Decade of British Housing '70s', *The Toshi-Jutaku*, Tokyo, October 1980
'London, Post-Modern Architecture – New House in Leighton Crescent', Abitare, Milan, July/August 1981

Ludgate Hill Sites

'Cullinans' Second City Chance', *Architects' Journal*, 8 December 1994

'Bright Spots – Designing the New Civic Realism', *London Architect*, January/February 1995

Mackintosh School of Art

'Master Visions' Installation at Glasgow School of Art, *Architects' Journal*, 22 and 29 August 1990

Manufacturing Centre

'Building Study – IMC building, Warwick University', RIBA Journal, May 1995

Minster Lovell

'Study Centre, Minster Lovell, Oxfordshire', *Architectural Review*, July 1976
'Study Centre in Minster Lovell, Oxfordshire', *Detail*, Nov/Dec 1983

Olivetti: conversions

'Olivetti Hove', *The Architectural Review*, September 1971
'Olivetti Branch Offices, Edinburgh', *The Architectural Review*, preview issue, January 1973
'Two for Olivetti', *The Architectural Review*, April 1974

Olivetti: new build

'Olivetti's New Branches in Britain', *Architectural Design*, April 1973
'Four Olivetti Branches', Building Study, *Architects' Journal*, 27 June 1973
'Quattro Filiali Olivetti in Inglitterra', *Domus*, Milan, November 1973
'Olivetti's New Branches', *Architecture & Urbanism*, Tokyo, February 1974
'Olivette Aujourd'hui', *L'Architecture d'Aujourd'hui*, Paris, December 1976

Petershill

'City Model' Petershill site (south of St Paul's Cathedral), *Architects' Journal*, 26 July 1989

Purcell School

'Cullinan: Harrow' and 'Cullinan: Fountains', *The Architectural Review*, February 1988

RMC

'RMC International HQ', *The Architectural Review*, preview issue, January 1986
'Cullinans in the Countryside', *Architects' Journal*, 20 May 1987
'HQ View', *New Civil Engineer*, 14 September 1989
'Vanishing Act', *Architects' Journal*, 18 July 1990
'Musique Concrète', *The Architectural Review*, September 1990, Volume CLXXXVIII No. 1123
'Buildings in Bloom', Marcus Binney, *Perspectives* (Green Architecture issue), October 1994

St John's College Library

Projects Preview, *Architects' Journal*, 8 and 15 January 1992
'Literary Device', *The Architectural Review*, April 1994, No. 1166.

'Cullinan's Key to Knowledge', Ironmongery and Security, *AJ Focus*, September 1994

St Mary's, Barnes

'St Mary Barnes' and 'A Question of Style', *Spazio e Societa*, Milan, Sep-Dec 1981
'Beautiful Barnes', *Architects' Journal*, March 1982
'St Barnes Church' (sic), *Arkitektnytt*, Oslo, 1983
'Saving Grace – Reformation of the Church at Barnes', *Architects' Journal*, April 1984
'Barnes Continuity', *The Architectural Review*, May 1984
'Barnes Church Construction', *Building Magazine*, June 1984
'St Mary Barnes', Exterior Wood Stain, *AJ Products in Practice*, August 1984
'Redeveloping Modernism', Royal Academy Magazine, September 1984
'Contemporary Architecture', Editions Anthony Krafft, Switzerland 1984
'St Mary's Church Barnes', *Detail*, Munich, March/April 1985
'International Interior Design Award 1985', *Interior Design*, April 1985
'Weideraufbau der Kirche St Mary's in Barnes, London', Deutsche Bauzeitung, Stuttgart, February 1986
'Construction Studies – Specialist Joinery', *Architects' Journal*, 2 April 1986
'St Mary's Church Barnes' Space Design, *Wooden Architecture Today*, Tokyo, January 1987
'Rotfast Modernisme' Byggekunst, *The Norwegian Review of Architecture*, No. 7 1987
'St Mary Barnes' *Building Design*, Timber Supplement, June 1987
'St Mary Barnes' and 'Lambeth Hospital' Ediciones Atrium SA, 1987
'Wiederaufbau de St Mary-Kirche in Barnes/GB' Edition Detail, Munich, 1988
'Pfarrkirche St Mary in Barnes', *Kunst und Kirche*, January 1992

Tama and Shimane, Japan

'The Hills are Alive' (University of North Carolina, Tama and Shimane and BP Inholmes), *Building Design*, 3 June 1994

University of North Carolina

'The Hills are Alive' (University of North Carolina, Tama and Shimane, and BP Inholmes), *Building Design*, 3 June 1994

Uplands Conference Centre

'Down at Uplands', *Architects' Journal*, August 1984
'Training and Conference Centre, High Wycombe, Bucks', *The Architectural Review*, July 1985
'Studien-und-Konferenzzentrum, High Wycombe, Bucks', *Detail*, Munich, March/April 1986
'Konferenzzentrum in High Wycombe'

Deutsche Bauzeitung, Stuttgart, April 1986
'Konferenzgebaude in High Wycombe' Baumeister, Munich, December 1986
'Rotfast Modernisme' Byggekunst, *The Norwegian Review of Architecture*, No. 7 1987
'Studien-und Konferenzzentrum High Wycombe, Bucks/GB', Edition Detail, Munich, 1988

Wembley Community Care Centre

'Webb-like in Wembley – Community Care Centre, Wembley, Middlesex', *The Architectural Review*, June 1988

Westmoreland Road

'Pleasing Planners', *Building Design*, 24th March 1978
'Cullinans' Bromley Block', *Architects' Journal*, 19th September 1979
'Unique Synthesis of Past & Present', *Building Design*, 5th October 1979
'A Decade of British Housing '70s', *The Toshi-Jutaku*, Tokyo, October 1980
'Housing in Bromley, Kent', *L'Industria Delle Costruzioni*, Rome, November 1981

Westoning Workshop

'Two Projects by Edward Cullinan Architects' (Workshop at Westoning and Charlie Chaplin Playground), *Architects' Journal*, June 1982
'Adventure Playground in London' and 'Workshops for the Handicapped at Westoning' Baumeister, Munich, August 1983

Whittington Centre

'Day Release', *Architects' Journal*, 23 October 1985
'Rotfast Modernisme' Byggekunst, *The Norwegian Review of Architecture*, No. 7 1987

Winchester College

'Gymnastic Conversions' (Theatre at Winchester College), *Architects' Journal*, March 1983
'Two School Refurbishments in Hampshire' (Winchester College and Fleet School), *The Architectural Review*, February 1985
'Une transformation à Winchester College, Hampshire' and 'Transformation d'une école a Fleet, Hampshire', *Architecture-Mouvement-Continuite*, Paris, October 1985
'Queen Elizabeth II Theatre, Winchester', *Deutsche Bauzeitung*, Stuttgart, December 1985

EDWARD CULLINAN ARCHITECTS

Name	Years	Name	Years	Name	Years
Ian Pickering	1965-66	Lyn Danvers	1983	Brian O'Brien	1988-89
Julyan Wickham	1965-71		& 1986	Richard Owers	1988-89
Julian Bicknell	1966-67	Angus Brown	1983-84	Wen Quek	1988-89
	& 1969-71	Ros Cullinan	1983-84	Peter Kirkham	1988-92
Alice Milo	1966-67	Dominic Cullinan	1983-84	Julia Mortimer	1988-92
Tchaik Chassay	1966-83		& 1986	John Cadell	1988-92
Giles Oliver	1969-70	Alex Freemantle	1983-85		& 1994-
	& 1979-82	Frances Holliss	1983-86	Steve Myers	1988
Mike Kozdon	1970-71	Wendy Garrett	1983	Jilly Watson	1988
Mariette Smith	1970-72	Julia Wilson Jones	1983	Michael McGrath	1989-
Ron Smith	1970-72	Bridie O'Dwyer	1984-	Joe Navin	1989-
Mark Beedle	1970-74	Tom Cullinan	1984-85	Ian Birksted	1989-90
	& 1976-	Angela Newman	1984-85	Boyanna Elks	1989-90
Glenn Shriver	1971-72	Seán Harrington	1984-95	Rebecca Hobbs	1989-90
Jasper Vaughan	1971-73	Atalanta Beaumont	1984	Cecily Horrocks	1989-90
Philip Tabor	1971-78	Liz Adams	1985-86	Matthew Letts	1989-90
Frans Nicholas	1971	David Linford	1985-88	Catherine Peake	1989-90
Deborah Strother	1972-75	Peter Bernamont	1985-88	Tom Fitzsimmons	1989-92
Anthony Peake	1972-86		& 1994	Jonathan Hale	1989-93
David Dennis	1973-74	Tony Belcher	1985	Mark Macek	1989
Charlie Wickham	1973-74	Noresh das Gupta	1986-87	Louise Potter	1990-
Brendan Woods	1973-78	Andrea Sinclair	1986-88	Ben Chamberlain	1990-91
Peter McGough	1973	Richard Gooden	1986-92	Jerome Partington	1990-91
Claire Herniman	1975-	Sasha Bhavan	1986-95	Steve Johnson	1990-91
Carlos Elsesser	1975-76	Barry Stanton	1986		& 1994
Susan Ford	1975-78	Roddy Langmuir	1987-	Simon Knox	1990-92
John Money-Kyrle	1976-81	John Romer	1987-	Diana Timbrell	1990-92
Sunand Prasad	1977-85	Gerald Adler	1987-88	Nick Turzynski	1990-92
Robin Nicholson	1979-	Miriam Fitzpatrick	1987-88	Carol Costello	1990-92
Victoria Manser	1979-80		& 1990-92		& 1994-
Julia Semler	1979-81	Helen Abadie	1987-89	Elizabeth Devas	1990-93
Keith Dabson	1979	Bert Stern	1987-89	Axel Dorner	1990
Carl Falck	1979	Jeremy Stacey	1987-91	Margaret McCafferty	1990
Peter St John	1979	Mary-Lou Arscott	1987-94	Deepak Rajani	1990
Mungo Smith	1980-85	Alec Gillies	1987-94	Louise Clayton	1991-92
Alan Short	1980-86	Kay Hughes	1987	Gaye Patel	1993-
Anne Brandon-Jones	1981	Annuka Pietella	1987	Niall Gault	1993-94
	& 1989	Colin Rice	1988-	Dennis Ho	1993-94
Hetty Startup	1982-83	John Winter	1988-	Anna Joynt	1993-94
Amanda Potts	1981	Dinah Bornat	1988-89	Tim Bradley	1994-
Gregory Penoyre	1982-87	Ian Goss	1988-89	Phillip Naylor	1994-95
Dennis Pierperz	1982	Michael Haslam	1988-89	Parul Rewal	1994
Elizabeth Shapiro	1982	Janet Marriner	1988-89	Karen Hughes	1995-